THE CINEMA OF MARÍA NOVARO

The Cinema of María Novaro

James Stratton

BearManor Media
2022

The Cinema of María Novaro

© 2022 James Stratton

All rights reserved.

No portion of this publication may be reproduced, stored, and/or copied electronically (except for academic use as a source), nor transmitted in any form or by any means without the prior written permission of the publisher and/or author.

Published in the United States of America by:

BearManor Media

4700 Millenia Blvd.
Suite 175 PMB 90497
Orlando, FL 32839

bearmanormedia.com

Printed in the United States.

Typesetting and layout by BearManor Media

ISBN—978-1-62933-969-6

For Family and Friends

in

Mexico and the United States

Also by James Stratton

Hitchcock's North by Northwest: The Man Who Had Too Much

*A Star Is Born and Born Again:
Variations on a Hollywood Archetype*

Picture Business: L.A. Stories, Poems and Portraits

Angie: The Life and Films of Angie Dickinson

Contents

Acknowledgments	xi
Introduction	1
Biographical Profile	5
Lola	49
Danzón	79
El jardín del Edén (*Garden of Eden*)	105
Sin dejar huella (*Without a Trace*; also, *Leaving No Trace*)	137
Las buenas hierbas (*The Good Herbs*)	162
Tesoros (*Treasures*)	187
Conclusion	207
Filmography (Major Works)	227
Notes	233
Sources	246
Index	253

Acknowledgments

As with each book I have written, this project would not have been possible without the generous assistance of Roberto Rangel, Robin Cresto, and Matt Severson. Roberto helped with design ideas, translation issues, and cultural background. In addition to preparing and formatting the manuscript, Robin assisted in the collection and transfer of photographs. Matt facilitated the gathering of various research materials. Each of them, particularly Roberto, was hugely supportive of the work at every stage of the process, and I am equally thankful for their encouragement and their contributions.

Ben Ohmart at BearManor Media was enthusiastic about the book from the beginning. His direction, patience, and support have been constant. He and his staff are models of professionalism, and I cannot imagine a more collaborative publisher. A very special note of appreciation to editor Stone Wallace for his careful reading of the book and to Sarah Joseph for her expert design of it.

This book is intended as a resource and research guide. Therefore, I am grateful to the many sources which provided information for the biographical profile and critical commentary for the analysis of the individual films.

Danzón photos courtesy the Collections of the Margaret Herrick Library. Sincere thanks to Elizabeth Youle and all the other dedicated staff members there. All images are reproduced for the purposes of critical analysis and historical reference only and remain the copyright of the production companies. Special gratitude to each of them for their support of film scholarship.

Finally, I would like to thank the following people for their encouragement and belief in the importance of this project: Patricia

Kondan Davis, Barbara Stewart Russell, Fernando Marquez, Richard Stratton, Marsha Watkins Stratton, Susan Boyd, and Corinne Venit. Thanks as well to Mark and staff at South Pasadena's Vidéothèque, one of the world's finest DVD rental stores.

Introduction

Beginning in the late 1980s, as the Mexican film industry began to reclaim an artistic reputation that had been undermined by government interference and economic austerity, an array of talented directors produced some of their best work. Veterans such as Arturo Ripstein, Jaime Humberto Hermosillo, Jorge Fons, and Felipe Cazals reached new creative heights, and an impressive group of newcomers including Luis Estrada, Julián Hernández, Carlos Carrera, and Juan Mora Catlett initiated their careers with a series of skillfully-made, uniquely personal documentaries, shorts, and feature films. Mexican movies attracted large domestic audiences and were screened at international film festivals in Berlin, Cannes, Venice, Havana, Toronto, and Chicago. Two films from this period, *Doña Herlinda and Her Son* (1985) and *Like Water for Chocolate* (1992), were big hits in multiple countries across the globe. Then early in the 2000s, directors Alejandro González Iñárritu and Alfonso Cuarón, both of whom would go on some years later to win Academy Awards, excited critics and audiences with their edgy, unconventional films *Amores perros* (2000) and *Y tu mamá también* (2001).

Many of these young filmmakers, notably Cuarón and future three-time Academy Award-winning cinematographer Emmanuel Lubezki, received their training at one of Mexico's two superb film schools, the Centro Universitario de Estudios Cinematográficos (CUEC) and the Centro de Capacitación (CCC). Both CUEC and CCC, founded in 1963 and 1975 respectively, boasted excellent faculty, professional facilities, and substantial financial support from the government. Their rigorous, multi-year programs began with general courses and advanced to specialization in directing, cinematography, screenwriting, editing, postproduction, and other areas of filmmaking.

Especially important to the resurgence in Mexican cinema but not always adequately recognized in histories of the period are the contributions of a closely bonded group of women filmmakers. The decline in the 1970s of the powerful, male-dominated industry unions made possible broader female participation behind the camera. For decades, explicitly sexist policies had restricted the kinds of jobs women could pursue; one union regulation prohibited them from serving as assistant directors and another barred them from even touching a camera. With the collapse of union controls, however, female crew members appeared more frequently on major industry productions. Women also took advantage of enrollment opportunities at the film schools. Only one female student had entered CUEC during its first year of operation; by the end of the 1980s, the majority of students at CCC were women. Many of them became working directors, writers, cinematographers, set designers, and editors.

Among the talented new women directors of that time were Busi Cortés, Dana Rotberg, Maryse Sistach, Guita Schyfter, María Elena Velasco, and—María Novaro. The daughter of a well-known publisher and poet, Novaro studied sociology at the national university before pursuing her longstanding interest in film. Like Cuarón (who was her classmate), she attended the five-year program at CUEC, where she fell in love with the mechanics of filmmaking. Coupled with the directing, she has written or co-written, edited or co-edited, and closely supervised the cinematography of each of her films. Two early short films, *Una isla rodeada de agua* (*An Island Surrounded by Water*, 1985) and *Azul celeste* (*Sky Blue*, 1987), gained her admittance to the directors' union (only the fourth woman to do so), received multiple awards, and helped to secure financing for her first feature film *Lola* (1989).

As was also the case with the other female directors, Novaro had not entered the industry to just continue making movies that relegated women to the stereotypical roles of suffering mother or treacherous harlot but rather to challenge all the outdated assumptions regarding gender expectations and national identity. *Lola* documents the struggles of a single working-class mother to raise a young daughter while *Danzón*, Novaro's second feature film from 1991, celebrates another working-class woman's assertion of social and sexual agency. Subsequent films, all of which center around strong women characters, deal with such subjects as violence against women, indigenous culture, Alzheimer's disease, herbal medicine, class disparity, and ecological awareness. Often Novaro intentionally references traditional film genres but always with a unique, personal approach.

In a career spanning five decades she has won three Ariel Awards (Mexico's Oscar equivalents), taught courses at CCC, and served as a governmental film agency official. Her body of work constitutes one of the hallmarks of the so-called New Mexican Cinema. This book, which includes a biographical profile, detailed reading of each feature film, and summary critical assessment, examines the films in terms of their thematic and stylistic cohesion. Hopefully it will increase the attention among English-speaking critics and audiences that María Novaro so clearly merits.

Biographical Profile

The fabled Golden Age of Mexican cinema was coming to a close just as María Novaro's young life was beginning. From the late 1930s to the early 1950s, Mexico's film industry enjoyed a burst of artistic creativity and popular success that rivaled the glories of Hollywood. An extraordinary gathering of talent came together on both sides of the camera to produce a steady flow of pictures that were technically polished, well-acted, and socially relevant. At its height, the Mexican moviemaking business constituted the nation's third largest industry, employed about 32,000 workers, occupied four major studios, and delivered product to approximately 1500 theaters throughout the country.[1] "Not only was Mexico the epicenter of cinematic production in Latin America," writes film scholar Chloe Roddick, "but films made during the period also garnered international recognition, as well as box-office success at home."[2]

Several different factors explain and define the achievements of the Golden Age. First and foremost was a combination of positive economic developments. General economic prosperity under the presidencies of Manuel Ávila Camacho (1940-46) and Miguel Alemán Valdéz (1946-52) encouraged more ticket buyers, and governmental support of the industry helped with production costs. International market trends related to World War II also played an important part. The disruption in wartime European film production and distribution, combined with Hollywood's increased emphasis on homefront pictures with limited international appeal, strengthened demand for Mexican films throughout Latin America. At the same time, the United States government, via the Office of the Coordinator for Inter-American Affairs (OCIAA) under the leadership of Nelson Rockefeller, provided material assistance in the hope that Mexico would produce anti-Axis films sympathetic to the Allies, an investment that paid off when Mexico declared war against the Axis powers on June 1, 1942. Not only did the United States help to modernize equipment and facilities, but so also did it release a valuable supply of raw film stock. According to historian Linda B. Hall, "The OCIAA gave the Mexican movie industry a huge boost by providing 45 million feet of virgin film at a time when celluloid was a strategic material and movie film a product almost completely monopolized, in terms of distribution to Latin America, by the United States."[3] In contrast to Mexico's windfall, production rival Argentina, which was seen as supportive of Nazi Germany, received no film at all.

Ready to take advantage of this fertile environment was a wealth of talent from theater, art, literature, and entertainment. Among the newly anointed movie stars who drew big audiences throughout the Golden Age were Pedro Armendáriz, Arturo de Córdoba, Mario Moreno ("Cantinflas"), María Félix, Pedro Infante, Jorge Negrete, Marga López, Columba Domínguez, Andrea Palma, David Silva, Roberto Cañedo, and Luis Aguilar. As the center of the Spanish-speaking film industry, Mexico also inspired top foreign performers to immigrate there in search of greater career opportunities, most notably Sara Montiel, Libertad Lamarque, and María Antonieta Pons from Spain, Argentina, and Cuba respectively. Even Dolores del Río, who had become a major star in Hollywood, returned home to make such classics of the period as *Flor Silvestre* (1943), *María Candelaria* (1943), *Las abandonadas* (1944), and *La otra* (1946).

Creating whole new genres for the actors were outstanding writers like José Revueltas, Mauricio Magdaleno, Luis Alcoriza, and Álvaro Custodio. The *ranchera* film combined rural settings with music, comedy, and romance to tell somewhat conservative stories celebrating agrarian harmony and patriarchal authority. Situated in an urban underworld of night clubs and brothels the *rum-*

bera or *cabaretera* genre, which María would humorously salute in her own film *Danzón*, blended tropical music performances with tales of romantic betrayal and revenge. Although not newly conceived, the Mexican *film noir* and melodrama pictures also dealt with social mores and conflicts in ways that engaged contemporary audiences.

Handling these stories with extraordinary skill and artistry was a corps of talented directors that included Julio Bracho, Juan Orol, Emilio "El Indio" Fernandez, Roberto Gavaldón, Alejandro Galindo, Matilde Landeta, Ismael Rodríguez, Alberto Gout, Gilberto Martínez Solares, and (toward the end of the era) Luis Buñuel. Aided by cinematographers such as Rosalío Solano, Alex Phillips, and the legendary Gabriel Figueroa, they developed distinctive personal styles linked loosely by their vivid imagery, flexible narrative design, and superior production values. They also initiated a collective exploration of Mexican identity (*Mexicanidad*) that has continued through the work of each generation of filmmakers that has followed.

Tangentially involved in his country's Golden Age of cinema was María Novaro's father Octavio, who wrote four motion picture screenplays for film comedian Tin Tan. Known also by his real name of Germán Valdéz, Tin Tan introduced the character of the *pachuco*, the zoot suit-wearing urban rogue who fractures language and decorum in the various schemes that propel him through one disaster after another. "He does not have a repertoire of tried and true jokes," explains cultural essayist Carlos Monsiváis, "nor has he timed the rhythm of his comical phrases. His allies are the ferocity of the gesture, the aggressiveness of the word, an enthusiasm for chaos, a sentimentality dissolved by irony, and a lack of respect for solemnity and its natural ally, the sense of propriety."[4] His films usually parodied classical literature or other contemporary films—takeoffs on everything from the Cinderella and

Sleeping Beauty fairy tales to *The Phantom of the Opera* and *María Candelaria*. Broadly constructed, the plots mostly provided opportunities for Tin Tan to sing, dance, gyrate, improvise, and engage in linguistically tortured verbal rants. A contemporary of Cantinflas, he developed a screen character decidedly more cynical, aggressive, insolent, and amorous. Crafting stories for that character to inhabit was fun and easy to do, like building a treehouse from a given set of directions.

But Octavio Novaro Fiora was more than just the occasional writer of Tin Tan comedies. Born on October 26, 1910, in Guadalajara, he was also a successful poet, publisher, professor, and diplomat. The son of Italian immigrants from Liguria, he studied law at the Universidad Nacional Autónoma de México (UNAM) and became a firm supporter of the reform-minded government of President Lázaro Cárdenas (1934-40). As part of his involvement in leftist politics, Octavio helped to establish several schools for the children of working-class families. Anti-clerical and progressive, they stressed science and the humanities and featured such special curricular components as sex education. Although the schools were later dismantled during the conservative, church-backed presidency of Miguel Alemán, Octavio's commitment to education and liberalism remained firm. "My dad was a socialist," María has stated with matter-of-fact pride.[5]

Around that same time, Octavio met and married María Luisa Peñalosa, whose own prosperous family had long been supporters of right-wing dictator Porfirio Díaz and his three decades of governmental control (1876-1911). Despite the differences in their backgrounds, the couple shared an independence of spirit, appreciation of the arts, and a devotion to each other. Also María Luisa's political views were much more liberal than those of her parents. Their first son, Octavio Augusto Novaro Peñalosa, was born on July 4, 1939, in Mexico City, followed quickly by two more sons, Luis and Gabriel, and a daughter who died in her infancy.

Octavio Novaro was a poet, publisher, teacher, and diplomat.

The Novaros valued education and culture; the children were encouraged to read widely and learn multiple languages. As the sibling role model, Octavio Augusto distinguished himself early in his schooling as an outstanding student especially skilled in science and mathematics. Ultimately graduating from UNAM with bachelor's, master's, and doctorate degrees, he would become honored and famous for his academic achievements to the same extent that María would for her artistic ones. A theoretical physicist, he developed several catalysts and patents used in the petrochemical industry, received the National Prize for Arts and Sciences and the UNESCO Science Prize, was named a lifetime member of The National College, taught for many years at UNAM, and conducted postdoctoral research in multiple foreign countries. Fluent in Spanish, French, English, Italian, and Portuguese, he also spoke some Chinese, Japanese, German, and Russian.

While beginning his illustrious young family, Octavio *père* worked as a staff writer for the prestigious Mexico City newspaper *La Prensa*. During World War II, he was one of the few Mexican reporters to cover events from Europe. Headquartered in London, he faced the very real dangers of the German Luftwaffe's blitz attack, which could bring death not only from the initial bomb explosions but also from the building collapses and fires which came afterwards. "In London, as the raids continued," writes historian Erik Larson, "the mundane challenges of daily life became wearing, like the endless dripping of rainwater through roofs perforated by shrapnel."[6] Food was rationed, electricity and gas outages happened regularly, and no one could ever get enough sleep during the nightly bombardments. Well aware of the situation, María Luisa worried about her husband's safety and struggled to care for their sons without him. Even with the help of her family, she found the separation to be stressful and was happily relieved when Octavio returned unscathed to Mexico City.

Sometime after the end of the war, Octavio wrote an article critical of the new president Miguel Alemán and was promptly fired from the newspaper. However, because *La Prensa* was a labor cooperative, Octavio and his brother Luis, who had been dismissed as well, were entitled to substantial financial compensation. Pooling the money, they founded a publishing company known at first as Novaro Editores-Impresores and later as Editorial Novaro. Almost immediately, the enterprise became hugely successful, specializing in comic books, both original Spanish-language series and translations of popular titles from DC, Dell, Gold Key, and Archie Comics. Among the American entries published by Editorial Novaro were Batman, Superman, Bugs Bunny, Tarzan, Popeye, Roy Rogers, Blondie, and Hopalong Cassidy; original characters included Kalimán, Fantômas, Starman el Libertario, and Chanoc.

With printing facilities located on three different continents, the company also published books, encyclopedias, technical manuals, paperbacks, coloring books, dictionaries, textbooks, and posters. Distinguished by their bright colors and lively text, the brothers' comic books dominated the market; many Spanish-speaking children around the world first engaged with the printed word courtesy of a Novaro publication. Resembling the imposing iron fortress of one of its superhero stories, the company headquarters spread over an entire city block in the industrial neighborhood of Naucalpan, and the main entrance logo consisted of a gigantic metal gear emblazoned with the letter "N." (During the late 60s, Octavio's old nemesis Miguel Alemán headed a financial group that took over a share of the business, but the family reasserted full control in the 80s with Octavio's sons Gabriel and Luis assuming responsibility for general interest and technical/educational publications respectively. The printing of comic books has been discontinued, but to this day, Novaro Editorial remains a family enterprise.)

Octavio may have been a socialist in theory, yet in practice he was also a savvy capitalist focused on profit and growth. Concurrent with the birth of his daughter María Novaro Peñalosa on September 11, 1950, was the acquisition of a considerable family fortune. "I was born at a time when my family started doing well, financially speaking . . . with a silver spoon in my mouth," María has admitted candidly.[7] Coupled with that material privilege was the fact that the brothers doted on her. Again, she confirms, "I was very spoiled by my three older brothers."[8] Like the boys, she was encouraged to be imaginative, independent, and curious about other people and places. When her sister Beatriz was born three years later on June 13, 1953, she had the perfect playmate and accomplice for her adventures. Similar in physical appearance and artistic inclinations, the sisters forged a bond that has endured from adolescence to adulthood, through overlapping careers and personal lives.

They also shared an early enthusiasm for movies. "As far back as I can remember," María told journalist Robert Ellsworth, "my favorite activity was filmgoing."[9] However, by the time she and Beatriz began to discover cinema, the Golden Age was nearly finished, done in by television, a weakening of government support, the reclaiming of post-war markets by the Motion Picture Association of America (MPAA), and the consolidation of Mexican theater ownership under the control of William Jenkins, a controversial American businessman who favored the importation of movies from the United States. According to Linda B. Hall, "The number of Mexican films [shown domestically] was back up to 85 in 1955, but these movies had more to do with formula than with art and were mostly silly comedies, weepy melodramas, U.S.-style westerns, and more Mexican *comedias rancheras*, dance features, and hero-style adventures about cowboys (and even wrestlers) as the principal productions."[10] Although the quality of new first-run features may have been quite poor, María watched the older classics on television, captivated by the camera work, the expansive plots, the bravura acting, the visual rhythms, and above all, the exploration of what it meant to be a Mexican. She may also have seen one or two pictures featuring her uncle, the "very handsome" actor Tito Novaro. María would remember all of it as she later learned to write, direct, photograph, and edit films herself.

María and Beatriz also found creative stimulation in the artistic and literary activity that surrounded their father because despite his status as an influential publishing mogul, Octavio Novaro was a poet at heart. Author of a book of verse titled *Inventario de cenizas* (*Inventory of Ashes*) with illustrations by Moreno Capdevila and vivid imagery forged from "palabras de fósforo" ("words like matches"), he was a member of the Group of Eight, an informal literary alliance that included Alejandro Avilés, Roberto Cabral del Hoyo, Honorato Magaloni Duarte, Efrén Hernández, and Rosario Castellanos. Javier Peñalosa Calderón, Maria Luisa's brother and a contributor to Editorial Novaro's "Illustrious Lives" book series, and his wife, the famous poet and literary critic Dolores Castro, were also members.

The group often met for spirited readings at the spacious Novaro residence, and María felt that it was all "very natural, let's say, the relationship of an intellectual, artistic world of good people, people with a good heart."[11] For an appreciative audience that frequently consisted of such prominent guests as future Nobel Prize-winning author Octavio Paz before he and the girls' father drifted apart, María and Beatriz would sing, dance, and recite verse, entirely comfortable amid the flow of adult debate and conversation.

With his resources and position, Octavio often financially supported those writers in need of help, what María characterized as "sheltering the others."[12] Many of the individuals within the circle went on to become pillars of academia, editing anthologies, serving on official arts committees, and like Dolores Castro and Octavio, teaching at various universities. María's own future involvement in academia as both film school professor and director of the Instituto Mexicano de Cinematografía (IMCINE) was almost inevitable given this intense early exposure.

An interruption in the Novaros' comfortable household routine occurred in the early 1960s when Octavio, who had never lost his interest in politics, was named by President Adolfo López Mateos (1958-64) as Mexico's Ambassador to Switzerland. While the older boys at university remained behind, the rest of the family, including María and Beatriz, made the journey to Europe. The culture shock was extreme. Because she spoke some French, María was sent to a Catholic boarding school in the western, French-speaking part of the country, and Beatriz stayed in the German-speaking capital of Bern with her mother and father.

María's educational experience was unpleasant, as bad as anything she had seen in movies about repressive convent schools. "Life with the nuns was a big shock," she has stated, recalling the harsh discipline, joyless demeanor, and narrow-minded beliefs of her teachers.[13] Since both her father and to a lesser degree her mother were atheists, the family had never practiced a religion, and

María's Swiss schooling drove her even further from the church. To ease her loneliness, she began to keep a diary, where she closely observed her surroundings, taking note of "other cultures, other modes, other climates."[14] She also used the journal to analyze her own culture from another perspective and to consider all the things she missed about Mexico and would be sure to celebrate in the films to come, including a kind of native folk spirituality at odds with strict religious dogma.

If María found life in Switzerland difficult, for ten-year-old Beatriz it was miserable. Not only did she miss her sister, but she also suffered from the cold, the prolonged winter darkness, and the brusqueness of the Swiss people. Her depression grew so severe that a child psychiatrist recommended a return to familiar faces and to the sun. Octavio agreed and brought the family home. Even though she was more than happy to leave the nuns, María always believed there had been some educational value in experiencing a different way of life and in learning to structure ideas in a different language.

Back in Mexico City, María entered *preparatoria*, the grades 10-12 high school program, which consisted of a general academic curriculum for the first two years and then a specialization in either the physical or social sciences for the last year. "I wanted to be an engineer," she has recollected. "I pictured myself making roads and bridges . . . flying over the country and making drawings of a great network of roads and bridges."[15] That dream foundered, however, when she checked out the UNAM engineering department as part of an exploratory visit. "UNAM was brutally close-minded about women in engineering," she discovered, as the male students howled in protest while she toured the facilities.[16] Rather than to just then fight the entrenched discrimination which she would later encounter again as a woman filmmaker, she decided to shift her academic focus to social science.

It was during her last year of *preparatoria*, on October 2, 1968, that María, like everyone else in the country, learned of the government massacre of hundreds of students (mostly from UNAM and the National Polytechnic Institute) at the Plaza de las Tres Culturas in the Tlatelolco section of Mexico City. Over 10,000 students and sympathetic neighborhood residents had gathered peacefully to protest President Gustavo Díaz Ordaz's violent suppression of previous demonstrations and his diversion of government funds to support the 1968 Mexico City Olympic Games scheduled for later in the month. With helicopters hovering overhead, soldiers from the Mexican Armed Forces along with members of a secret government security force called the Olympia Battalion sealed off the plaza and began firing indiscriminately. For several hours they continued the assault, which included machine guns from the rooftops, sniper shooting, and door to door searches of the nearby apartment buildings. Among the hundreds killed were innocent bystanders, neighbors, and people in the wrong place at the wrong time. State-controlled media reported that armed demonstrators had begun the firefight, but most independent observers knew the truth. For María, the events of October, 1968, acted as an accelerant in her growing disgust with the ruling Partido Revolucinario Institucional (PRI) and her steady movement toward political radicalization.

The following year, María like her father and brothers before her, entered UNAM, still reeling from the massacre of its students. Enrolling in the College of Political and Social Sciences, she chose sociology as her major field of study. "I was eager to change the world for real, and sociology seemed like a way to do it," she has explained.[17] In between reading Comte and Durkheim, she attended student political meetings and cultural events. More than the formal classes, she loved the social fieldwork—the research and the interviews. Learning to interact constructively with others, she always felt, was excellent preparation for making movies.

After graduation from UNAM, María's interests in film and leftist politics followed along parallel lines. Career possibilities for her particular discipline were limited to working in a government agency or teaching, and she was not interested in either option. "Job opportunities as a sociologist were dreadful to me," is how she characterized the dilemma.[18] Instead, she found a related job helping a documentary crew research a film about the women of a poor Mexico City neighborhood. Delighted with the work, she realized that filmmaking could be a real vocational possibility: "I fell in love with film. And I thought if these people can make movies, so can I."[19] That experience led her to join the film collective Cine-Mujer, begun by Rosa Marta Fernández in 1975 as an association between student filmmakers and feminists from the fields of sociology, anthropology, and political science. "Made up exclusively of women and focused on women's issues," writes Elissa J. Rashkin in her book *Women Filmmakers in Mexico: The Country of Which We Dream*, "the collective was also strongly Marxist in orientation, locating the oppression suffered by women within the broader context of class struggle."[20] The group made films dealing with abortion, rape, prostitution, community activism, workers' unions, and domestic labor. In addition to Fernández, collective members included Beatriz Mira, Maricarmen de Lara, and María Eugenia Tamés. As teachers and role models, the women introduced María to the mechanics of filmmaking. "I fell in love with the camera, I fell in love with the Nagra, I fell in love with the Moviola," she has remarked, referring to the cinematic apparatus by which 16mm films were shot, recorded, and edited.[21]

Thoroughly hooked, María decided to attend film school for more detailed and comprehensive instruction. Starting over in a new professional training program is hard enough but for María, in her mid-20s and the mother of two young children, it was especially challenging. Throughout the many print and video interviews María has given over the years, she has mentioned nothing—other than the surname Chávez—about the father of her son Santiago and daughter Mara. Clearly, however, he was not in the picture at this time, and she was raising the children without any paternal help. A solution emerged from within the alternative lifestyle she had adopted.

During the 70s, María's left-leaning politics had grown increasingly more radical. After helping to organize peasant groups in rural Mexico, she became a full-blown Maoist. "I was a clandestine militant," she confirmed with a degree of self-deprecating humor many years later. "I had my alias. There was a moment when I was very, very seriously involved."[22] Along with the adoption of a *nom de guerre* and the doctrinaire discipline, she learned valuably to exist without her bourgeois privilege and to share rudimentary living conditions with all types of people. By the time she decided on film school, María was living in a commune, and it was that arrangement that made her study possible. She would work in the mornings and attend class in the afternoons while other commune members looked after Santiago and Mara. "And my kids have reproached me for it my entire life," she has said only half-jokingly.[23]

The program she entered at the Centro Universitario de Estudios Cinematográficos (CUEC) was founded in 1963 as part of UNAM's cultural affairs division and became a separate department seven years later with its own budget and faculty. Again according to Rashkin, "the school emphasized social responsibility, film as a means of critical inquiry and research, and collective rather than individual (auteur) production."[24] It was a rigorous five-year program with intensive training in all aspects of film production—from cinematography to editing—and with the expectation that students would work on classmates' films in various capacities. Esther Morales Gávez was the first and only woman admitted to the program in its founding year; she was followed in 1964 by Marcela Fernández Violante. They were the exceptions, the only women students to enter CUEC during the 60s, but upon María's admission over a decade later, fully 40% of the student enrollment was female.

Having collaborated successfully with other women in Cine-Mujer, María quickly bonded with a tight peer group composed of Marie-Christine Camus, Silvia Otero, Guadalupe Sánchez, and Rosa María Mendez. Because they were outgoing and attractive, the male students took to calling them the "Celluloid Nymphs," a name they shortened and appropriated in referring to themselves as the "Nymphs." Completing many of the school assignments together, they shared areas of expertise and supported each other's ambitions. María has credited Marie-Christine Camus in particular with showing her how to properly frame a composition.

María's film school training inspired a love for the mechanics of moviemaking.

As in most film schools of that period, students at CUEC progressed from scripting exercises through super 8mm to the production of sound-synced 16mm films. María's first four films, all from 1981 and all shot in the 8mm format, were *Lavaderos* (*The Washing Places*), *Sobre las olas* (*Above the Waves*), *De encaje y azúcar* (*Of Lace and Sugar*), and *Es la primera vez* (*It's the First Time*).

Combining lyrical imagery with documentary realism, they were well photographed and crisply edited. Over the next two years, she wrote, directed, photographed, and edited two 16mm black and white short films titled *7AM* and *Querida Carmen* (*Dear Carmen*) and co-directed/photographed the three-minute black and white 16mm film *Conmigo la pasarás muy bien* (*You'll Have a Good Time with Me*) with her friend Marie-Christine Camus. As per CUEC program requirements, she also joined the crews of several other student productions. Between 1982 and 1983, she edited one film, photographed two, and both photographed as well as edited four others. It was essential training, and the instructors' insistence on technical mastery helps to explain the superior production values that would distinguish all the Novaro feature films to come.

María's fourth-year student film, completed in 1985, was titled *Una isla rodeada de agua* (*An Island Surrounded by Water*). A feminist variation on Juan Rulfo's novel *Pedro Páramo* in which a man journeys to his deceased mother's hometown to find his unknown father, it tells the story of a young girl who travels from the Guerrero coast to the mountains in search of the mother who abandoned her. María's own daughter Mara Chávez played the girl, and friends Silvia Otero, Conchis Arroyo, Yolanda Ocampo, and Alejandro Marín also appeared as cast members. With synchronized sound, color photography, and a running time of 28 minutes, the film was a considerable advancement over the earlier projects and gave clear evidence of a budding cinematic talent. María wrote, directed, and edited the film while frequent collaborator Marie-Christine Camus provided the cinematography. Conforming to María's newly realized preference for the narrative format, *Una isla* introduces several themes and motifs that would be developed further in the feature films—the self-actualizing journey, the assertion of female agency, the question of identity, and the exploration of motherhood. Similarly, the Novaro penchant for lyrical interludes surfaces memorably here through the viewpoint of the little girl. Because she has blue eyes, she sees everything in different colors—the sea in purple, the sky in yellow—during fantasy-like sequences beautifully photographed by Camus. This was also the first of many times she would set the story in a politically volatile location and let the camera linger on street graffiti saluting the government opposition (in this case, the leftist leaders Lucio Cabañas and Genaro Vásquez, who led armed uprisings in Guerrero throughout the 70s).

Although only a student production, *Una isla* received a great deal of positive critical attention. Earning María the first of three Ariel Awards (Mexico's equivalent of the Academy Awards), it was named Best Short Fiction Film by the Mexican Academy of Cinematographic Arts and Sciences. Purchased by the Museum of Modern Art in New York for its permanent collection, it also won a special jury award at the Clermont-Ferrand International Short Film Festival. Equally important for her professional career, its success brought job offers and opportunities to work within the industry. "That little short film opened several doors for me," María has gratefully acknowledged.[25]

Meanwhile, as she prepared her tentatively titled fifth-year thesis film *La Pervertida* (*The Pervert*), María ran into problems with CUEC's administration. Marcela Fernández Violante, recently named department dean, had issues with María and several other students including Alfonso Cuarón, Emmanuel "Chivo" Lubezki, and Luis Estrada. The dynamic was fraught with intergenerational tension. Fernández Violante, whom María has described as a "very, very conflictive person,"[26] had directed two short films and four features before taking over the CUEC leadership but was finding it difficult to obtain funding and distribution for new projects. The students, with more flexible, less politically rigid styles than her own, were clearly on the rise. Cuarón would go on to win four Academy Awards, including two as Best Director, for *Gravity* (2013) and *Roma* (2018); Lubezki would win three consecutive Best Cinematography Academy Awards for *Gravity* (2013), *Birdman* (2014), and *The Revenant* (2015); and multiple Ariel Award-winning director Luis Estrada would make such critical and commercial hits as *A Wonderful World* (2006), *Infierno* (2010), and *The Perfect Dictatorship* (2014). But in 1985, each was one of six students whose formal graduation was blocked by Fernández Violante for a variety of spurious bureaucratic reasons.

One can only surmise that professional jealousy played an operative part in her actions. Fernández Violante made two more features, both of which were ignored by audiences and dismissed by critics. Her final picture, *Golpe de suerte* (*Stroke of Luck*), in 1991 had to be personally financed and was denied distribution through official artistic channels. Today Fernández Violante's reputation is contestable. Rather than receiving recognition solely for her own accomplishments, she also figures negatively in the professional backstories of the students whose careers she tried to thwart. To be remembered as the grim martinet who denied CUEC certification to some of your country's most promising cinematic talent because of a few unreturned tripod screws (Novaro's alleged offense) or a frayed sound cable is to not fully be remembered at all.

Despite her inability to complete *La Pervertida* and to receive a diploma, María finished film school in 1985 and went to work immediately as an editor and sound mixer. Impressed with the student films, director Alberto Cortés hired her to be assistant director on his 1986 feature *Amor a la vuelta de la esquina* (*Love Around the Corner*), which won an Ariel for Best First Work. The story of a prostitute on the run from prison, it gave María plenty of experience with nighttime shooting in Mexico City and brought her together with future collaborator Rodrigo García, who was working as assistant to cinematographer Guillermo Navarro. They bonded over a shared family background in the arts (Rodrigo was the son of Nobel Prize-winning author Gabriel García Márquez) and vowed to work together again in the near future.

Then, in a touch of irony, another department at UNAM, the Dirección de Actividades Cinematográficas (Division of Cinematic Activities), asked María to contribute a half hour film to the anthology picture called *Historias de ciudad* (*Tales of the City*) which it was producing. The fact that the university would finance a film for commercial distribution gives a sense of Mexico's multi-faceted funding model for film production, a system that combined investments from educational institutions, independent producers, and government agencies (the Instituto Mexicano de Cinematografía or IMCINE, the Fondo de Fomento a la Calidad Cinematográfica or FFCC, and the Banco Cinematográfico before it was privatized). At one time or another, María would tap each of these sources for her feature films, but the budget for what would become *Azul celeste* (*Sky Blue*) was a relatively simple matter. And because María had been admitted to the directors' union on the basis of *Una isla rodeada de agua*, there was no problem in hiring her as director. The issue was with women elsewhere on the crew. Since the bylaws of the major filmworkers' union Sindicato de Trabajadores de la Producción Cinematográfica (STPC) stated that women literally could not touch the camera, she was not able to hire Marie-Christine Camus as cinematographer and went with Santiago Navarrete instead. It would not be the last such trouble with STPC.

There were no similar kinds of restrictions on women screenwriters, and María asked her sister Beatriz to help with a re-write on *Azul celeste*. Following an educational path similar to María's, Beatriz had studied theater as an undergraduate at UNAM before entering film school. In her case, it was the Centro de Capacitación Cinematográfica (CCC), founded in 1975 as the country's second national center for film study, and the area of concentration was screenwriting. She and María worked well together in polishing the story of a young woman, eight months pregnant, who comes to Mexico City looking for the baby's father. Knowing only the color of his house, she wanders randomly through the streets in an exploration of the city that would be extended in the sisters' first feature film script *Lola*. As with *Una isla*, María touched on the themes of identity, discovery, abandonment, and motherhood. Completed in 1987, *Azul celeste* gave María her first experience managing a professional crew and directing in 35mm. Among the cast members were Cheli Godínez, who would also appear in *Lola* and *Danzón*, and Gabriela Roel, who would co-star in *El jardín del Edén*.

Almost immediately the sisters went to work on their next project, the screenplay for *Lola*. Once again, it was the story of an abandoned mother, this time a young street vendor named Lola whose rock singer boyfriend has left her to care for their six-year-old daughter alone. Ill-equipped to handle the responsibilities, she struggles to provide proper food, supervision, and safety. Several bad decisions later, Lola leaves the little girl in the care of her grandmother before having second thoughts and returning to make another, inconclusive attempt at motherhood.

Deciding she needed more help in shaping the final script, María applied for and received a scholarship to attend the International School for Cinema and Television (EICTV) located just outside Havana, Cuba. A dream project of President Fidel Castro and Gabriel García Márquez, the EICTV was launched in December, 1986, as a center for seminars, lectures, workshops, and actual film production. According to his biographer Gerald Martin, García Márquez "came to specialize in story-telling and script-writing at the new school— he gave a regular course on how to write a story, then how to turn the story into a film script. Visitors and teachers over the next few years would include Francis Ford Coppola, Gillo Pontecorvo, Fernando Solanas, and Robert Redford."[27] María was there during the residencies of both García Márquez and Redford, and she considered each man to be a much-valued mentor. Explaining their differences in an interview a few years later, she recalled that one day García Márquez (or "Gabo" as he was nicknamed) shared how he had attempted unsuccessfully three times to shoot a complicated underwater scene for a movie that he himself was making and how he was about to try again. "We have to fight for our dreams," he insisted.[28] Asked if he would do the same, Redford answered that he would look for an equally effective alternate scene and shoot that. María professed to understand both viewpoints—the stubborn determination and the practical flexibility. "I want Redford and I want Gabo in my life, in my imagination," she concluded.[29]

Skilled in English and familiar with the technical vocabulary of filmmaking, María became Redford's unofficial translator, accompanying him on trips around the country. During one of those excursions, Redford decided they could unobtrusively venture out among the spectators at a political event to soak up local atmosphere. Not only was he immediately recognized, but the crowd chanted his name so loudly that the noise drowned out the words of the speakers. It was one more lesson for María, in case she needed it, on the power of cinema.

Over the course of their time together, Redford became so impressed with María's talent and dedication that he invited her to attend the young directors' workshop at his own Sundance Institute the following summer. Founded personally by Redford in 1981 and located far away from Hollywood in Park City, Utah, Sundance was designed to support independent filmmakers through informal classes, curated resources, expert advice, and personalized feedback from established artists. Prominent among the faculty members during María's visit were directors Sydney Pollack and Paul Mazursky, screenwriter Ivan Passer, and actress Sigourney Weaver; as a personal reciprocal favor to Redford, García Márquez was also there conducting a seminar on story design. Redford himself taught a class in directing actors, the nuances of which were enlightening to Novaro. "I never had one class at CUEC in directing actors," she remarked. "They didn't exist."[30]

Strange as it seemed at first to be talking to Hollywood celebrities about mutual production concerns, María ultimately found the dialogues to be insightful and useful. "In Sundance they regard Redford as a god, but I was very cynical," she admitted to a writer from the *Los Angeles Times*. "But I was wrong. He read my script for *Lola* and spent three afternoons with me. He gave me some brilliant ideas on how to direct the child in my film. I was very impressed. He really wants to help people."[31] There was also valuable advice from the other directors. "You can't make a mistake in casting," Mazursky told her, "it is primordial . . .80% of your characters' success is that you do a good casting."[32] Although Mexican film production at the time had no formal casting structure beyond the director telephoning actors with an offer, María took Mazursky's counsel to heart and would later conduct a major search for the young woman and little girl to play Lola and her daughter. (Her first choice for Lola was Elizabeth Peña, who was also attending Sundance after appearing in Mazursky's 1986 hit *Down and Out in Beverly Hills*, but although the two became good friends, schedules and budget did not permit them working together on María's first feature).

With the screenplay for *Lola* now having been workshopped and revised, María returned to Mexico to secure funding. Part of the money came from a Spanish Fifth Centennial cash prize she had won for *Azul celeste* and some more from a prize for *Lola*'s script. It was not the full amount needed but enough to start production. The producers were María's friend Dulce Kuri and husband Jorge Sánchez, the father of María's newest family member, a baby daughter named Lucero born in 1986. While Kuri and Sánchez sought the additional funding, María began to assemble her crew.

That was when the old trouble with STPC surfaced again. To clear the women she wanted, María arranged a meeting with union boss Sr. Palomino, whose first question to her was "What's gotten into you hags to make you want to do filmmaking?"[33] Rather than tolerate the misogyny, María excused herself immediately and vowed to work around the union opposition. Making use of a special industry provision, she registered her film under the authority of a labor cooperative, in this case the Cooperativa José Revueltas, and proceeded without the STPC sanction. Ultimately, Novaro's crew included women working as assistant directors, makeup artists, lighting technicians, art director, wardrobe designer, and assistant editor. For her cinematographer, she made good on that *Love Around the Corner* pledge and hired close friend Rodrigo García.

With Mazursky's casting advice firmly in mind, María had found just the right pair of actresses to play the tightly bonded mother and daughter of her story. Deciding wisely to cast the little girl first, she tested many experienced child performers before discovering a talented non-professional named Alejandra Vargas who was completely natural and unaffected in front of the camera. For Lola, she selected Leticia Huijara, a formally trained theater actress who nevertheless had unstudied presence and the right screen chemistry with Alejandra. "Since the tests with Leticia went well," recounted María, "I began to put her together with Alejandra. I wanted to see if they looked like mother and child . . . I took them both for ice cream in the park and saw that, in fact, they did make a good pair."[34]

In preparation for the actual filming, she initiated a series of video exercises to get the actors loose and relaxed in front of the camera. The goal was to counter what she saw as an inherent weakness in Mexican film performances: "This acting tradition that is very Mexican and Latin American, and that originally we inherited from Spain, is very exaggerated, very melodramatic. For many people in our countries good acting is considered being very spirited, saying things well, and not so much sincerity or making the character believable."[35] Instead, she showed her actors how to use body movement, gaze, and underplayed delivery to make their performances more authentic.

After more than two years of workshops, rewrites, funding quests, crew decisions, and casting searches, actual filming finally began in 1989. At Novaro's insistence, the settings were all real places rather than studio fabrications, and location shooting centered around Mexico City's Doctores and Roma neighborhoods. Still heavily damaged from the 1985 earthquake, the areas chosen for the movie mirrored the same collapse facing Lola. The result was a film that looked like a sociologically viable study of real life. "I love that in newer films since the 80s the frontiers between documentary and fiction are almost erased," María remarked in describing the film's narrative intent."[36]

By the time filming concluded, Jorge Sánchez had combined personal funds with a sufficient enough investment from IMCINE to finance postproduction. International and domestic distribution of the finished film was spaced out over several months. *Lola* premiered in December, 1989, at the Havana Film Festival, where it won a Coral Award for Best First Work. It also screened at the Toronto Festival of Festivals (1990), the Santa Barbara Film Festival (1991), and the Berlin International Film Festival (1991), winning that event's Forum of New Cinema Award. In his program notes for the Toronto festival, Piers Handling declared, "María Novaro's first feature is a simple and eloquent story of a relationship between a young mother and her daughter. Told with great sensitivity and understatement, the film is a stark and uncompromising take on modern Mexico and the problems that a modern, independent woman confronts in the face of a harsh and uncaring society."[37] After he saw the film in Havana, a reporter for *Variety* predicted, "If handled carefully, pic stands a fair chance on the arthouse circuit.[38]

Although it was not released for general distribution in Mexico until February of 1991, *Lola* was nominated for five Ariel Awards, winning in the categories of Best Supporting Actor (Roberto Sosa), Best Screenplay (Beatriz and María), and Best First Work (María). Initial critical reaction, however, was unfavorable; according to María, "The critics whacked me, they treated me really badly . . . all of them were male, they were absolutely tinged with a value judgment."[39] Reviewers objected to a vision of motherhood that did not fit the traditional notions of propriety. Alejandro Leal of the journal *El Universal* wrote that *Lola* was a glorification of "maternal irresponsibility."[40] Audiences also split along gender lines. Women tended to like the picture, but men did not. Because ticket prices were set by law just then at eight pesos, a film had to fill the massive theaters to do well, and *Lola* never achieved that kind of box office. Ironically, during its rerelease three years later after the huge success of *Danzón*, María's debut feature was warmly received by audiences and by some of the same critics who had disparaged it previously.

María in an informal publicity photo.

While still editing *Lola*, María had decided that her next film with Beatriz would be a total reversal in tone, an upbeat picture with a joyously independent woman at its center. "After all the emotions we had touched upon in Lola's story," she elaborated, "my heart was torn apart, and I felt like doing something completely the opposite. One of the first things we talked about was that it had to be a movie with a lot of color, with music, with dancing, with laughter."[41] Almost immediately they decided to take the old Golden Age *cabaretera* or dance hall genre and have fun with some of its more melodramatic elements. In the story they conceived, a single mother named Julia Solórzano, somewhat older than Lola and with a grown daughter, spends the evenings away from her job as a Mexico City telephone operator at the Salón Colonia indulging her passion for *danzón*, a seductive, formally partnered dance with Caribbean roots. When her regular partner Carmelo fails to appear one night, she takes a leave of absence and journeys to Veracruz to find him. Befriended by some drag queens she meets and by the prostitutes who reside at her hotel, Julia fails to locate Carmelo but enjoys a romantic fling with a handsome young seaman. Having grown from her experiences, she returns to Mexico City with renewed confidence and agency.

Novaro also knew that she wanted popular actress María Rojo to play Julia. Not only had the two women met a couple of years earlier at the Cuban film center, but also María had very much admired Rojo's performance in *Maria de mi corazón* (*Mary My Dearest*), a 1979 film directed by Jaime Humberto Hermosillo and written by García Márquez. "In *Danzón's* case, ever since we wrote the script, I had María Rojo in mind," María has confirmed. "I never stopped having her image in mind, her shape, her smile . . . her aura of being very real, of being a real woman."[42] However, IMCINE, which was providing a major piece of the funding, believed a younger actress would work better in the part; María insisted on her first choice, and María Rojo ultimately was selected. Additional financing came from Televisión Española, whose executives were content to let the director make her own casting decisions.

Once Rojo was on board, María began the familiar video exercises, not to get such an experienced actress comfortable in front of the camera but to study her movements, gestures, and reactions. As María remembered it, "I spent months going to the Salón Colonia, taping her dancing, watching her expressions, her smile, the angles of her face, her moods, knowing when she was uncomfortable, when she could be spontaneous, when something was bothering her."[43] Like Beatriz and María had done while writing the script, Rojo also carefully studied the *danzón*, becoming a highly skilled, elegantly assured dancer. That mastery coupled with Novaro's sense of how to best present her on film made for a very convincing portrayal.

With Rodrigo García again behind the camera, location shooting in Mexico City and Veracruz proceeded smoothly on what continued to be a happy and harmonious production. The film championed diversity, and that was the norm on set as well. When a dolly operator expressed discomfort with the drag queens, María playfully crowned him with a wig and suggested he get over it. Lightness of touch was the key to everything. The treacherous harlots of the *cabaretera* became hard-working prostitutes with children to raise, the *vedette* became a sweet-natured drag performer named Susy, and the violently macho Casanova morphed into a gentle young sailor heartbroken over the loss of Julia, who was herself neither victim nor manipulator but rather an intelligent working-class woman open to life's unexpected opportunities. "The part I enjoyed the most was getting Julia to meet people she normally wouldn't have known or come in touch with," explained María. "She is so open-minded and innocent that she doesn't have any preconceived ideas about people like prostitutes and transvestites. She learned things from them she may haven't learned living in her own sheltered world."[44]

As with all of her films, *Danzón* also afforded María the chance to further explore the Golden Age interest in Mexican identity, in the cultural traditions and social behaviors that make the country unique. Additionally, Julia's reverence for *danzón* is a kind of nostalgia for a more civil, more refined way of life. "Not simply a nostalgia for the heyday of the dance halls and the music," agreed María, "but for a Mexico that is being lost—thanks to the process of Americanization we are undergoing. I believe that it is Mexico, and a pride for what is Mexican, that must be defended."[45]

Danzón, in fact, packs a lot of ideas into what seems like a simple story. In the end, Novaro manages to celebrate artistic heritage, reflect on filmic conventions, and promote the personally important themes of female empowerment and solidarity. Novaro knew from the beginning that the project was special, buoyed throughout by a sense of elation that collapsed suddenly during postproduction editing when her father passed away. She was only somewhat consoled by the fact that he had lived to see his beloved daughters succeed in an art form that he himself had both practiced and appreciated.

In keeping with that success, *Danzón* soon began to roll up an impressive record of honors and awards. Included in the 1991 Directors' Fortnight section, it was the first Mexican film in fourteen years to be shown at the Cannes Film Festival. It also screened at the Chicago, Telluride, Toronto, Miami, Seattle, San Francisco, and Valladolid Film Festivals, won the Best Film award at New York City's Latin Film Festival, earned five ACE Awards (including Best Film, Director, and Actress) from the Association of Latin Entertainment Critics, and was nominated for three Ariel Awards. Sold for distribution in 45 countries, it attracted positive reviews from around the world. Joking that the plot "plays a bit like the Good Housekeeping version of a Pedro Almodóvar story," Janet Maslin of *The New York Times* also praised *Danzón* for its "eloquence" and the "unexpected sweetness" of María Rojo's performance.[46] Michael Wilmington, in the *Los Angeles Times*, wrote, "The colors shimmer, the actors play with warmth and sophistication, the entire movie seems to glide by. When the camera moves, which is in nearly every shot, it moves with an effortless grace and bewitching airiness that recalls a master musical-maker like Vincente Minnelli."[47] María's friend and mentor García Márquez pronounced that in grappling with Latin American problems, "she has been able to express them in a tone that is traditional."[48]

While Mexican cultural critics dithered over whether *Danzón* was feminist enough, domestic audiences fully embraced it. Released in Mexico toward the end of June, 1991, the film quickly became one of the top five box office hits of the year, outpacing

Robin Hood: Prince of Thieves and doing nearly as well as the first Tim Burton *Batman* picture. By the time its first run ended, *Danzón* had attracted nine million Mexican viewers, an extraordinary total for that period. María enjoyed visiting theaters where it was playing to talk with audiences about their reactions. "I wanted to take the men by surprise with this film—and they laughed a lot," she proudly recalled.[49] *Danzón* remains the film by which María Novaro is still mostly fondly remembered today in Mexico.

María Rojo and Daniel Rergis in a scene from *Danzón* (1991), Novaro's most popular film.

Given such financial success at home, it was not long before distributors in the United States took notice. After marketing reps caught the film at Telluride, Orion Classics picked up all U.S. rights to *Danzón* in a deal announced by *Variety* in October of 1991. Several months later, prior to a bankruptcy filing, Orion sold those rights to Sony Classics. To promote the subsequent mid-1992 U.S. release, María traveled with Jorge to both coasts for a round of interviews. In New York, she talked about the challenges of being a woman director, and in Los Angeles she discussed cultural differences between the two countries. Providing copy for the press packet, she wrote, "I know very well that things are going badly in the world today. I know very well that the future of all of us is full of dark clouds. Perhaps precisely for that reason I made *Danzón*."[50] While staying at the Bel Age Hotel in West Hollywood, she had preliminary conversations with studio executives about possibly making films in the United States but unlike her contemporaries Cuaron and Iñárritu, she never seriously pursued the overtures. Announcing a new movie to be shot in Mexico, she told *The Hollywood Reporter*, "I've been able to make the films I want, non-formula films, and I wouldn't lose that for anything."[51] Personal vision would always trump Hollywood production values.

Before embarking on that announced project, María shot *Otoñal* (*Autumnal*), a six minute, 35mm color short based on an idea by Argentinian cartoonist Joaquín Salvador Lavado Tejón (pen named Quino) and written by Dharma Reyes. Fanciful and somewhat impressionistic, it concerned ghosts and a woman who prefers to live in an imagined rather than a real world. The cast included Delia Casanova, Alicia del Lago, Miguel Angel Rodríguez, and, as a favor to the director, María Rojo. *Lola* alum Sigfrido Barjau returned as editor and against the wishes of her producers, María selected a woman, Lucia Olguín, to be cinematographer. The choice did not turn out exactly the way she had hoped. "The result wasn't very good," she confirmed. "It was her first filming, and it was a very complicated film ... which required a certain technical ability."[52] To make certain that women could obtain the experience needed for such work, she insisted in the future that each of her male cinematographers take on female assistants.

The next major production following *Otoñal* was a complex, overlapping narrative about three young women, two single mothers and an unattached American adventurer, who restart their lives in Tijuana. Liz, a Chicana art curator with limited Spanish-speaking ability, is there with her daughter to organize an exhibit on Chicano identity. Her friend Jane, a well-meaning but naïve American, arrives with notions of exotic lands and colorful customs while Serena, the recently widowed mother of two teenaged sons and a younger daughter, has moved north from Mexico City to earn a living as a portrait photographer. After meeting a handsome would-be migrant named Felipe, Jane decides to smuggle him across the border in a scheme that also involves Serena's oldest son. The title, *El jardín del Edén* (*The Garden of Eden*), refers to Felipe's as well as the various other characters' quests for sanctuary and fulfillment. A deep dive into border culture, the film also touched on issues of language, art, national identity, sisterhood, family, and frontier politics.

Beatriz Novaro co-wrote three feature films with her older sister María.

Just like their fictional characters, María and Beatriz lived in Tijuana for several months while they were writing the film, accompanied by Beatriz's two children and María's younger daughter Lucero. Mara and Santiago, who did not want to leave their school friends, stayed behind in Mexico City. In conducting the research essential to each of her films, María traveled widely throughout the region, crossing over into San Diego to scout locations for Felipe and Jane's time together "on the other side." It was an area that she had also visited as a young girl with her maternal grandmother to see aunts who had married American husbands whose inability to speak Spanish never stopped the older woman from addressing them in the language she assumed everyone could understand. What had changed over the years since then was the newly felt vibrancy of the border zone, the galvanic cultural hybridization that María captures so well in the film. "This is the future," she declared, "it is a dazzling thing."[53] In addition to research, the stay in Tijuana also provided a respite from the invasive public interest that had descended on María as a result of *Danzón's* overwhelming success. The media's obsession with her private life and with her husbands, so intense that it caused her to change phone numbers, had begun to interfere with her work.

The funding to begin actual production on *El jardín del Edén* came primarily from Canadian independent producers with Jorge Sánchez and Dulce Kuri cobbling together much of the rest of the two million dollar budget from IMCINE and other governmental sources. The easily secured Canadian investment was a mixed blessing. Along with their profit percentages, the producers wanted a substantial voice in casting and scripting decisions. Besides the appropriately selected Canadian actress Renée Coleman in the role of blond-haired, English-speaking Jane, they pushed for more Canadians in the other parts, even that of Felipe, the Mexican migrant eventually played by Bruno Bichir, brother of actors Demián and Odiseo Bichir. Another suggestion from the producers was to place less emphasis on the undocumented workers. María successfully resisted this misguided interference but failed to negotiate a contract provision giving her approval of the final edit—an oversight she would soon come to regret.

Despite the pressures on Novaro, Renée Coleman remembers the shoot as a congenial, collaborative affair. "It was all very civilized," she has stated. "The lunches were longer, and everything was slower, more casual."⁵⁴ As usual, there were also plenty of familiar faces among the relaxed company. Beatriz was still in Tijuana, María's daughter Lucero was playing Serena's daughter Paloma, and good friend Gabriela Roel, who had starred in *Azul celeste*, had the part of Serena. The presence of so many children on set made it all seem even more like an extended family. Since most of the cast and crew were staying at the same hotel, they quickly bonded into a tight professional unit fiercely loyal to Novaro. Although María was working with a new cinematographer, Eric Edwards, he was just as eager as she to set up complicated tracking shots in challenging terrain. The nighttime border photography and the city sequences are stunning.

Once filming had wrapped, however, María became concerned about the rough cut she and her veteran editor Sigfrido Barjau had assembled. "When she put the film together," says Coleman, "she was mortified. She realized it was her first failure."⁵⁵ There was too much emphasis on the Felipe-Jane relationship and too little connectivity between the various other plotlines. Rather than to share her reservations, the producers instead wanted to focus even more tightly on the romance angle. Without contractual approval of the final cut, María was unable to achieve the narrative balance she intended. Twenty minutes were ultimately cut from the reworked version she and Bajau submitted. "I love the movie, I love many things from that movie," María has confessed, "but I do see it and I feel there are things that remain a little bit disconnected."⁵⁶ Attentive viewing of *El jardín del Edén* reveals a much more successfully complex and cohesive film than María imagines, but she always remained dissatisfied: "It's not a movie about which I would say, 'I did the movie I wanted.' No."⁵⁷ Scholars, on the other hand, have continued to find it one of her most culturally and politically significant works.

El jardín del Edén was also adversely affected by an unfortunate new distribution/exhibition framework linked to the North American Free Trade Agreement. Signed in December, 1992, and implemented on January 1, 1994, NAFTA lifted tariffs on the majority of goods traded between the United States, Mexico, and Canada. Included in the list of products were motion pictures; neither quotas nor taxes of any kind would prevent American and Mexican films from competing under the same marketing parameters. Because domestic theaters were controlled by only three organizations and because those owners favored the big ticket sales of Hollywood blockbusters, Mexican pictures were squeezed. María was one of a group of prominent artists who petitioned the government for film industry exemptions but was told that movies were like T-shirts—if they were made well, they would sell. However, since the budget for an average Mexican film was exponentially smaller than that of a comparable American picture, it was difficult to match the scope, technology, and spectacle that attracted moviegoers. (Several years later filmmakers attempted to have the Mexican Congress pass a law to increase ticket prices so that a portion could be earmarked for domestic movie production, but Jack Valenti, the hard-charging CEO of the Motion Picture Association of America, and the Mexican theater owners successfully lobbied President Vicente Fox to oppose the legislation.)

Shot in 1993 and released domestically nearly two years later, *El jardín* suffered under the new system. With a handful of theater executives deciding if and when a picture would be shown, viewing opportunities were limited. "Released," in fact, paints too rosy a picture; "restricted" is a more accurate description of *El jardín*'s handling. María remembers that it screened at one Cinemark theater in Mexico City at two o'clock in the afternoon for two weeks only. "It's like it didn't exist in Mexico," she has noted with a mixture of resignation and regret.[58] Despite the abbreviated release, *El jardín del Edén* was nominated for six Ariel Awards, including Best Picture, Director, Original Story, and Actor (Bichir). International distribution, particularly in Spain, France, and Italy, yielded a much wider audience, a fact which prompted María and other Mexican moviemakers to tailor future films for export to Europe, South America, and Asia. That new marketing strategy allowed domestic production to eventually climb back to 100 films per annum from the low of four or five during the lean years of 1994-96.

Discouraged and disillusioned by the treatment of her third feature, María searched about for new projects. She made plans to film *Succulents*, an original script by Beatriz and Rosa Inicial, but abandoned the project after failing to find adequate funding. The Mexican financial crisis, brought about by President Ernesto Zedillo's mismanagement of the economy, had made the always scarce investment sources even harder to locate. "There was no money for films, funds weren't working out, everything was very, very, depressed," she explained.[59] On her own, María wrote a film adaptation of Carlos Montemayor's novel *War in Paradise*, a satirical treatment of the Mexican military that Montemayor told her would never get past the authorities. She also wrote an original screenplay titled *The List*, which brought a comic tone to her past as a militant leftist and which won two international awards. Nether project, however, was ever filmed.

Just as she had resigned herself after this five-year dry spell to not making any more movies, two separate incidents reaffirmed her career commitment. One was being asked to contribute a short segment to the 1998 documentary anthology *Enredando sombras* (*Entangling Shadows*), a 90 minute survey of Latin America's first century of cinema. Composed of eleven sections and two round-table discussions, the film boasted the participation of such directors as Ivan Trujillo, Edmundo Array, David Rodriguez, Juan Carlos Tabío, María's film school antagonist Marcela Fernández Violante, and Orlando Senna. María's segment was titled *Cuando comenzamos a hablar* (*When We Started Talking*) and dealt with the earliest Mexican sound films of the 1930s. Among the personalities interviewed for the anthology were her old friends García Márquez and Redford, Costa-Gavras, Pilar Miró, Maria Bethânia, and René Monclova.

The second and more material development was a grant she received from the Herbert Bals Fund. Founded in 1988 by the International Film Festival Rotterdam and named after its first director, the fund was designed to help young independent filmmakers, especially those from developing countries, move their projects from conceptualization to realization. María's grant was to facilitate completion of a script she had begun about two women on a road trip from Juarez to Belize. Tentatively titled *Rice and Beans* (after Belize's national dish), it would ultimately become her fourth feature, *Sin dejar huella* (*Without a Trace*).

Using part of the money to buy a truck, she left the children at home and set off on a two month journey that mirrored the route laid out in the script. The timing was significant. It was 1999, her marriage to Jorge Sánchez, which Renée Coleman remembered as strained during *El jardín,* had ended, and she was feeling, by her own account, "premenopausal."[60] Loaded up with cameras and notebooks, she found it restorative to routinely document everything seen and felt along the way. Gradually, the story took on new dimensions. "I thought of course of *Thelma and Louise*, which is a movie that I love," María revealed, "but confronting Thelma and Louise's tragic destiny and the punishment they receive for being two reckless women, my movie was obviously not going to be like that. It was the Mexican style, I had to give it a twist."[61] The women became a highly educated art counterfeiter on the run from corrupt authorities and a single working-class mother who has made off with her cartel member boyfriend's drug stash. Mutually distrustful at first, they grow to respect and support each other by the film's conclusion.

Surprisingly, María had no trouble obtaining financing for the film. Spanish producers (Tornasol Films with an assist from Mexico's Altavista Films) provided the biggest budget ($2.4 million) and the largest crew with which she would ever work. Shooting on location from October to December, 1999, in Yucatán, Tabasco, Veracruz, Chihuahua, Quintana Roo, and elsewhere throughout Mexico, María commanded a well-supplied legion that included 30 moving vehicles and 100 crew members. Referring to the company as an "elephant caravan," she became overwhelmed with the scale of it all. "There was too much movement," she claimed. "There were too many people, it was too much logistics."[62] In addition, she was working in Super 35 and with anamorphic lenses—elaborate technology that demanded even more of her attention. And rather than being surrounded by the familiar faces of her earlier films, she was directing freshly assembled personnel, including a new cinematographer, editor, art director, costume designer, sound engineer, wardrobe supervisor, and assistant. There was even, for the first and only time, a special effects coordinator. Missing, however, were Beatriz and Rodrigo.

Along with their abundant resources and perks, the producers also brought plenty of editorial suggestions. An early recommendation was that to avoid comparisons with *Thelma and Louise*, María should change one of the characters to a man. Firmly declining, she argued that there are probably close to a thousand male-oriented road movies, and no one has seemed to care about the similarities. More vigorous was their insistence that María cast Spanish actress Aitana Sánchez-Gijón as the art smuggler, a request with which she complied. Ana became a cosmopolitan sophisticate who had been born in Mexico but educated in Spain. Although María was pleased with Sánchez-Gijón's excellent (and well-compensated) performance, she always felt both characters should have been Mexican.

"I don't like action films. I don't like following formulas. I abhor violence," María has emphatically told more than one interviewer.[63] Surprisingly then, as if to show male audiences that she could pull out the heavy guns if she wanted to, *Sin dejar huella* delivers both action and violence. There are car chases, a stunt crash, a murder, and plenty of onscreen threat, all of it expertly staged and photographed. Moreover, this being a Novaro picture, there is also a great deal of humor blended into her treatment of recurrent themes such as female empowerment, the self-actualizing journey, motherhood, class disparity, and patriarchal authority.

With its wide international distribution, *Sin dejar huella* did much better at the box office than its predecessor, advanced the careers of its two stars, Sánchez-Gijón and Tiaré Scanda, and solidified María's professional reputation as a versatile, accomplished director. In a review for *Variety*, David Rooney called the picture "a warm, breezy film with an agreeable grasp of light comedy and a generous share of winning observations."[64] *The New York Times* movie critic Elvis Mitchell praised its "provocative and dark-humored" sensibility.[65] Some members of the press at the San Sebastian Film Festival dismissively referred to *Sin dejar huella* as *Thelmita y Luisita*, but at Sundance it tied with *Possible Lovers* for Best Latin American Film. A major contender at the Ariel Awards, it received five nominations, including wins for Serguei Saldívar Tanaka's cinematography and Alejandro Vazquez's special effects. Although María was never fully satisfied ("it's not the movie that should have been, it's not"[66]), *Sin dejar huella* is an exciting, well-crafted film that shows how familiar action genre tropes can be repurposed to support a personally consistent artistic vision.

Resolved to stay off the elephant caravan, María faced a new problem. How to maintain a love of filmmaking given the ever-increasing challenges of financing, shooting, and distributing personal movies? One solution, besides making the 2006 short films *La morena* (*The Dark Complected Woman*) and *Traducción simultánea* (*Simultaneous Translation*), was to begin teaching film production at the university level. She first substituted for a sick instructor at CUEC and then was invited to teach as a full-time faculty member at CCC, a position she held for ten years. Recognized today as one of the world's best film schools, CCC had been founded in 1975 by the federal government as a training ground for directors, sound experts, cinematographers, screenwriters, editors, and all manner of film technicians. The curriculum emphasized both theory and practical experience; all students were expected to participate in any school-sponsored projects in production during their attendance. As the program grew, it recruited outstanding professional faculty and received substantial financial backing from the state. Both major film schools also attracted an increasingly diverse student body. According to historians David Maciel and Joanne Hershfield, "The contemporary generations of graduates in film studies included a record number of women students who specialized not only in film direction but also in other spheres of filmmaking."[67] By 1987, CCC was admitting more female than male students. Among the notable filmmakers mentored there by María were director Elisa Miller and cinematographer María Secco. Her own daughter, Lucero Sánchez Novaro graduated summa cum laude from CCC with a specialty in screenwriting.

The teaching experience was as enriching as she had hoped. "What I discovered is that the one learning the most was me," she has acknowledged. "I learned to renew my language . . . and I think that that opportunity to confront myself, rethink, relocate myself, recognize the changes in film has been given to me by being a film teacher."[68] Above all, she also learned that the new digital technology provided another solution to the question of how to produce films on a more personal, economical, and less cumbersome level.

Encouraged by her students to make a movie in the same flexible way she was showing them, María began shooting *Las buenas hierbas* (*The Good Herbs*), a script she wrote in 2000. A somber mother-daughter tale, it starred Ofelia Medina as an ethnobotanist with early onset Alzheimer's, Úrsula Pruneda as the daughter who comes home to help her, and Ana Ofelia Murguía, who had appeared in *El jardín del Edén,* as a care-giving neighbor tormented by guilt over her failure to prevent the murder of her granddaughter on the occasion of her *quinceañera*. More experimental even than *El jardín*, it featured multiple plotlines, animated chapter headings, and a touch of García Márquez-inspired magical realism (the dead fifteen-year-old girl appears as a recurrent spirit). Beyond María's serious interest in biology, there was an additional, more intense, personal connection to the film's subject matter—her own mother María Luisa had died several years earlier from Alzheimer's.

Supported initially by a Guggenheim Fellowship, María raised money while she was shooting. Current and former students comprised the crew, including Gerardo Barroso as cinematographer and Sebastián Garza (with María) as co-editor. Daughter Lucero worked as a set dresser, and son Santiago contributed a couple of onscreen song performances. The fixed company totaled about ten members with four or five extra added for special scenes. Much of the picture was filmed exclusively in María's own house and neighborhood. "And we shot it like that, here in my house, in my garden," she revealed. "I mean the furthest we went was Ciudad Universitaria, we also shot there, in the Jardín Botanico, in a couple of other places, a little bit in Huautla, Oaxaca, but well it was like a homemade movie that was being made in that new way, in a very radical way."[69] It was almost like being a student filmmaker again herself.

Although she was a major star with over sixty movie and television credits, Ofelia Medina easily adapted to the guerrilla-style filmmaking. It helped that she and María shared similar left-leaning politics. Just as María had given film workshops in the Zapatista rebel-controlled territory of Chiapas so too had Ofelia Medina and María Rojo hosted a 1994 charity night of *danzón* in which guests paid to dance with celebrities and the proceeds went to the indigenous children of Chiapas. The intertextual connections were such that Elissa Rashkin has called it a "political act . . . staged via the integration of a popular cultural practice with mass-media star discourse, enhanced not only by Medina's activist reputation but by Rojo's prior association with *Danzón*."⁷⁰ Happy to be working with Novaro, both Medina and Ofelia Murguía were equally comfortable with the young, relatively inexperienced crew.

Wrapping at a budget well under a million dollars, *Las buenas hierbas* opened in 2010 at the Amazonas, Havana, Guadalajara, and Rome Film Festivals. The Italian festival jury was so impressed that it gave the entire female cast the award for best actress, an enthusiastic reception that was followed by exceptionally strong notices from the Italian critics. The film's interlocking treatment of herbal healing, Alzheimer's, and euthanasia also resonated strongly with audiences in Japan, where it played in theaters for over a year. The release in Mexico, however, followed a by-now familiar pattern: Ariel Awards (Best Supporting Actress Ofelia Medina) and recognition from the Mexican Cinema journalists (Best Actress Úrsula Pruneda and Best Supporting Actress Medina) but limited theatrical distribution. It played in Mexico City's Cineteca for six weeks plus in a few theaters throughout the country for three weeks. Overall, it was seen by very few Mexicans.

Having turned sixty, María was now enjoying a life that productively combined academia, family, and the film community. There was nothing left to prove, explain, or defend. Deeply affected by the sudden death of Úrsula Pruneda's young daughter during the filming of *Las buenas hierbas*, she focused more attention on her children and grandchildren. "Life is always more important than the film," she realized.⁷¹ When the next film project came together, it blended several of María's most passionate interests—family, travel, digital technology, children, marine biology, and Mexican culture. With a streamlined crew that included several student interns, she journeyed to Costa Grande de Guerrero to make a movie about a group of children searching for the buried treasure of Sir Francis Drake. More than just an adventure story, *Tesoros* (*Treasures*) is a record of how the young and old residents of Barra de Potosí interact with each other and with the natural riches surrounding them.

It is also an elaborate home movie. María's daughter Mara Chávez, son-in-law Martin Sutton, and grandchildren Dylan and Andrea Sutton Chávez play the newly arrived family who have come to the village in pursuit of a simpler life. The biologists who manage the nature preserve are portrayed by María's son Santiago Chávez and his wife Judith de León; their daughter Jacinta appears as the film's engaging onscreen narrator Jaci. Santiago also designed the sound and visuals for the computer pirate game played by the children, and María's daughter Lucero served as second unit director and author of an illustrated story book that Jaci reads throughout the movie. Dylan and Andrea's angelic little brother Lucas, who steals each of his scenes, is actually the son of co-cinematographers Gerardo Barroso and wife Lisa Tillinger. With all of these connections, cast and crew meals had all the joyousness of family picnics at the beach.

Although *Tesoros*, which was filmed during January and February of 2015, has a definite overall narrative, it is also very documentary-like. "I shot it a lot like a documentary," María agreed. "It's a fiction, there's a clear story that I included, but I shot it the way you shoot a documentary."[72] There are plenty of extended takes, lyrical vignettes of the children at play, and handheld camera set-ups. To get the coverage and development she needed, María shot an immense amount of raw footage and then retreated to her home editing room for several months to assemble a final cut. Slow-paced and beautifully photographed, it is one of the most authentic movies about children ever made.

Miami-based FiGa Films, after acquiring world sales rights to the picture, premiered *Tesoros* in March, 2017, at the Berlin International Film Festival, where it was nominated for a Crystal Bear Award as Best Film in the Generation Kplus (Young Audience) division. Noting some of the correspondences with her earlier work,

Variety's John Hopewell wrote, "Novaro's sixth feature 'Tesoros' puts kids center stage; grown-ups hardly appear in frame. In its visuals, it may be more of a piece with Novaro's 2000 road movie 'Leaving No Trace,' which captured stunning but off-the-beaten-track scenery and featured bright, warm colors. As with Novaro's 2010 'The Good Herbs,' it also plumbs the pleasure of nature, here in a community complete with an animal reserve, a shanty beach café, crab-fishing, whales in the bay, sandbars and local songs sung by a local couple."[73] *Tesoros* also screened at the Miami and Providence Film Festivals and was purchased by Amazon Prime for online streaming. That wide Internet availability helped to realize María's goal of stoking children's imaginations with creative visual material beyond just the products of Hollywood animation studios.

Novaro during an outreach event for IMCINE.

Having succeeded as a professional moviemaker and a university instructor, it seemed natural that María should also become involved in one of the governmental agencies that constitute the third pillar of the Mexican film community. In December, 2018, President Andrés Manuel López Obrador appointed her Director of the Instituto Mexicano de Cinematografía (IMCINE); her predecessor, coincidentally enough, was her ex-husband and former producer Jorge Sánchez. Inaugurated in 1983, IMCINE was designed to oversee official government policy related to the film industry, encourage artistic innovation, and even financially support specific productions. Both of Novaro's first two feature films, *Lola* and *Danzón*, were partially funded by IMCINE. Over the years, the agency had moved through periods of progress, corruption, and reform, attempting to establish itself as a reputable champion of Mexico's cinematic culture. Under the brief but effective leadership of film director Diego López Rivera, it had made great strides forward. According to historian David Maciel, "In his short tenure, certain positive changes occurred: a solid staff in charge of the various divisions of IMCINE was hired, an aggressive campaign to secure additional resources for production was launched, and decisions of production were made quickly and filming began on important projects."[74] A new research center for the study of Mexican film history was also established. As IMCINE's first woman director general, María has continued López Rivera's same dedicated and hands-on management of the mission. During her first year in office, María opened up new opportunities for indigenous filmmakers, including the construction of a new postproduction center in Chiapas. "This is a fully-equipped center that includes a recording and dubbing studio and facilities for Foley, editing, color corrections, etc.," she told *Variety*. "It will give local filmmakers a fighting chance to make first-rate films."[75] Accompanied by her mostly female team of assistants, she also traveled throughout the country explaining the various outreach programs available to qualified applicants.

Shortly after her sixty-fifth birthday, María sat down for an extended, wide-ranging interview with Lourdes Portillo as part of "From Latin America to Hollywood: Latino Film Culture in Los Angeles 1967-2017," the Academy of Motion Picture Arts and Sciences' contribution to the Getty Foundation's *Pacific Standard Time: LA/LA* cultural initiative. She discussed her childhood, family, education, professional training, and career. Saluting the "emblematic" pioneering director Matilde Landeta, she applauded her contemporaries Busi Cortés, Marisa Sistach, and Dana Rothberg before praising a new generation of filmmakers such as Elisa

Miller, Yulene Olaizola, Lucia Daja, Yohanna Escamilla, and Alejandra Sánchez. She revealed that she might like to have been a botanist and mentioned that she still wanted to make *The List*, the film that would humorously revisit her militant past. When questioned about her contribution to Mexican film, she answered that she and other women had opened up a dialogue of new voices, a conversation that previously had been "monolithic." Asked to describe the most important attribute of a good director, she replied, "Well, it's authenticity, it's having an authentic voice—be clear about what you want to say and why."[76] The multiple references to a unique voice are instructive. They suggest the careful observation, behavioral insight, cultural analysis, and personal vision that María Novaro has always believed to be the characteristics of a good film. One can only hope that her own voice, as one of the premier film artists of her generation, will continue to find new and unexpected ways to make itself heard.

María reflected on her life and career in a lengthy filmed interview.

Lola

Jacques Demy (1961), Richard Donner (1969), and Rainer Werner Fassbinder (1982) all made movies titled *Lola*. Marlene Dietrich introduced herself to American audiences in 1930 as coldhearted cabaret singer Lola-Lola in Josef von Sternberg's *The Blue Angel*, and Max Ophüls's final masterpiece, the tragic story of a notorious courtesan turned circus performer, was *Lola Montès*. What each of these pictures has in common, besides nomenclature, is the fact that every one of them was conceived and directed by a man. Their Lolas are dangerous sirens who lure troubled males to destruction and disgrace. For her first feature film, María Novaro was determined to abolish the stereotype, reclaim the name, and create a more realistic portrayal of "an imperfect woman with all of her possibilities, weaknesses, limitations."[1]

Co-written with sister Beatriz, the script was workshopped at the New Latin American Film Foundation in Cuba and the Sundance Institute in Utah, where Novaro was mentored and befriended by both Gabriel García Márquez and Robert Redford. Budgeted at around $300,000, the picture was financed through money from two Spanish awards María had received and a grant from the Instituto Mexicano de Cinematografía. Preparation and shooting occurred throughout 1988-89; locations included many Mexico City neighborhoods still recovering from the devastating 1985 earthquake.

Lola premiered in December, 1989, at the Havana Film Festival where it won a Coral Award for Best First Work. Screenings followed at the Toronto and Berlin International Film Festivals. Although the film's initial commercial release in Mexico met with minimal financial and critical success, it was nominated for five Silver Ariel Awards, winning in the categories of Best Screenplay, Best

First Work, and Best Supporting Actor. A rerelease after the huge success of Novaro's second feature film *Danzón* garnered strong reviews and larger audiences.

Much discussed and analyzed by academics, *Lola* introduces many of the themes, images, settings, and character types that will continue to interest Novaro in subsequent films. Speaking of *Lola's* significance, literary scholar Óscar Robles has written, "Ésta pelicula reconfigura a la familia Mexicana y articula una nueva subjetividad feminina más dinámica, moderna e independiente a partir del personaje de la madre, figura clave en el cine y la cultura de Mexico" ("This film reconfigures the Mexican family and articulates a new feminine subjectivity more dynamic, modern and independent, starting with the character of the mother, the key figure in Mexican cinema and culture" [author's translation]).[2] Fitting neither of Mexican cinema's traditional binary options for female characters, fallen harlot or saintly, suffering mother, Lola is a flesh and blood woman with real flaws and virtues.

Story

Lola is a young unmarried mother living on her own in Mexico City with her six-year-old daughter Ana. She makes a marginal living as an unlicensed street vendor of clothes. It is Christmas, and Lola and Ana are planning to celebrate with Ana's father Omar, the handsome, long-haired lead singer of a rock group called the Fabulous Thunderbirds. While waiting, they lip-sync songs and pretend to play guitar on stage. When Omar calls to cancel, Lola curses at him and takes Ana out into the city. They wander the streets for a while and return late to the apartment where they eat holiday cake and fall asleep on the couch. Omar calls, but Lola refuses to answer the phone.

Back at work after Christmas, Lola and the other vendors are forced to quickly dismantle their stalls and scatter when the police van makes one of its regular raids. Playing at home alone, Ana is joined by Omar, who arrives unexpectedly with a color television. They watch an old musical together and wait for Lola. Having gotten over her anger at the Christmas cancellation, Lola greets Omar warmly and they make up again.

Lola attends a Thunderbirds performance with one of the bandmembers' girlfriends and watches Omar sing in front of some adoring female fans. Her happiness turns to discomfort which is magnified back in the apartment when Omar prepares to leave on a tour. As he packs his suitcase, Lola takes pieces of clothing and throws them out the window. They stare silently at each other while Ana sings to herself in a corner of the bedroom.

With Omar gone, Lola's closest contacts are the other young people who work in the street stalls. In addition to her mannish friend Dora, there are Duende, the gentle, shaggy-haired guy who is painfully in love with Lola; Mudo, Duende's silent companion and protector; and Mario, a married Romeo nicknamed Mr. Congeniality for his smooth, would-be seductions. Supportive and generous by nature, Dora invites Ana to choose a doll from her merchandise, and Duende intervenes when Mario tries to put the make on Lola. Out of loneliness, Lola agrees to accompany Duende to a show at a local rock club.

On the night of their date, Ana balks at staying with a babysitter, and Lola remains at home. They play Barbie dolls together like two best friends, and it becomes increasingly clear that Lola is more effective at entertaining her daughter than at parenting her. Ana walks home from school alone, stopping on an overpass to drop teabags onto the traffic below. She enters the empty apartment by herself and scrapes together whatever she can find to eat in the kitchen. At a school conference, her teacher tells Lola that the other children are unsettled by how dirty and unkempt Ana always appears. Even her homework, she says, is sloppy.

Making an effort to do better, Lola irons Ana's clothes, checks for dirty hands, and supervises her homework. At a dance recital in honor of Mother's Day, she watches Ana perform the hula with a group of other little girls. Also in the audience is Lola's own mother Chelo, an attractive, well-dressed, middle-class woman who obviously enjoys being around her granddaughter. The three of them have refreshments afterwards, and Lola's mother criticizes her for not making a costume that looks like the ones worn by the rest of the children.

After some trouble at work with her clothes supplier, Lola takes up another brief interlude with Omar, who has returned from his tour and has brought some rollerskates for Ana. They reconcile, fight, make love, and then split decisively when he announces that the band is going to Los Angeles for a year. Out of anger, Lola sleeps with Mario. Abandoned by Omar, she drifts through her regular routine, taking Ana to school and then sitting outside on the curb. A typical day finds Ana relying on lunches brought to school by Chelo or making ketchup sandwiches for herself; Lola takes long baths and drinks more and more beer. Her tenuous efforts at parenting seem to collapse as she reverts again to mostly playing with her daughter. During some time together on a sand pile outside the apartment, they disagree over whether to be ballerinas or exotic dancers, and Lola gets lost in her own dancing as Ana watches from the side.

One day a friend takes Ana and some neighborhood kids to the beach. Instead of cleaning the messy apartment, Lola wanders around the city, dyes a locket of her hair blond, and drinks steadily throughout the day. When Ana returns from her outing, Lola gets her to fall asleep by stuffing her with chips and giving her sips of beer. The following afternoon, Ana dyes a strip of her own hair to copy her mother. Despite her natural cheerfulness, Ana is negatively affected by Omar's absence as well. She crumbles up a postcard from her father and tells Lola to stop calling her "Little Mouse," the nickname both parents previously have used for her.

After she notices Ana studying a cookbook photograph of a juicy-looking meatloaf, Lola tries to make the dish herself. Complaining that it doesn't smell good and that she doesn't like the olives on top, Ana refuses to eat. When Lola cuts up a piece and tries to feed Ana, she spits the mouthful onto her plate. In anger, Lola grabs a jar of honey from the table and smashes it against the wall.

Cut to mother and daughter shopping for groceries at the supermarket. As they select items from the shelves, Ana advises Lola to get a plastic bear-shaped bottle of honey because it won't break. Lola slips the container into her shoulder bag but not before attracting the attention of a clerk. Detained in the manager's office for shoplifting, Lola empties a bra, panties, candy bars, and other stolen goods from the bag. Stepping apprehensively behind her mother, Ana hands over a package of snacks. When the manager asks if there is anything else, Lola unbuttons her blouse and stares suggestively into his eyes. Some time later, while Lola services the manager in the front seat of his parked car, Ana sits at home by herself watching a *telenovela* on TV. There is a sudden power outage, and after dropping a cup on the floor, she manages to light a candle from the gas stove. Lola arrives home and finds Mario waiting for her in the stairwell. Stumbling into the apartment, she sees the broken china and the still-burning gas flame and frantically pushes Mario out the door. Asleep in her bedroom, Ana lies tangled among some singed bedsheets while still holding the extinguished candle.

Shaken by what has happened, Lola bundles Ana into warm clothes and carries her out into the city. They trudge through the nearly deserted, early morning streets before arriving at Chelo's house. With no explanation of the near disaster, Lola asks her mother to take care of Ana. Knowing that she is incapable of ensuring the basic security of her child, Lola sinks further into depression. The drinking now finds her swilling beer at night in the neighborhood playground and sharing her cigarettes with a disoriented vagrant.

One of the poster advertisements for *Lola* (1989).

Ana, by contrast, seems to be thriving with her grandmother, who prepares nourishing meals and clothes her in new dresses with matching socks and ribbons. They exercise together and Chelo uses Ana as a model for her clay sculptures. Ana's daily routine is regulated and well supervised. The only thing missing is the loose spontaneity that Lola provided. One day during a trip to the bakery, Chelo disciplines Ana for playing with a stray dog on the street, and Ana responds, "I don't love you anymore."

After another police raid of the vendors, Duende decides to cheer up Lola by driving her to the beach. Also along on the trip are Mudo and Dora. During a stop to fix a tire and stock up on beer, Mario unexpectedly joins the group as well. Around an ocean-front campfire that evening, everyone drinks heavily, and Duende watches anxiously as Mario tries to ingratiate himself with Lola. When she walks off alone along the shore, Mario follows after her. Drunk and aggressive, he pours tequila on her while attempting a sexual embrace. In a moment of anger, Lola smashes the bottle against his head. Realizing how seriously injured he is, the other three drive him to a nearby clinic.

Left by herself on the beach, Lola curls up in a hammock and sobs; at the same moment, Ana wakes up at Chelo's house from a bad dream and calls for her mother. The next morning Lola watches a large extended family enjoy time together at the beach. Little children play in the sand as their parents look on from the shoreline. A wiry, bearded old man, the clan's grandfather, jumps around in the waves, losing his shorts and exposing some full frontal nudity. Overcome with laughter, one of the adult daughters wades into the water to help him cover up. Duende and the others, including a heavily bandaged Mario, arrive in his sedan. The tone turns solemn as they all gaze self-consciously at one another and say nothing.

Back in Mexico City, Lola retrieves Ana from her mother's house. There is no conversation, and Chelo watches sadly as Lola carries away her granddaughter. Exhausted from all that has happened, Lola falls asleep in the apartment next to Ana. An indefinite amount of time passes, and Ana and Lola are next seen sitting on a different beach watching the clouds.

"Let's go up on a cloud," says Ana.

"Where will we go?" asks Lola.

"Wherever the wind takes us."

In the film's final shot, mother and daughter walk along the shore, gathering up shells.

Themes

Lola constitutes the first sustained look at the issue of *maternidad* (motherhood) that will occupy María Novaro to some degree in each of the feature films to follow. "To make movies," she remarked in an interview included with the picture's video release, "is a pretext to explore, to look at yourself and ask questions and look for answers . . . to explore who we are as mothers."[3] That exploration can be difficult, she added, "because there is a lot of pain involved in being a mom."[4]

Lola's challenge is not that she does not adequately love her daughter Ana but that she does not know how to raise her. She is much more comfortable as playmate than parent. The opening scene, in fact, has Lola and Ana pretending to be rock stars, lip-syncing to Lola's boombox and using a toy guitar and improvised spotlight as props. When Lola cancels her date to stay home with Ana, they play with the Barbie dolls and Ana objects when Lola uses a King Kong action figure to ask Barbie for a dance. Lost in the playtime fantasy, Lola continues on her own, just as she does later when they disagree on whether to be ballerinas or hula dancers. While Ana watches, Lola sways back and forth in a dance that she makes up on the spot.

Lola is equally oblivious to the more serious responsibility of providing her daughter with regular nutritious meals. Ana is almost always hungry. In a dozen different scenes, she either looks for or consumes food. When she is with Lola, she eats chips, cake, cereal, and ketchup sandwiches. Playing alone on the roof of her apartment building, Ana gets on her toy telephone and orders "a pound of eggs." Only grandmother Chelo keeps her properly fed, bringing lunches to school and serving complete meals when Ana comes to stay with her.

In contrast to Chelo's immaculate, well-ordered apartment, Lola's place is a mess. There are clothes on the floor and unwashed dishes on the table. No cleaning takes place, and Ana is only occasionally asked to scrub her hands. She goes to school so ill-groomed that Lola is called in by the teacher to discuss her general "unhygienic" condition. Although she is motivated to change, those efforts never succeed. She quickly abandons the careful ironing of Ana's clothes and gives up on cooking when Ana refuses to eat her dried-out meatloaf. As if in ironic reproach, a "Happy Mother's Day" banner flies above the dance recital and Lola drinks beer under an "Homage to Mothers" statue while she waits for Duende to change the tire on his car.

Lola (Leticia Huijara) is more comfortable playing with her daughter Ana (Alejandra Vargas) than parenting her in *Lola* (1989).

"The challenges are too big for her," Novaro has explained, "and hence many difficult features of the character are worsened."⁵ Among those features is the bad judgment that leads Lola to give Ana beer and to involve her in shoplifting. Equally careless is the decision to leave Ana home by herself while she pays off the store manager with a sexual tryst in his car. The power blackout that follows puts Ana in real physical danger when she fumbles to light a candle from the open gas burner of the stove.

All of this would suggest Lola's complete failure as a mother, but Novaro sees a wider context to the issue. As film scholar Traci Roberts-Camps has noted, "To begin with, *Lola* is set against the backdrop of [the] political and socio-economic crisis in Mexico, and Novaro portrays her protagonist, Lola, as a woman struggling to survive this crisis. Lola works as a street vendor who has to hide her wares and flee the police each time they arrive."[6] Earning barely enough to afford her run-down apartment, she has no extra money for after-school daycare or tutors. There are no state agencies to help her with health care, psychological support, and food assistance. The only government institutions she comes in contact with, the public school and the police, are either disapproving or aggressively hostile. If Lola does not work the stalls, she does not survive, but the garment factory boss overcharges her for merchandise and fines her heavily for soiled returns.

Commenting on the economic forces at work, comparative cultures professor Diane Sippl has written that "Lola, a refugee from the exploitation and abuses of class and gender, is a reactive subject. Her reaction, however, is to participate in an alternative world of subcultural affiliations and practices, of youthful fantasies in the face of disemployment within the world market economy."[7] Some critics have faulted Novaro for not more fully analyzing Lola's struggle to stay afloat within a patriarchal, capitalist society. Like the sewing machine operators at the garment factory but with even less financial security, she is subject to one-sided working conditions set by the manager and a scope of operation circumscribed by the civil authorities. Her economic alienation is so severe that she is forced to commodify her own body in the exchange value sexual payoff to the grocery store manager.

Apart from this general class exploitation, however, the major factor in Lola's deterioration is the abandonment by Omar. "For me the trigger is not the economic situation," Novaro revealed in an interview with women's studies professor Isabel Arredondo. "The crisis really occurs because Omar leaves and Lola experiences a brutal, emotional vacuum. She is not experiencing an economic crisis. She goes on selling clothes, just as before; she was screwed before and she is still screwed economically."[8] Omar is the first in a string of Novaro feature film male characters who either vacate or complicate the lives of the women. More devoted to his career than his family, he drops in on Lola and Ana as his touring schedule allows. Slim and handsome, he substitutes charm for responsibility. Even when present, he is not very effective at parenting his daughter. Like Lola, he is more of a playmate, bringing a color television and roller skates as gifts to keep Ana entertained. All of the material needs he leaves to Lola, sending an occasional postcard but never any kind of financial support. Lola's connection to him is physical and emotional; he satisfies her sexually and he makes her feel less isolated in an increasingly hostile environment. When he abandons her completely for Los Angeles, she experiences an emotional loss beyond logic and reason. Commenting in the Arredondo interview on this dynamic, Novaro described Lola as "a woman who, when she thought about things, thought about them afterward, who was constantly acting out of rage, anger, jealousy, desperation, emptiness, loneliness, sexual desire."[9] When asked if Lola might have resolved her dilemma more strategically, Novaro replied that "to have Lola in control of her emotions would have been to ask her to have an attitude toward her life that would be more male than female."[10]

Omar is not an exception; none of the men she encounters is able to provide much comfort or assistance. Lola's own father is out of the picture and although little of Chelo's backstory is provided, he seems to have been absent for some time. As mentioned, both the garment factory and grocery store managers prey on Lola's powerlessness, and the plainclothes police harass her continually. She is not physically attracted to hapless, would-be suitor Duende or to Mudo, both of whom have trouble managing their own affairs anyway. Finally, fellow street vendor Mario is an unctuous, infrequent sexual partner whose poorly timed advances ultimately provoke a violent response.

Male support is basically nonexistent but so also are the salutary female friendships that become important to the Novaro characters who follow after Lola. "What is lacking in this film," contends Roberts-Camps, "which we find in subsequent films, is the group of women—or at least the one friend—who serves as a support network."[11] In fact, Lola's predicament suggests the necessity of such solidarity. Clearly she could use help meeting all of Ana's needs. Dora is sympathetic but in no position to provide much support, and the other bandmember girlfriends are as marginalized as she is. Although Lola's mother Chelo looks after Ana during her absence, she is hypercritical of her daughter's actions and would prefer to raise Ana herself. The extensive female support system that fellow Mexico City native Julia Solórzano will enjoy in *Danzón* is exactly what Lola needs.

Without it, she steadily crumbles, her collapse mirrored in the earthquake damaged streets through which she wanders. The city emerges as a character itself, equally hurt and struggling to survive. "Mexico Sigue en Pie" ("Mexico is Still Standing") read multiple signs that Lola passes on her journeys through neighborhoods where ruined buildings are visible in the background. The sounds of demolition echo plaintively like scraps of mechanical dialogue. "Even though it's true that the character of Lola was planned from the beginning," confirms Novaro, "the other character, the city, came out slowly in a parallel way."[12] The two characters merge when Lola realizes she can no longer safely care for Ana and carries her through deserted streets to her mother's house. According to Novaro, "The woman was so broken she had to leave her daughter. She was as broken as the city."[13] In a wordless extended sequence, Lola trudges through block after block of abandoned, half-intact structures while the *Stabat Mater*, Antonio Vivaldi's baroque meditation on Mary's suffering during the crucifixion, accompanies her on the soundtrack. "That's where the two characters come together," explains the director. "That's also the reason for the *Stabat Mater*, which evoked for me the mother in pain, the suffering that appears in Vivaldi's lyrics."[14] It is intended as and realized as one of the most poignant moments in the film. "Can the human heart refrain from partaking in her pain, in that Mother's pain untold?" ask the

English language lyrics in a tone appropriate to the traditional suffering mother of Mexican cinema, an image that Novaro only partially embraces as one of Lola's many shifting personas.

Lola would seem at this point to be stripped of agency and paralyzed with despair. Her drinking has accelerated to include public consumption in an empty playground at night, and she takes little interest in matters of work. When the police raid the vendors again, she barely manages to dismantle the stall and conceal the merchandise. Her loneliness is palpable. Unwilling to leave her in such a hopeless state, Novaro introduces a rudimentary version of what will become a more fully developed narrative trope in later films—the self-actualizing journey to the ocean. "I had to send them to the sea," Novaro has admitted unabashedly.[15]

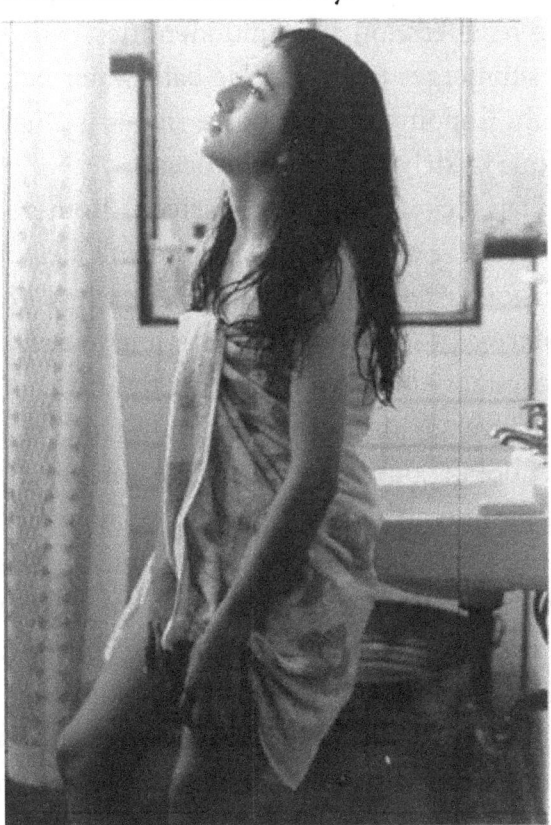

Water as restorative force in *Lola* (1989).

The thematic importance of water is established early. Dominating the wall of Lola's livingroom is a colorful mural that depicts a tropical beach complete with blue skies, palm trees, and waves. Under its calming influence, she often curls up on the couch as if cradled next to the ocean. When Lola takes over Ana's letter printing homework, a series of transitions leads from the repeated "O's" on the page to the waves of the mural and then outside to a water tank and finally to the painted ocean backdrop of the stage on which Ana and the other little girls are performing the hula. Linked by their association with tropical waters, the mural, stage, and dance (which Lola later performs by herself outside the apartment) represent alternative spaces free of economic and emotional burdens. There is also a restorative power to water, what Diane Sippl calls "a mode for proposing recuperation and fluid identities,"[16] that Lola experiences as she submerges herself in the bath water before gratifying herself sexually. Capping these curative rituals is Duende's decision to cheer up Lola by driving her to the ocean.

At first that idea seems misconceived. Bothered by Mario's uninvited presence, Lola and the others drink steadily and brood over their misfortunes. Things turn violent when Lola smashes a bottle over Mario's head to stop his harassment, and he gets carted off to the hospital. Alone overnight on the beach, Lola is more depressed than ever. With the morning, however, comes an epiphanic moment. Looking out at the ocean, she watches the beach come alive with simple human activity—children playing in the sand, fruit vendors pulling a cart, parents chatting among themselves. Of particular delight is the adventures of the old man who loses his shorts in the water, requiring the efforts of his daughter to retrieve them. "There she has the opportunity to witness something external to her," Novaro has revealed. "I thought the scene was very important for Lola to make a change, for understanding something that wasn't very clear, very profound, but moved her to return to her child."[17] That something is the validation of family ties, the simple joy of caring for another. "It's a reflection on the life that surrounds Lola to which Lola has access and is worthwhile," added Novaro in her commentary on the scene.[18]

Thus inspired, Lola returns to Mexico City, reclaims Ana, and relocates both of them to another pristine beach like the one pictured in the mural. Reunited mother and daughter would appear to have established a new, less fragmented beginning, but questions remain as to how Lola will earn a living and provide materially for Ana. As Romy Sutherland notes in a brief analysis of the film, "Clearly Novaro is suggesting an optimistic future, but after the relentless social realism of the narrative to this point, we cannot be confident that their circumstances will necessarily improve."[19] Lola and Ana walk into the distance together like Chaplin and Paulette Goddard at the close of *Modern Times* (1936), but there is no conclusive end to their journey.

A measure of ambiguity reaches all throughout the film. Diane Sippl has cited the reversal of mother-daughter roles and the singing of the *Stabat Mater* by a male countertenor instead of the female contralto for which it was intended as evidence of shifting identities and gender expectations. To those examples I would add the many instances of performance and the contrast between masculine Dora and feminine featured Duende. Although Omar is the professional performer in the family, both Lola and Ana dance, lip-sync, and play act. The layering of divergent roles is a constant factor in Lola's behavior, the key to her personality. She is a nuanced character who is struggling with all of her virtues and flaws to survive in a gray area of modern life.

Multidimensionality, finally then, is the key point that Novaro is making about motherhood. As Elissa Rashkin writes, "Unlike the mother archetypes of the classic cinema, Lola is shown as a complex human being who experiences pleasure and desire, ambivalence toward motherhood, depression, frustration, and longing for escape."[20] There is no single ideal model for how to handle the responsibility of raising a child. Novaro will create other memorable mother characters, less conflicted and overwhelmed, but none who is any more realistic than Lola.

Style and Structure

María Novaro has stated that many Mexican critics considered *Lola* too "Europeanized," characterized by less dialogue than usual in a Mexican film, subdued action, and naturalistic acting.[21] All of these descriptors are true, but many viewers have seen the likeness to European cinema as an aesthetic plus rather than a minus.

Several important scenes are almost completely wordless. After Omar fails to show up for Christmas, Lola and Ana take a silent trek around the city, dark and devoid of its normal bustle. When Omar brings the color television as an apology, he and Ana watch an old movie without talking. Lola arrives home and exchanges only a few words with Omar before they make up with an extended embrace. The subsequent scene where he packs and she tosses his clothes out the window has no dialogue at all.

Failure to communicate is a large part of their problem. Even as Lola and Omar inflict needless pain on one another, they make no effort to explain their feelings or explore remedies. He announces his trip to Los Angeles, and Lola storms out of the apartment for a tryst with Mario. When she returns, Omar pushes her against the wall, leaves without a word, and ends up alone in an empty cafe. Back together in the apartment, they make silent love and Lola sobs quietly to herself. All told, Novaro gives them no more than a couple dozen lines together throughout the picture.

Two of the most pivotal episodes in Lola's emotional life are staged with barely any speech. Aware that she cannot properly care for Ana, Lola carries her through the city to Chelo's house. For two minutes, a succession of tracking shots and pans, preceded by a tilt down from three strings of sneakers hanging from the utility wires, follows her down one street after another. The buildings she passes are still heavily damaged from the earthquake and appear ghostly in the pre-dawn light. Bundled in multi-colored coats, caps, and sweaters, she and Ana are framed mostly in long shots and look like a single misshapen creature. The only sounds are the *Stabat Mater* and some ambient street noise. From the left edge of an exterior side angle, Lola slowly approaches her mother's gated entrance. Finally, Chelo opens the door to her flat, and Lola speaks the sequence's only line of dialogue: "Can Ana stay with you?" The somber tone is reenforced by the Vivaldi hymn, the stark setting, the pacing, and the silence.

Slightly longer, at approximately three minutes, is the dialogue-free beach sequence. It is a lyrical interlude, like the ship-viewing harbor walk that Julia will take in *Danzón*, but it is also one that prompts Lola's emotional recovery. From Lola's middle-distanced point of view on a sandbank above the water, the family-affirming vignettes unfold like events in a home movie. The only fragment of dialogue is when the mother asks her daughter to help grandpa pull his shorts up out of the water. Framed separately in medium close-up, Lola never intrudes on the activities, but cross-cuts reveal her growing interest. The insight she gains remains unexpressed, as does whatever remorse she may feel when Duende and the others arrive with bandaged Mario. The five co-workers gather awkwardly around the car without speaking a word to one another. Equally silent is the following scene where Lola returns to her mother's apartment and carries a soundly sleeping Ana away with her. All that Lola feels remains closed inside, revealed neither to her friends nor her mother.

Novaro's structural design here and in subsequent films is to arrange the narrative sequentially, moving from one scene to another by way of direct cuts rather than fades or dissolves. There are no flashbacks, dream sequences, or special effects. Within the immediate present, the juxtaposition of two scenes often emphasizes the mood swings that Lola experiences. Watching Omar perform at a club is followed by watching him pack for a tour, listening to the teacher detail Ana's untidiness results in ironing her clothes and supervising her homework, and the smashed honey jar leads to the shopping spree which ends with a shoplifting pinch. The cross-cutting indicates the same kinds of thematic or emotional contrasts. At the same time that Lola suffers through her long night alone on the beach, for example, Ana wakens from a bad dream which her grandmother relieves with tea and snacks.

How Novaro frames and moves her characters within a shot is as important as what they say or don't say to one another. Inhabiting markedly different visual space (he a public performative one, she a private feminine one), Omar and Lola rarely appear together in the same shot. More often they are framed separately as when she watches him perform on stage with the Thunderbirds or he tries to reach her on the phone. Even in two-shots they only occasionally maintain a direct eyeline to eyeline gaze. Typical are the scenes where Omar returns to the apartment after Christmas and after the fight over the trip to Los Angeles. In both instances, he approaches Lola from behind, hugging her tentatively but avoiding eye contact.

The same distancing occurs between Lola and her co-workers. Duende accompanies her to the merchandise supplier's factory but remains waiting outside while she conducts her business inside. Showing up at Mario's gym, Lola signals her sexual interest without ever sharing a two-shot with the guy she will later hit over the head with a bottle. In addition, the trip to the beach in Duende's car, an event which would seem to promise harmony, is actually very fragmented visually. Framed separately, the four passengers drive, listen to music, drink beer, and sleep but with no social engagement between one another. "Although they are in the same car," writes Traci Roberts-Camps, "their loneliness is still palpable. Moreover, from the camera and viewer's perspective, it is as if we are seeing each character from another character's perspective in the car but there is not interaction among them in the scene, just individual shots of the four passengers."[22] When they gather despondently around the campfire later in the evening, they continue to be divided visually into discrete personal spaces.

By contrast, Lola and Ana are almost always framed side by side in the same shot. Their closeness is evident in the many different scenes where they play, eat, sleep, and converse together. Exceptions are rare and are meant to indicate temporary fractures in their relationship. The outdoor play-acting dance scene, where Novaro makes masterful use of blocking and camera movement, provides a good example. In an opening two-shot, mother and daughter stand on a dirt mound outside the apartment and pretend to be dancers. Despite Ana's insistence that they portray ballerinas, Lola begins to perform an exotic hula variation. Unhappy with her mother's behavior, Ana exits the frame and goes to sit on a nearby swing. There is a cut back to Lola who closes her eyes as the camera slowly tracks around her impromptu dance and the offscreen creaking of the swing grows louder on the soundtrack. For a moment, she is lost in a fantasy beyond the parenting cares and responsibilities which continue to intrude aurally. Ana once again signals her displeasure by leaving the frame of a two-shot when Lola reads her a Disneyland postcard from Omar. "I hate Minnie Mouse," she says, crumpling the card and abruptly walking out of the shot in rejection of the pet nickname that cannot smooth over Omar's disappearance from her life.

Lola (Leticia Huijara) and Ana (Alejandra Vargas) in a bonded two-shot as Lola attempts to bring order to the daily routine.

Moving the camera, as with the lateral tracking shot for Lola's hula, is a key element of Novaro's visual style. At various times, the technique suggests scope (tracking along the line of sewing machine operators), punctuates a key plot point (tracking in on Lola's meeting with the teacher), or keeps pace with the characters' actions (tracking across the roof terrace with Ana). Most effectively, the moving camera visually emphasizes Lola's isolation amid an indifferent urban landscape. The morning after Omar leaves for Los Angeles, Lola drops Ana off at school in a kind of daze; the camera tracks along the exterior fence with her until she sits down in front of the iron bars to calm the pain she is feeling. Similarly, the scene that follows the one in which Lola relinquishes Ana to Chelo's safekeeping opens with a shot of a vagrant propped against the wall of a deserted nighttime playground. In a single long take, the camera tracks laterally as he crosses the yard, passes a mysteriously moving yet unoccupied swing, and approaches Lola, "discovered" sitting on the ground and smoking by herself. He bums a cigarette, muttering over and over that "they're all a bunch of bastards." She nods and watches while he returns to his position against the wall; the camera holds on Lola, who takes a long swig from the bottle of beer she has carried with her and stares off into space. Despite coming together for a brief moment, Lola and the stranger ultimately retreat back into their private grief, two equally lost souls in the city.

The dangling swing is one of several visual motifs that Novaro associates with a particular character or location. Appearing on two separate occasions, it alternately signifies both the demands that Ana's presence makes and the sense of loss brought on by her absence. The toys and dolls, which an extended pan through the apartment catalogues at the beginning of the film, represent the playfulness that binds Ana so tightly to her mother. Lola's signifiers, the red boombox and the sequined denim jacket, indicate her own youthfulness and desire for self-expression. They are emblematic reminders of the blurred demarcation between mother and daughter, the adult correlatives to Ana's roller skates and Barbie dolls. And as the thematically related character that Novaro intends it to be, the city itself is defined through the ever-present motifs of darkened streets and devastated buildings, both of which are documented by the expansively panning camera that accompanies Lola on her urban journeys.

Mexico City's brokenness is also conveyed through the omnipresent sound of pickaxes pounding away at the rubble. That persistent background clamor is there in many of the exterior scenes, swelling noticeably during the first vendor raid, the sharing of refreshments after the dance recital, and Chelo's exercises on the terrace with Ana. Constant reminders of the earthquake's lasting effect, the demolition noises are also Polanski-like projections of the shattering inner despair that Lola confronts each day. Other inventive uses of sound give the sense of a first-time feature film director exploring all the creative possibilities of the medium. These include the transition from the humming of a fan inside the sweatshop to Duende scratching Lola's name into a metal plate outside as well as several offscreen sound overlaps. One is the creaking of the swing that encroaches on Lola's solitary hula dance and another is the street musicians' saxophone and drum duet that carries up into Lola's apartment as Ana leaves for her day at the beach.

Street signs provide thematic commentary in *Lola* (1989).

Related to this collage-like sound design is the artistic practice Novaro begins here of incorporating fragments of printed text to broaden the discourse. From the opening scenes where Lola and Ana first venture out into the city, we see signs that read "El Fenix" and "Mexico Sigue en Pie" ("Mexico is Still Standing"), a placard that appears again later in the film. The official government message they communicate is that Mexico is recovering, that President Miguel de la Madrid and his successor Carlos Salinas de Gortari, despite 20% unemployment and massive emigration to *el norte*, have stabilized the economy. Against this politically-driven optimism is a general socioeconomic malaise that Novaro reveals in the graffiti scrawled by disillusioned citizens—"Santa Clos es Puto" ("Santa Claus is a Gay Whore") and "Partido de Trabajadores Zapatistas" ("Socialist Workers' Party"). It is out of this same economic disenfranchisement that Lola and her co-workers try to make a living in the hidden economy of street vending, an illegal, underpaid labor system minus benefits, protection, and regulation. The disparity between the aspirational and the real also characterizes the examination of motherhood that Novaro has been making all throughout the film, an analysis encapsulated by the shot of Lola, guilt-stricken over the abandonment of her daughter, drinking beer under a statue that reads "In Honor of Motherhood."

Lola's intertextuality, another consistent feature of Novaro's style, involves the characters' participation as either consumers or producers in the mass entertainment industry. Bringing the gift of a color television upon his return from touring, Omar sits down with Ana to watch an old Mexican movie musical. In it, an actor in an Arabic robe sings new lyrics to the Calypso "Banana Boat" song in which he asks Allah to overturn the jail sentence he has been given for being too "macho." Cavorting on a gaudy set and surrounded by scantily-clad belly dancers, he simultaneously exoticizes and trivializes the very behavior that Lola resents Omar for displaying. Left home alone in a later scene, Ana watches a steamy *telenovela*. "You'll regret it," says an impassioned actor. "You'll be the most miserable woman in the world." In both cases, the campy stereotypes of the popular culture industry devaluate the authentic emotional turmoil that Lola is experiencing—as opposed to the "high culture" *Mater Dolorosa* and *Pietà* poses that ennoble Lola's painful viewing of Omar's performance at the nightclub. Omar's own music is self-generated and highly personal. Lyrics such as "A great violence cannot be kept down/With just a little love between your legs," "Love, sometimes like a death bullet, ends life," and "I want to scream and spit this in your face" speak to the nihilism and egoism that characterize his approach to romantic involvement. With his tight jeans and scarves, he is much more comfortable in the persona of rock performer than in the role of partner and father. Related expressions of media self-reflexivity include the Madonna photo which conspicuously replaces the Fabulous Thunderbirds posters on Lola's wall and the "Sobre las Solas" license plate that the vendors see on their way to the beach—a misspelled reference to ocean waves and to a well-known Pedro Infante movie about composer Juventino Rosas.

As she will in every subsequent film, Novaro has carefully chosen the songs that appear on the soundtrack. Most of the music is diegetic, performed by the Thunderbirds or played on Lola's boombox. Very much in the style of Eighties New Wave, the music helps to anchor the film temporally and to augment the themes of identity and alienation. The key non-diegetic selections are the *Stabat Mater* and the jaunty pop tune "Si tú te vás" ("If You Should Leave"), first heard during the car ride to the beach and reprised for Lola and Ana's walk along the shore at the end. Its romantic lyrics ("If you leave me, I will die") are recalibrated to celebrate the invincible bond between mother and daughter rather than the compact between a traditional male-female couple.

The intimate, low-key finale beside the ocean is indicative of the film's overall structure. This is a small-scale picture with a limited budget, simple narrative, minimalist mise-en-scène, and small cast. It is also a remarkably accomplished first feature film from a young director—tightly constructed, inventive, ludic, and packed with fresh ideas.

Cast and Crew

Novaro's first and most important casting imperative was finding the right child actor to play Ana. "I wanted a girl who was not an actress," Novaro explained in an interview some years later, "because I had seen how the children who have worked in commercials or movies are little monsters; they are children with little spontaneity who think that acting is reciting."[23] In Alejandra Vargas she found exactly the precocious yet credible child performer she needed. Although the daughter of a professional actress, Alejandra was herself untrained and behaved very naturally in front of the camera. To prepare, Novaro spent hours recording her on video, playing games and responding to imaginary situations. "At times I asked her very open-ended things—to do whatever she felt like," elaborated the director. "Other times I asked her to do specific things. But the condition was always that she couldn't look at the camera; if she looked at the camera, she lost. I realized that Alejandra was fantastic because she could go for hours without looking at the camera."[24] The strategy was always to help the little girl feel she was having fun in a protected environment.

Once she had found her ideal Ana, Novaro searched for a Lola who could embody the character's disparate personality traits and also be a believable match with Alejandra. "I wanted to see if they looked like mother and child," she disclosed, "because I hate this cinematic convention that the mother and daughter don't seem to know each other at all but you're supposed to believe that they're related."[25] Settling tentatively on Leticia Huijara, a stage actress with only one major film credit, Novaro put her together with Alejandra and discovered that they made a compelling pair. There followed dozens more hours of videotaping in which the two new friends played in the park, went for ice cream, and travelled around the city. "I worked with Leticia and Ale for months . . . shooting video in the streets and subway,"[26] recalled Novaro, who would use the same extensive video preparation for her next film as well. "Alejandra was a little disappointed her mom would not be blond," admitted Huijara good-naturedly but otherwise they bonded as a tight family unit.[27]

Throughout the actual filming, Novaro remained sensitive to this chemistry and permitted her two lead performers to stray as necessary from the script. "I was in the mood to change any scene that Ale proposed in her play," she confirmed.[28] Whether the camera was running or not, Alejandra was encouraged to go wherever her imagination led her. According to the young actress as she remembered the Barbie dolls scene a few years later, "María said 'Do whatever you want, say whatever you want, move wherever you want, look wherever you want.'"[29] Even the simple little song that Ana sings to herself in the film came from something Alejandra was doing in real life. For the scenes where Ana becomes upset with her mother, Novaro (who credited Robert Redford with giving her "brilliant ideas"[30] at Sundance on how to direct children) did not ask Alejandra to "act those scenes like the adult actors, who work with their own experiences" but rather told her, "We are going to play that you are angry."[31] The result was a completely natural, unself-conscious performance that does not seem like a performance at all.

Novaro invited the same loose spontaneity from Leticia Huijara, pleased with the way she was interpreting the character of Lola. "We had to create a dark character which could bring out darkness from a vital woman," the actress said of her performance.[32] She made Lola more volatile, more prone to dramatic mood swings. The original beach scene as written in the script, for example, did not include Lola smashing the tequila bottle over Mario's head, but both Novaro and Huijara agreed that it was the more likely way that Lola would express her pent-up anger at that moment. "Sometimes I had the impression that Leticia didn't adjust to the character that was written," corroborated Novaro, "and sometimes that is like a confrontation, a pain, but I believe that it was lucky that finally the true Lola arose from the script, the direction, and Leticia's work."[33] No physical detail was overlooked in her focused internalization of the part. Knowing beforehand, for instance, that the long walk to Chelo's house would be overlaid with the *Stabat Mater*, she keyed her movements to the Vivaldi hymn playing out in her head. "Leticia projects a lot of force and hardness . . . I like all the tones [she] achieved," concluded Novaro.[34]

Both Leticia Huijara and Alejandra Vargas (as Alejandra Cerrillo) went on to build successful careers in Mexican film and television. Appearing in nearly twenty feature films and over a dozen television series, Huijara has been nominated twice for a Silver Ariel Best Supporting Actress Award (*Dos crímenes* in 1995 and *Ciudades oscuras* in 2003) and won the Silver Ariel Best Actress Award in 1998 for her performance in *Por si no te vuelvo a ver*. She is especially well known as Charo Banegas de Uriarte on the popular *telenovela Los Sanchez*, for which she won a National Circle of Journalists award for lead actress in a television series. She has also continued to work in theater as an actress, director, and playwright. Equally comfortable on both sides of the camera, Alejandra Cerrillo has earned credits as an actress (*Los años de Greta*, 1992), cinematographer (*De noche*, 2008), writer-director (*La araña*, 2008), art director (*Nunca creí*, 2008), and production coordinator (*Post Tenebras Lux*, 2012). Her portrayal of Ana remains one of the finest, most unaffected child performances in Mexican cinema.

Lola's supporting characters were all as well cast as the two female leads. Nineteen-year-old Roberto Sosa, who won a Silver Ariel Best Supporting Actor Award as Duende, had been acting in Mexican and American film and television since he was ten. With minor roles in John Huston's *Under the Volcano* (1984) and Oliver Stone's *Salvador* (1986), he had also appeared in the popular Mexican TV series *Chispita* (1982-83) and about a dozen feature films. Boyish and almost delicate-looking despite the character's jagged facial scar, he was one of the most experienced actors (and crew members in general) on the entire project. Working with only a few lines of dialogue, he manages to create a visceral portrait of a lonely young man torn apart by his inability either to win Lola's love or ease her unhappiness. Currently still very much active in the business, he has amassed over 150 lifetime credits to date, including his Silver Ariel Best Supporting Actor Award-winning performance in *El fantástico mundo de Juan Orol* (2012).

Ana (Alejandra Vargas) is temporarily cared for by her grandmother Chelo (Martha Navarro) in this scene from *Lola* (1989).

Also well-known to audiences was Martha Navarro as Lola's mother Chelo. Having already won a Silver Ariel Best Supporting Actress Award in Jaime Humberto Hermosillo's *La pasión segun Berenice* (1976), she was the veteran of several *telenovelas* and nearly twenty feature films. She would be closely associated with director Hermosillo throughout her career, often referred to as his muse and the star of his hit films *Intimidades de un cuarto de baño* (1991) and *De noche vienes, Esmeralda* (1997). Although the part of

Chelo is a small one, she effectively conveys the quiet conformity and middle-class propriety that Lola has rejected. Upon Martha Navarro's death in 2020, Leticia Huijara praised her co-star for "the fierce defense she made of the motivations of her character" and the "exquisite duel" between Lola and Chelo.[35] Delighted with her performance, Novaro asked her to take the role of the card reader in the follow-up film *Danzón*.

In his first major film role, handsome singer-actor Mauricio Rivera is appropriately out-of-touch as Omar. Neither cruel nor conniving, he is just too caught up in his own rock star mythos to be much of a father or spouse. It is Mario who is the unlikable man in Lola's life, and character actor Javier Zaragoza gives him the right combination of smarminess and threat. Novaro's friend Cheli Godínez, who had appeared in the director's short film *Azul celeste* (1988), portrays Dora as the same brusque but loyal friend she will reprise for the part of Tere in *Danzón*.

Another good friend involved in the production was cinematographer Rodrigo García, son of Nobel Prize-winning author and Novaro mentor Gabriel García Márquez. Rodrigo and María had met while both working as crew members on the Alberto Cortés film *Amor a la vuelta de la esquina* (1986) and had remained close ever since then. Intending him always as her first choice to photograph the film, she considered García to be "the perfect accomplice" and "a great observer of human nature."[36] They shared a fondness for intricately orchestrated tracking shots and lyrical, documentary-like interludes that complemented the narrative. García would return as cinematographer on *Danzón*.

A second close collaboration begun during *Lola* was with Sigfrido Barjau, a former student and later professor of editing at the Centro de Capacitación Cinematográfica. In addition to his solo credit on *Lola*, he would co-edit *Danzón* (the "extra" version) and *El jardín del Edén* with Novaro and again singly edit her short film *Otoñal*. In actual practice, for *Lola* and the other projects, they worked side by side in the editing room, sorting through the alternate take acting experiments that Novaro encouraged to assemble the seamless performances and sequential structure of the finished films.

The art director was Marisa Pecanins, who received a Silver Ariel Award nomination for Best Set Design. In keeping with Novaro's preference for location shooting, she made use of settings in the still-damaged Doctores and Roma neighborhoods of Mexico City. Her interior design for Lola's apartment splashed fluorescent color against the drab walls and emphasized the huge tropical beach mural, details that help Lola and Ana lose themselves in playful fantasy.

Novaro's producers were then-husband Jorge Sánchez and good friend Dulce Kuri, both of whom actively assisted with developing a budget and hiring the crew. Her co-writer, as she would be on all of the first three feature films, was sister Beatriz. Not only had she also studied sociology at the university, but so too was she a fan of the Golden Age genres that she and María played with in their scripts. Sensitive to the economic forces influencing the characters, she helped to root the narratives in a specific social milieu. Like María, she was also flexible in altering what had been written to meet the variable demands of shooting—e.g., changing Lola's marijuana smoking to beer drinking for censorship purposes and including the bottle smashing scene for story purposes. Together, María and Beatriz shared a Silver Award for Best Screenplay.

Despite the presence of family and friends, *Lola* was not an easy shoot. There were location difficulties, the challenges of directing a first feature film, the downbeat subject matter, and resistance from the misogynistic Sindicato de Trabajadores de la Producción Cinematográfica (STPC). To circumvent the open hostility of the male union bosses, Novaro utilized the legal loophole of working under the umbrella of an existing labor co-op (perhaps for political reasons, the end credits also included a formal thank-you to the rival Sindicato de Trabajadores de la Industria Cinematográfica, or STIP, union). Altogether, Novaro has remembered the production as "both physically and emotionally draining," entirely unlike the joyful experience of *Danzón* that was to come next.[37]

Danzón

Novaro's second feature remains her most popular and well-known picture both domestically and internationally. Rushed through postproduction to meet the entrance deadline, it was the first Mexican film in fourteen years to be screened in the Directors' Fortnight division of the Cannes Film Festival, playing alongside movies by Atom Egoyan, Ken Loach, Jaco Van Dormael and Jocelyn Moorhouse. Commercially released immediately afterward in France, it circulated through various other film festivals, including the Toronto International Film Festival and the Chicago International Film Festival, where it was nominated for a Gold Hugo Best Feature award. The Association of Latin Entertainment Critics honored it with five ACE awards for Best Film, Best Director, Best Actress (María Rojo), Best Supporting Actor (Tito Vasconcelos) and Best Supporting Actress (Carmen Salinas).

Following its successful international release, Sony Classics acquired *Danzón* for distribution in the United States, opening it on September 25, 1992, in New York City. Critical reception remained consistently positive as it screened in major cities across the country. In his review for the *Los Angeles Times*, critic Michael Wilmington wrote, "Novaro's movie is one of the best 'women's pictures' of the year. It has a delicate, playful intelligence; it's done with brilliant lyricism and rich dollops of character and humor."[1]

Story

Julia Solórzano is a Mexico City telephone operator who spends her free evenings at a dance hall called Salón Colonia. Like all of the regulars there, she prefers the *danzón*, a Cuban ballroom dance in which the partners maneuver through a formal square of steps, holding each other in erect postures and making only occasional eye contact. Julia's partner of choice is Carmelo Benitez, an impeccably dressed, silver-haired gentleman who has teamed with her in many a winning dance competition but whom she meets only every Wednesday evening at the salon. Best friend Silvia shares her passion for dancing and also works as a switchboard operator, along with another good pal named Tere and Julia's young, recently hired daughter Perla.

One evening Carmelo fails to appear at the Colonia and Julia begins a desperate search for him. Following her unsuccessful visits to other dance halls and to the restaurant where Carmelo was employed as a cook, Julia overhears Silvia tell Tere that Carmelo apparently has returned to his native Veracruz after being wrongly accused of a workplace theft. A subsequent encounter with a tarot card reader convinces Julia to follow in pursuit. Leaving Perla in the care of her friends, she boards a train for Veracruz.

Upon arrival, she checks into a slightly seedy hotel near the station that is run by Doña Tí and is home to several young prostitutes. Gruff and unfriendly at first, Doña Tí soon becomes mother figure cum confidante. While listening to Julia's carefully edited backstory, Doña Tí serves coffee and explains where the city's most devoted *danzón* performers gather. So informed, Julia finds dancers at open-air cantinas and at the famous Zamora Park pavilion, but no Carmelo.

During one of her nighttime excursions, Julia meets a friendly, endearingly optimistic drag queen named Susy. In addition to helping with the search, Susy invites Julia to her apartment overlooking the ocean and to the nightclub where she performs. The two quickly become friends as Susy offers makeup advice and Julia gives *danzón* instruction. Julia also gets to know La Colorada, a strong-willed prostitute who lives with her two young sons at Doña Tí's hotel.

Acting on tips from Susy and La Colorada, Julia checks out the harbor, where Carmelo may or may not have signed on to a Greek cargo vessel. Although she finds neither the ship nor Carmelo, she begins a flirtation with handsome, long-haired tugboat crew member Rubén that soon develops into a romantic fling. They go out dancing and spend nights together on his boat and in her hotel room. Ultimately, however, Julia decides that he is too young for her and that she needs to return to her real home. Saying good-bye to Doña Tí, she leaves a note for Susy but no message of any kind for Rubén.

Back in Mexico City, Julia distributes gifts to her friends and daughter, hinting slyly at her romantic adventure. One night she and Silvia return to the Colonia, and she is warmly greeted by the patrons and the band leader. Having reappeared as mysteriously as he departed, Carmelo cuts in on her dance partner. They expertly perform the *danzón* as the no longer shy Julia gazes directly into Carmelo's eyes.

Themes

The idea of a transformative journey, one that is both literal and figurative, is central to Novaro's work. Here, Julia travels to Veracruz to locate Carmelo Benitez but instead obtains a keener understanding of community, gender identity, and her own sense of self. The actual train trip is narratively insignificant, occurring almost entirely off screen. Checking her reflection in the mirror of a dance hall restroom, Julia tells her friends she has decided to take a work leave, and in the next shot, the camera pulls back from a painting of a locomotive and pans across to Julia looking out the window of her train compartment as it glides into Veracruz's central station. What matters is the life-changing destination.

The Julia Solórzano of Mexico City goes through the motions of a romance. Quiet and reserved, she enjoys the rigid conventions of *danzón*, averting her eyes and barely speaking. Although she hardly knows him, she has invested considerable emotional energy in her dance partner Carmelo. Because he is tall, soft-spoken, and graceful, she considers him to be the ideal man. Correspondingly, during their weekly ballroom trysts, she is content to play the part of unassertive admirer, hesitant to ask too many questions or make too many demands.

In Veracruz, however, she sees other options. "Something that I think is constant in my work," Novaro remarked during an interview shot concurrently with the film's production, "is the question about what it is to be a woman and what it is to be a man."[2] Starting with the permanent residents of Doña Tí's hotel, Julia meets a variety of powerful women whose agency transcends their economic marginalization. La Colorada earns her living as a sex worker yet also cares for two very young children. She refuses to be taken advantage of or to let anyone control her. In a scene witnessed by Julia, she argues violently with a man who is either her boyfriend or pimp, but Doña Tí advises that "she can take care of herself." Sympathetic to Julia's search, she gives recommendations on how to navigate Veracruz.

Even more important as a role model, ironically enough, is Susy the drag performer. She encourages Julia to embrace her physical attractiveness by wearing bright clothes and boldly applied makeup. When she hesitates, fearing that people will think that she too is a prostitute, Susy tells her not to worry about how others picture her.

Julia's concern is underscored by the fact that throughout the film men directly and aggressively stare at her. When she disembarks at Veracruz in high heels and carrying a single suitcase, several men watch her traverse the platform and then a dozen more outside the station scrutinize her long walk across the plaza. The sustained silence is broken by a shrill wolf's whistle. Later, as she wanders through the cantina, the male patrons follow her every movement. One of them, a Russian sailor named Piotr, sits down at her table and keeps repeating "I love you, I love you" until she is forced to leave. Exemplary to the point of exaggeration is the scene where Julia goes down to the harbor in the red dress and bright red lipstick suggested by Susy; some twenty dockworkers line up outside a warehouse to leer at her and a huge forklift appears from off screen to follow menacingly behind her. She has come for information but instead encounters only uninvited sexual appraisal.

"In a world ordered by sexual imbalance," Laura Mulvey first noted in her influential essay "Visual Pleasure and Narrative Cinema," "pleasure in looking has been split between active/male and passive/female. The determining male gaze projects its fantasy onto the female figure, which is stylized accordingly. In their traditional exhibitionist role women are simultaneously looked at and displayed, with their appearance coded for strong visual and erotic impact so that they can be said to connote *to-be-looked-at-ness*."[3] Such is the privilege claimed by the men who meet Julia in public—the assumption that she is there for them to ogle and assess. As a man who makes his living and interacts socially in women's clothes, Susy (we are never given his male birth name) has learned to control the gaze. On stage, she satirizes the notion of feminine display with her Carmen Miranda-ish costumes and her overtly flirtatious advances to the audience. Out in the community, she simply ignores the hostile stares of those who dismiss her as sexually transgressive.

Chameleon-like, Susy shifts easily between male and female identities. She is so convincing in drag that at their first meeting Julia assumes she is an actual female cabaret performer. As the friendship develops, Susy appears regularly in casual men's clothes and during a restaurant scene together playfully suggests that they should pretend to be a couple. Even the strict conventions of *danzón* exist to be upended. In teaching Susy the steps, Julia intuitively adopts the female role, averting her eyes and signaling passivity. A woman's glance, she explains, should never be a "golpe," a punch. Susy, however, insists on learning both parts and in having Julia lead. For her, gender roles are always fluid, never fixed.

Julia (María Rojo) teaches Susy (Tito Vasconcelos) to dance in *Danzón* (1991).

That attitude helps Julia to reexamine her behavior. When she first sees handsome young Rubén on the deck of his tug boat, her immediate reaction is to drop her eyes but then she looks up to observe his stance, a pose that is more traditionally associated with female display. Leaning back against the railing in cut-off shorts and a tank top, Rubén shakes his long hair into the wind and flashes a seductive smile that Julia returns. Although during their first encounter he tries to unnerve her with probing questions, she manages with some slight embarrassment to hold his gaze. When they meet again for a second time at an outdoor café, extreme close-ups of Julia's eyes indicate her heightened romantic interest in Rubén. From that moment on, in fact, Novaro reverses the usual male/female power dynamics, making Julia the dominant partner. She decides when and where they will get together, instructs Rubén in the fine points of *danzón* and controls the narrative arc of their affair. In the film's most sexually explicit scene, Julia wakens in bed, smokes a cigarette and takes "full pleasure in looking" at Rubén's half-naked body lying next to her. It is Julia who decides to end their romance, abruptly departing Veracruz and leaving the much younger man to wait forlornly for her in the rain. The Julia Solórzano who returns to Mexico City is a different, more empowered woman, one who not only dances again with Carmelo but now also looks directly in his eyes and initiates real conversation. She is finally able to enjoy being both initiator and recipient of the admiring gaze.

In *Danzón*'s reversal of traditional sexual dynamics, Julia (María Rojo) considers Rubén's (Victor Carpinteiro's) erotic appeal.

What links Julia's experience in both cities is her participation in a female support system, another recurrent Novaro theme. All of the Mexico City phone operators are women, including Julia's friends Silvia and Tere and her daughter Perla. They cover for each other at work, spend social time together, and share intimate personal stories. When Julia loses contact with Carmelo, Silvia helps her look for him in the dance halls. When she makes the possibly misguided decision to extend the search to a distant city, Silvia and Tere back the plan and promise to look after Perla.

Upon arrival in Veracruz, Julia encounters similar support. Although she appears for a while to be antagonistic, Doña Tí softens up after witnessing Julia's tearful disappointment at not finding Carmelo and invites the younger woman into her kitchen for coffee and sympathy. As the two become friends, Doña Tí admits Julia into her makeshift family and openly accepts the relationship with

Rubén, the kind of fling with a younger man that Julia herself had criticized back in Mexico City. Despite their obvious differences, Julia also bonds with La Colorada, who is equally nonjudgmental and willing to offer suggestions on where to find Carmelo. Presented in a conventional feminized way, Susy becomes the Veracruz version of Silvia, the close friend who accompanies Julia around the city. Fiercely loyal, she indulges every whim, from posting a missing person announcement on the radio to putting a message in a bottle and tossing it into the ocean. The only other men are Susy's fellow "artistes" Karla and Yadira plus all the missing, temporary, or unreliable boyfriends. As Traci Roberts-Camps observes in her book *Latin American Women Filmmakers: Social and Cultural Perspectives*, "Essentially, absence defines the role of men in Novaro's films; when faced with this absence, Novaro's protagonists rely on female solidarity."[4] Citing the same tendency, film scholar Elissa Rashkin writes, "Julia's fate rests on the generous assistance and complicity of those who surround her."[5]

The space in which Julia operates is markedly feminine. Apart from the dance salons and restaurants, much of the action takes place in the phone company break room and overnight dormitory, Julia's apartment, women's restrooms, Doña Tí's kitchen, and the hotel's communal cooking/laundry areas. Even Susy's apartment is coded as heavily feminine, a colorfully decorated space where she prepares food for visitors, grooms Julia, and listens to sentimental popular music. Julia and her friends are not the privileged ladies of an upper class melodrama chatting over an elegant lunch but working women who must balance their personal lives with job and family responsibilities. In their discussion of Novaro and other women directors of 1990s Mexico, film historians Joanne Hershfield and David Maciel assert, "*Danzón* shares with other recent women's films a focus on women's daily lives. *Lola, Los Pasos de Ana*, and *Danzón* document, narrativize, and represent the distinctive unconscious and social realities of women's experiences. Meaningful change does not usually occur in the wider areas of social or political relations for women, especially for lower-class women who typically lack access to political and social power, but in the narrower and more personal realm of everyday life. Thus these films emphasize the spaces in which women's lives take place . . . ."[6.] The hotel, in fact, is completely organized around the business and labor of women.

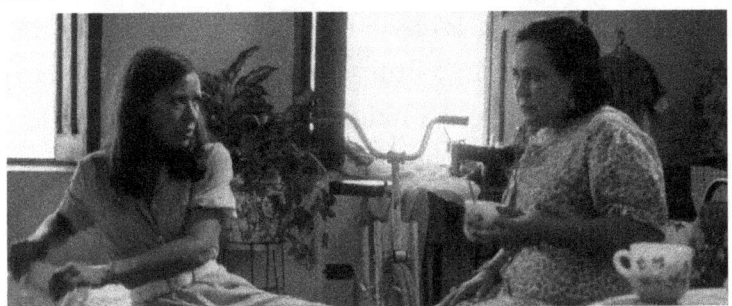

Julia (María Rojo) bonds with Doña Tí (Carmen Salinas) in the hotel kitchen of *Danzón* (1991).

Typically present along with their mothers in these domestic spaces are various young children, and their emergence as major characters will become more significant in later Novaro films such as *Las buenas hierbas* and *Tesoros*. Julia has raised a teenage daughter despite the never explained absence of the father and Doña Tí has suffered estrangement from her adult children, but there are much younger kids involved throughout the film as well. Arriving in Veracruz, Julia happily watches a woman bathe her child under a water control valve next to the train tracks. The same act is repeated when La Colorada gives her youngest son a bath in a large basin from Doña Tí's interior courtyard. Caring for the children is communal; Doña Tí helps to dry the boy in a towel and Julia later joins La Colorada in covering both of her sons with mosquito netting before they go to sleep. The children are part of the women's everyday routines, one more aspect of their domestic labor, yet they also embody an innocence that leavens the adult world's emotional and economic turmoil. In several of the *danzón* scenes, young boys and girls join the dancers, and during one such moment, a little girl circles the stage to ask an old woman to dance with her—an artful, unforced symbol of the familial and cultural continuity that Novaro will explore more fully in her subsequent work.

The *danzón* itself, which opens and closes the film and threads its way throughout, is as important to the overall message here as the tango is to *Scent of a Woman* (1992), *The Tango Lesson* (1997) and *Our Last Tango* (2015). Both are intricately expressive dances popular in the working-class neighborhoods of large cities. In his history of tango, Robert Farris Thompson states, "Tango is timeless, mixing love and action in the motion of the people."[7] The same is true for the part *danzón* plays in Julia's life; as explained previously, it is the vehicle through which she expresses her feelings about love and sexuality. Its conventions first appeal to her as a substitute for love, as contact with neither engagement nor passion. She is perfectly content to be led elegantly around the dance floor by Carmelo, waist lightly clasped and eyes cast mostly to the side. After the intensely physical affair with Rubén, her dancing becomes more joyful and animated, an expression of her awakened sexuality. After studying *danzón* in detail, actress María Rojo described the effect she was attempting in Julia's new style as one in which "women sway like palm trees. It's lovely."[8]

There are ten different scenes involving a performance of *danzón*, reminding us that like *The Turning Point* (1977) and *Center Stage* (2000) this is a dance film as well as a drama. We see Julia's dedication to *danzón* when she teaches steps to first Perla and then later to Susy and Rubén. Private and intimate, these moments communicate the romantic yearning that motivates so many of her actions. By contrast, the large ensemble pieces concentrate on the spectacle of performance. As a kind of documentary chronicle, the Zamora Park sequence shows real *danzóneros* gliding around the outdoor pavilion in a display of authentic local style. "The man must start dancing with his left foot and the woman with her right. He moves forward and she moves backward," explained Rojo. "The man leads but the woman shines."⁹ The Colonia dance hall sequences, shot on location with real patrons, also concentrate on the elegance of the steps and movements. Most of the couples are older and very average looking, their faces slightly weathered but reflecting natural grace and dignity. In the dancers, said Novaro, "there was a Mexican identity, a pride in our own ways," and the *danzón* itself expressed an attempt "to hold on to things that are being lost."¹⁰

In *Danzón* (1991), Julia (María Rojo) and Carmelo (Daniel Rergis) use dance as a vehicle for courtship.

Music is essential in every Novaro movie but especially so in this case. Not only does it provide appropriate accompaniment to the dancing but so also does it reinforce the overall tone of longing and loss. "I kissed you and then I lost you . . . maybe I'll die without you," lament the words of one song. "Love is an anguish, a question," warn those of another. Julia's melancholy is reflected in both sound and image. As Rashkin correctly notes, the chosen music "is as stylized, romantic, sentimental, and emotionally cathartic as the story we are watching."[11]

Much of the music is diegetic—the Colonia and Zamora park dance bands, Susy's "Coconut Vendor" drag routine, the Toña La Negra songs that Doña Tí sings to herself, and the vintage records that Susy and Julia play. The bands in particular lend historical authenticity to the contemporary settings, affirming the tradition so important to Novaro. During their first real date, Julia and Rubén watch a band perform a call and response number; the trumpet player separates himself from the others, moving throughout the dance floor to exchange melodic lines in a suggestion of courtship and pursuit. Doña Tí's songs and the records also evoke a romantic, half-illusory past that speaks to those challenged or confused by the present. "There's a lot of that," Novaro has agreed, "illusion and reality, not as contradictions, but as two sides of a coin."[12]

The non-diegetic music accompanies Julia's travel time, her walks along the harbor, and her reflective moods. Two instances stand out as representative. Stopping on the dock, Julia watches a graceful progression of ships slide in and out of view as woodwinds on the soundtrack turn the interlude into a lyrical encapsulation of her search and the film's overall tone. Similarly, when she wakes in the middle of the night and gazes at Rubén's body, a clarinet solo captures the fleeting, bittersweet pleasure of the moment.

On her first night in Veracruz with the band music playing in her head, Julia goes down to the beach and traces *danzón* steps in the sand with her bare feet. "I associate *danzón* with the movement of the sea," explained Rojo of the gesture.[13] She looks out at the ocean, where she will later spend an amorous night with Rubén and which will come to signify freedom, adventure, self-discovery, and creative potential. It is a location that will figure predominantly in three of Novaro's next four films.

Style and Structure

Although on the surface *Danzón* may seem like a conventional romantic drama, stylistically it is anything but that. Novaro has replaced the narrative seamlessness of classic Hollywood and Mexican cinema with a story framework full of gaps and pauses. Accumulation of information and character revelations usually occur off screen rather than on screen as the dramatically plotted pay-offs to individual scenes. Julia appears at Carmelo's restaurant in Mexico City to check on his whereabouts, but we never hear the conversation she has with the employees there. Susy talks to the cooks at a cantina and comes away with a vague clue about a Greek ship in the harbor, but we never learn why he has approached the men and what specifically they have told him. In one scene Julia announces that she has decided to look for Carmelo in Veracruz and in the next scene she is arriving at the station there. Nothing about the trip itself is ever mentioned. The history of Julia's relationship with Carmelo and with Perla's father is also left unexplored. There is not a single flashback in the entire film.

Even surprise revelations are excluded from what we see on screen. When Julia first meets Susy, she is in full public drag, and Julia seems to believe she is an actual female entertainer, an impression that is further supported when she visits Susy's cabaret and watches one of her performances. Several scenes later, however, the two are in Susy's apartment, where Susy appears dressed as a man in tank top and shorts. Somewhere along the way, Julia obviously has learned more about her identity, but that new knowledge is not presented as some disruptive shock. For Novaro, the issue of Susy's sexuality is immaterial; what is important are her strength, her generosity, and her supportive network of friends. As Hershfield and Maciel argue, the essential point is that Susy "is portrayed as a person whose self-reliance is not dependent on the whims of men" and whose independence is sustained by the "transvestite friends who confirm the identity that she has chosen for herself."[14] Carmelo's exit and return are also unexplained. He simply shows up again one night at the Colonia with no exposition and no backstory. More significant than the details of Carmelo's disappearance are the empowerment and self-awareness that Julia has gained during his absence.

Novaro has counted Michelangelo Antonioni among her artistic influences[15], and indeed the pursuit of Carmelo has the same randomness about it as does the search for Anna in *L'Avventura* (1960). Julia follows a hunch to Veracruz, drifts through the nightspots there, meets a string of unrelated characters, and fixates on a passing reference to a Greek ship in the harbor. After a short while, she abandons the search and embarks on a new relationship. Having failed to locate any trace of Carmelo, she departs Veracruz as abruptly as she arrived. In a brief essay on Antonioni for the *St. James Film Directors Encyclopedia*, Kimball Lockhart notes that "the dramatic or the narrative aspect of his films—telling a story in the manner of literary narrative—comes to be of less and less importance."[16] So it is with *Danzón*, where Novaro replaces conventional dramaturgy with a lyrical examination of emotional growth.

"The truth is that I'm not concerned about things happening," Novaro admitted in an interview with film scholar Isabel Arredondo, "but I feel somewhat forced to put in more action, because I know if I don't, people will miss it and will feel disconnected or think that what I am doing is weird." Further commenting on her narrative approach, she explained, "I've come to the conclusion that often the most significant memories of a person in real life or in the life of the character I'm writing are not powerful actions or events. Sometimes things are more subtle, almost imperceptible. What is important is how we are affected by them and what our reception of them is."[17]

Equally unconventional is Novaro's practice of not opening her scenes with an establishing shot. Rather than orienting viewers spatially, as per the classic Hollywood model, and then moving in for close-ups, Novaro often works here in the opposite direction—focusing first on a detail and later placing that detail in a wider spatial context. The film opens on an extreme close-up of silver ankle-strapped high heels that are soon joined by a pair of men's shoes entering the right side of the frame. Brassy instrumental music announces a *danzón*, which the partners begin to perform as a ground-level camera tracks laterally with them across the dance floor. More dancing feet come into view during the extended single take before there is a cut to a waist-high medium shot of dancers, whom we will later identify as Julia and Carmelo, maneuvering within a crowd of other couples. There are further cuts into the orchestra and among the *danzóneros*, and not until the end of the opening sequence is there finally a long shot of the entire ballroom, which still has not been identified by name.

Similarly, the telephone company is entered through a medium shot of Julia and Perla examining timesheets rather than a long shot, which comes afterward, of the switchboards lined up next to each other. Other Mexico City settings introduced minus an establishing shot include Julia's house, the phone company dormitory, the card reader's chamber, and the Salón Los Angeles. In Veracruz, several scenes take place in Susy's apartment, but none of them begins with a master shot. During Julia's first visit there, we see her looking out a window at the harbor and then teaching Susy dance steps in an area that is probably the living room. In subsequent scenes, Susy applies makeup to Julia in front of a large mirror and serves breakfast to a friend in the kitchen. Never, however, do we get a sense of the apartment's overall floor plan by referencing related establishing shots.

The intention is not to disorient viewers but rather to quickly associate a character with an emblematic object or activity. The close-up of Julia's high heels on the train steps in Veracruz illustrates the point. "When I have Julia get off the train in Veracruz," Novaro has explained, "I use a classic framing to indicate that she has arrived at her destination: I put the camera on the steps of the train and the character gets off. However, I also add an important detail: Julia's high heels ... Julia's very high heels, which are characteristic of her throughout the movie, symbolize the way she sees the world. The high heels let me link her descent from the train with her feeling that the men are looking at her; so much so that it seems that when Julia arrives in Veracruz, the station is full of no one but men."[18]

Julia's iconic high heels are featured in a poster for *Danzón* (1991).

The film also accrues meaning through camera movement and character placement. Julia's state of mind is often revealed by how and where she is positioned within the frame. At the Los Angeles Salón, Silvia and Tere accompany Julia into the restroom, where the three friends adjust their makeup in front of a wall-to-wall mirror and an attendant sits silently to the side. When Julia announces her decision to look for Carmelo in Veracruz, the other two react skeptically, and Julia angrily breaks away and enters a stall, the camera panning to the right with her and isolating her in the reframed shot. There is a cut back to the mirrored space, which Julia eventually reenters to continue the discussion. Still sensing resistance, she again walks away, again the camera pans to reframe, and again she occupies the shot by herself. This time, however, Silvia enters from the left side of the frame, says, "You know what, little one, just go," and embraces Julia, restoring the sense of loyal solidarity essential to their friendship.

A related expression of visual and emotional unity occurs toward the end of the film, after Julia has returned to Mexico City. She is in her living room, distributing gifts to Silvia, Tere, and daughter Perla. All four characters are grouped together in the shot; Julia and Silvia step forward to prepare drinks at a counter in the foreground and to share a conversation about Julia's trip. As they finish and the single extended take continues, they return and regroup around a table with Tere and Perla. Each of the women has her back to the camera in the reframed four-shot, and Silvia presses, "Tell me, tell me." Huddled tightly within the protective group that has continually supported her, Julia presumably begins to share the story of her Veracruz romance.

Novaro's adroit use of the moving camera is evident in several of the dance hall / cantina sequences as well. Looking for Carmelo at the nearly empty Colonia, Julia enters the left edge of the frame as the camera tracks right past a solitary dancer and a few seated guests. Having circled around behind the camera, Julia reenters screen right and steps up on the stage to have an unheard conversation with the manager. An even more complicated shot involves Julia and Rubén's dance date. The camera tracks back from a medium close-up of a little girl standing beside a cantina stage and then pans across the dance floor to "pick up" several dancing couples including Julia and Rubén who enter screen right. Reversing direction, the camera tracks to the left with them as they stop and position themselves against a railing to watch the other dancers. A trumpet player enters the frame, exchanging musical cues with the band and crossing right to descend steps and finish his solo outside on the terrace. Through a combination of blocking and camera movement worthy of Max Ophüls, the extended take sequence effectively captures the fluidity of both the *danzón* and of Julia's journey itself.

Another way that Novaro the author comments on her action is to thematically link images by directly panning or cutting from one to another. To critique the fetishistic commodification of femininity, she pans off a wooden wall carving of a woman's bare breasts to a shot of Julia watching Susy perform in elaborate tropical drag and then cuts to a pair of falsies on Susy's makeup table. To situate Julia in a broader socioeconomic context, Novaro pans from Julia's switchboard back and forth across an entire row of identical operator stations and toward the end of the film pans off of Julia and Rubén's conversation at the seawall to show a long line of embracing couples who have come down to the public beach for a similar moment of inexpensive intimacy. When Julia accepts Rubén's invitation to board his tugboat for the night, they leave the frame and the camera pans slowly to the left to focus suggestively on the hull rocking gently against its moorage. Panning the camera for mood or meaning becomes one of Novaro's signature stylistic traits—across the travel posters to reference Julia's journey, past the male faces watching her in the cantinas, onto the women doing chores at Doña Tí's hotel. Nowhere, however, is the technique used for greater effect than in the lyrical interlude where Julia watches the ships cross through the harbor. As the camera pans across names like "Lágrimas Negras" (Black Tears), "Amour Fou" (Crazy Love), and "Amor Perdido" (Lost Love), ships glide into and out of the frame, their reflections sparkling against the water. There is total silence except for a soft flute melody on the soundtrack. Overcome by the beauty of it all, Julia watches with a joy made even more piercing when she glimpses Rubén sail into view on the bow of a tug named "Me Ves y Sufres" (You See Me and Suffer).

Like a collage artist, Novaro pastes these foregrounded words, fragments of text, and still photos into the filmic composition. Every detail is significant. The ship names evoke romantic melancholy, the restaurant where Carmelo works is called Esperanza (Hope), and a plaque on one of the dance club walls reads, "No conoce Mexico" (You don't know Mexico). Julia's visit to the card reader is introduced by a printed newspaper advertisement and accompanied by close-ups of the tarot cards, cards that signify ships, trains, and trips. Among the photos Julia is seen examining are the childhood pictures in her living room, the vintage portraits of women at Esperanza, and the movie-star pin-ups tucked into Susy's makeup mirror; each image offers her a different model of femininity. Novaro's open field messaging will expand later in her career to include passages from books and bits of animation.

One of the thematically significant ship names in *Danzón* (1991).

The film's color palette is also heavily coded. "There's lots of color in the locations," remarked her cinematographer. "Color variety and saturation."[19] The most distinct, deliberately applied colors are cerulean blue and bright red. Associated mainly with the seaside Veracruz settings, blue is used for the walls of Susy's apartment, the exterior of the tugboat office, and the interiors of various cantinas. Although the effect cannot be reduced to some simple symbolic correspondence between color and emotion, the blues tend to reflect the soothing influence of the ocean and of Veracruz's relaxed lifestyle, particularly in comparison to the more frenetic pace of Mexico City. "A sad world bathed in blue," goes the song played over Julia's contemplation of Rubén asleep in her bed, and there is melancholy to the color as well.

On the other hand, somewhat more dramatically, atmospheric red light bathes the interior of the Salón Los Angeles and Susy's cabaret. Susy recommends bright red for Julia's makeover, and La Colorada wears a tight red dress with black stockings when she goes to work on the streets. For the scene where Susy and Julia toss the bottled message into the sea, Julia's dress, the lighthouse, and the portable radio are all done in bright red. "Using red, which has nothing to do with the rest of the movie, helps us to tell the story," clarified the cameraman at the time of filming.[20] The reds emphasize the more chaotic eruption of passion into Julia's life. "This use of color," comments Elissa Rashkin on the reds, "reinforces the link between passion and masquerade and posits desire as a kind of pre-existent free-floating quality as well as a force belonging to or felt by individuals."[21]

As the attention to color indicates, Novaro has carefully coordinated each element of the cinematic process to support a narrative that proceeds in unexpected, unconventional directions. There is obvious mastery of mise-en-scène, sound, blocking, and camera movement but never a stylistic flourish for the sake of technique alone.

Cast and Crew

"I thought María Rojo's passion for cinema is the same as Julia's passion for dancing *danzón*," Novaro has revealed. "This script was written for her and no one else."[22] In 1991, Rojo, nearing the age of fifty, was already a major star of Mexican films and *telenovelas*, having won Ariel Awards for *Naufragio* (1978), *Lo que importa es vivir* (1987), and *Rojo amanecer* (1989). As such, she was the most important actress that Novaro had yet worked with, bringing her box office clout and critical prestige to the production. An active member of the left-leaning Party of the Democratic Revolution (PRD) who later would be elected as Coyoacán Borough Chief of Mexico City, member of the Legislative Assembly, and Senator of the Republic, she also brought political credibility to her portrayal of working class Julia Solórzano. We see not only the intelligence and independence that make Julia unique but also the single mother challenges and workplace tensions that place her in a specific socio-economic context.

María Rojo as Julia searches along the oceanfront for Carmelo in one of *Danzón's* memorable lyrical interludes (1991).

Elaborating on their professional preparation together, Novaro commented, "With María Rojo, for example, it really helped me get to know her. I spent months going to the Salón Colonia, taping her dancing, watching her expressions, her smile, the angles of her face, her moods, knowing when she was uncomfortable, when she could be spontaneous, when something was bothering her. Knowing her was important because she's a very intelligent woman and very sincere in her work, and if she didn't like what she was doing, it showed."[23] The careful study paid off, allowing Novaro to capture such candid moments as Julia quarreling with Perla over each other's appearance, erupting in giggles at the Russian sailor's clumsy attempt to seduce her, or squirming uncomfortably as Rubén catches her in a series of conflicting white lies about her age and her romantic history. Elissa Rashkin notes that Rojo's expressive acting conveys each of the "dazzled, confused, and delighted reactions" that mark Julia's transformation.[24]

Equally experienced were Carmen Salinas (Doña Tí), Tito Vasconcelos (Susy), Margarita Isabel (Silvia) and Blanca Guerra (La Colorada). To make everyone comfortable, Novaro again used a rehearsal technique that had worked well for her in her first feature film *Lola*: videotaping the cast in various dramatic games and exercises before the start of production. "Since the actors had a lot of experience," clarified Novaro, "I was afraid that they would feel that they knew more than I did and would be hesitant to let me direct them. In contrast to *Lola*, in *Danzón* the games with the video camera beforehand and the casting helped, not so the actors could face the camera, but rather, so I could face them."[25] The cast members appreciated Novaro's overall approach in developing their characters. "We all want to work with her," confessed Carmen Salinas, "she's very gentle."[26] Popular with audiences since the 60s and the star of such risqué hit movies as *Bellas de noche* (1975) and *Noches de cabaret* (1978), she saw Doña Tí as the savvy survivor of the kinds of hard-living demimonde exploits she had endured in those earlier roles. Indeed, her iconic presence here links the film historically with the entire tradition of Mexican cabaret pictures. "A bit rough," she envisioned the character, yet always able to find "that human connection."[27] Her idea was that Doña Tí would wear no makeup but always look like she has just emerged from a shower. Capturing the character's duality, she gives her a hard, clipped edge at the reception counter and a more chatty affability while tending to the women and their children in the courtyard.

Tito Vasconcelos, who had been an early member of the theatrical movement known as Mexican political cabaret and who would later become a professor of theatre at the National University of Mexico, believed Susy to be the most rewarding role he had been given up to that point in his career. Named after the title character in the popular 60s comic book series *Susy, secretos del corazón* (published, not coincidentally, by Novaro's family's press), she is Julia's major ally, and Vasconcelos perceived her as a generous fairy tale "godmother" steeped in fantasy.[28] But rather than present her as some kind of decadent joke, he imbues her with an everyday dignity unmarred by broad gesturality or vocalization. Never settling for one-note caricature, he creates a believable human being who can be offended as easily as delighted and whose lifestyle Julia comes to understand as perfectly normal. In their roles as best girlfriend and seasoned prostitute respectively, Margarita Isabel and Blanca Guerra also avoid stereotyping by projecting a combination of humor, frankness, and weariness. Daniel Rergis's authenticity as Carmelo derives from his origins as an actual Veracruz dockworker and long-time *danzónero*.

Novaro's care with the actors was matched by her detailed instructions to the crew. To achieve the proper resonance for Julia's lyrical harbor interlude, she directed her set designers to repaint the names of the passing ships (if you look closely, you can see the original lettering underneath). According to Novaro, "changing the names of the ships to film them was torture: we had to get the captain's permission, permission from the ship's country of origin, permission from the harbormaster—it was an awful lot of red tape! In addition, we could barely afford to paint the names, film them, and repaint them. The producers tried to convince me, they told me, 'María, film the ships with the names they have. Look it's a pretty name, it's called *Milano*,' but I said, 'No, it has to be called *Puras Ilusiones* (Pure Illusions) or *Amor Perdido* (Lost Love). That's got to be the name.'"[29] In a similar attention to detail, she insisted that the extras for Julia's arrival at the Veracruz train station not include women or children; for thematic purposes, only men had to be scrutinizing her walk through the terminal and across the street to the hotel. Julia sees this unfamiliar city with a mixture of surprise and wonder that Novaro wanted to be reflected in the repainted walls and reconfigured furnishings of each setting. "I constructed the movie in terms of specific locations," she explained.[30]

Her cinematographer once again, as in *Lola*, was good friend and colleague Rodrigo García. True to form, she was very hands-on, directly involved in the set-up and execution of every shot. For the scene where Julia awakens next to Rubén in her hotel room, Novaro recalled, "I told Rodrigo to have the camera linger over the half-naked body of a man: 'It's as if you were caressing his thigh, his calf; you move up his naked back and then move back to María Rojo.' But Rodrigo couldn't get the camera movement I was asking him for . . . When I got up on the camera and showed him graphically—so he could see on the monitor the movement I wanted—he almost died laughing, because it was almost as if he couldn't get it. He wasn't willing to caress the body of a man with the camera."[31] Despite that glitch, they forged a working relationship which Novaro characterized as one where "we have constantly talked things over, discussed them."[32] The successful results of their collaboration are evident in the lush tracking shots for the dance sequences and in the uninterrupted long takes for several of the ensemble scenes. García, who has acknowledged Novaro's early support, has since gone on to write and direct his own pictures, including the English language films *Passengers* (2008), *Mother and Child* (2009) and *Albert Nobbs* (2011).

Editing credit is shared between Sigfrido Barjau, Nelson Rodriguez, and Novaro herself. Like Novaro, both men came from formal film school training, Barjau with the Centro de Capacitación Cinematográfica and Rodriguez with the Cuban Film Institute, and both also bring the same wide-ranging, multi-faceted production experience that eventually would include the writing and directing of their own personal projects. The three filmmakers' shared background in experimental shorts and documentaries also helps to explain the unconventional editing of *Danzón*, specifically the minimal use of master shots and the reliance on reframing rather than cross-cutting to handle much of the dialogue.

Also back with Novaro from *Lola* is her sister Beatriz, with whom she again co-wrote the script. In fact, they both intended *Danzón* to be an upbeat response to the hardships faced by the young single mother of that first film. The idea was to take an old formula, the *cabaretera* or dance hall film, and rejuvenate it with humor, intertextual references, and more enlightened characters. In place of pimps, killers, and duplicitous prostitutes there would be irrepressible Julia Solórzano and all her likeable friends.

As Novaro saw it, "The script for *Danzón* was the opposite of the script for *Lola*—it concerned a woman who could forge her own path, virtually without limits. Although she was a woman from as limited an environment as Lola was, she was able to do almost whatever she wanted, because of her fantasy, her generosity, her openness to life."[33] In telling Julia's story, she and Beatriz used some of the narrative tropes of melodrama but satirized them at the same time. "What we do is work with the genre," she confirmed, "make fun of the forms melodrama takes. In *Danzón* we certainly were playing constantly with a melodramatic form, but then we took another tack and the movie ended up going in a different direction."[34]

Straightforward as all this sounds, the film generated a great deal of contemporaneous critical debate over whether or not it constituted a truly feminist statement. In an interview with the journal *Cine Mundial*, María Rojo quickly announced that the film was "intimist, but above all highly feminist."[35] Some writers suggested that although not polemical, the film validated women's everyday reality and celebrated a feminine if not strictly feminist sensibility. Others argued that the preoccupation with *danzón* was by its nature nonfeminist given the strictly assigned gender roles. The most virulent critics insisted that Novaro's use of melodramatic clichés was not nearly as nuanced as she professed and that Julia's return to her work routine and to Carmelo represented a restoration of patriarchal order. Social researcher Norma Iglesias even conducted a focus group study to gauge the different reactions of male and female viewers to the film.[36] Novaro herself declared, "There isn't a feminist stance, I only stand beside women and take their side."[37]

In retrospect, the frenzy over political labels seems more or less superfluous. While Novaro may or may not fit a rigidly defined notion of feminism, what is clear is that her film is progressive in both intent and delivery, an unconventionally crafted document of one woman's journey of self discovery and empowerment.

El jardín del Edén (*Garden of Eden*)

María Novaro's third feature production in five years, *El jardín del Edén* is a narratively demanding and complex film about three women whose lives intertwine on the border between Mexico and the United States. At a cost of around $2 million, the Canadian/Mexican/French co-production was financed by a labyrinthine consortium of government agencies, private foundations, and independent production companies. Shooting took place in Tijuana, Mexico, and San Diego County, California, with postproduction work completed in Mexico City.

Once again, Novaro co-wrote, directed, and co-edited the film with husband Jorge Sánchez and friend Dulce Kuri as producers. The cast, her largest to date, included established performers such as Bruno Bichir and Ana Ofelia Murguía plus a host of relative newcomers. Several scenes were written and performed in English, as necessitated by the characters' and actors' language backgrounds.

In what was becoming a standard Novaro marketing strategy, the picture was screened first on the film festival circuit—Cannes in May of 1994, Venice and Toronto in September, Sundance in January of 1995, San Francisco in April. Reception at each event was positive. Program notes for Toronto, Sundance, and San Francisco emphasized how effectively the individual stories overlapped.

Commercial release in Europe, Mexico, and the United States began in the spring and continued through the autumn of 1995. As evidence of Novaro's solid critical reputation in Mexico, the film was nominated for six Ariel Awards, including the Golden Ariel for Best Film and Silver Ariels for direction and original screenplay. Although not as successful at the box office as *Danzón*, *El jardín del Edén* has drawn the same kind of intense social and cultural commentary.

Story

Three very different young women adjust to their newly established lives in Tijuana, Mexico. Naive, blond-haired American Jane arrives on a bus with bags, backpack, and romantic notions of an exotic land south of the border. Recently widowed Serena comes from Mexico City with her sons Sergio and Julián and her young daughter Paloma. Liz, a highly educated Latina from the United States, is there with her daughter Lupe to curate an exhibit on Chicano art.

One of Jane's first actions is to reunite with her friend Liz and get a preview of the cultural exhibit. She also telephones her brother Frank, a former writer and amateur whale researcher who lives by himself in a house at the beach. Although Frank ignores the message on his answering machine, Jane shows up at his house, declaring her intention to become a writer. He dismisses the idea as just one more of his sister's ill-conceived fantasies.

Intending to make a living as a wedding and portrait photographer, Serena has installed her family in a small house above the border that she rents from her Aunt Juana, who also runs a secondhand goods shop and plays cards with the children. Everyone misses their recently deceased husband/father, but Serena does not know best how to talk about the loss, and there is tension between her and her oldest teenage son Julián. Silent and moody, Julián wanders around the city taking pictures with a used camera he has purchased.

Serena (Gabriela Roel) arrives in Tijuana as the widowed mother of three children in *El jardín del Edén* (1993).

In preparation for the exhibit, Liz spends a great deal of time watching videos where the interviewees talk about cultural dislocation and Mexican identity. She also worries about her little daughter Lupe, who is slow to acclimate and reluctant to speak in either English or Spanish. Like Serena, Liz is renting a small house from Juana, and as neighbors the two women watch their daughters play together and share details from their private lives.

Driven by her fascination with Mexican culture and a genuine desire to help other people, Jane meets a beautiful young indigenous Huave woman named Margarita Luna working at El Pescado Mojado seaside restaurant and brings her to Frank's place for possible employment as his housekeeper. He angrily rejects the "harebrained scheme" but ultimately introduces Margarita Luna to his affluent American neighbors who themselves hire her as a domestic helper. That evening a young boy, who turns out to be Serena's younger son Sergio, slips while playing on the rocks with Frank's dog, and Frank bandages his leg. They talk about whales and baseball, opening up an unlikely friendship. Although he is as reserved as the brother with whom he often quarrels, Sergio begins to draw highly accomplished pictures of whales and to show an interest in playing baseball again.

While out driving around town in Liz's SUV, Liz and Jane pretend to need help with a flat tire so that Jane can meet a scruffily handsome *norteño* named Felipe who happens to be walking down the highway. They treat him to a meal at a nearby restaurant, where he tells about his birthplace and his desire to cross the border. He and Jane flirt with each other, and she embarrasses him with the gift of a flower. Later that night, Felipe gathers with other would-be migrants at a stretch of beach divided by the border wall. He meets Julián, who is exploring the area with his camera, and asks to have his picture taken. Saying that Julián reminds him of his own younger brother back home, Felipe strikes up a friendship and asks an acquaintance to snap a photo of them together.

One day soon after, Sergio is up to bat during a baseball game at a ballpark whose outfield abuts the border fence. Aided by the tips Frank gives from behind the backstop, he hits a homerun that draws high-fives from border patrolmen who have stopped to observe. Watching from the bleachers, Serena asks Juana who the stranger is, and she explains that he is the gringo who lives by the ocean.

Jane and Liz return to El Pescado Mojado restaurant for updated information on how Margarita Luna is doing in her new job. Walking along the beach, they stop to look through a catalogue of photos of women from Juchután, Oaxaca, and Jane asks, "Which one is you?" After spending a night together, Jane and Felipe tour the seawall border area and watch an unsuccessful attempt by a *pollero* (guide) and several "chickens" to cross. Felipe reaffirms his intention to make it to the United States.

Pleased with the photos that were taken, Felipe has brought Julián to a grungy bar where they drink beer and watch some couples dance to *norteño* music. Felipe meets there with a *pollero* named El Maleno and agrees to pay him $500 for help in crossing the border. On the night of his departure, Felipe packs his few belongings and joins a small group that El Maleno intends to escort across the frontier. As they creep silently through the hills, the group is attacked by thieves, scattering chaotically in the darkness. Separated from the others, Felipe is robbed, badly beaten, and left for dead. Julián, who has stormed away from home after quarreling with his mother over use of the darkroom and intentionally spoiling some of her wedding portraits, comes across Felipe being assisted by another migrant and manages to get him to Jane's hotel room.

Upset by her son's disappearance, Serena drives around town looking for him. Acting decisively, Jane gets medical attention for Felipe and begins to nurse him back to health in her room. Julián remains there as well watching over Felipe in a vigil that tearfully reminds him of his own father's recent death. Once Felipe is out of danger, Jane spends an afternoon with Liz, updating her on all that has happened. She also announces that she plans to help Felipe even further, to do more than just stand and watch as Liz is doing with her exhibit videos. Visibly angered, Liz argues that the search for cultural identity is personally important to her, and Jane apologizes. Reconciled, Liz drives Jane back to her hotel with an assortment of new clothes she has bought for Felipe.

As Felipe models his *norteño* hat and embroidered shirt, Jane and Julián watch him admiring himself in the mirror. Together all three visit a popular folk shrine where hopeful migrants leave photos and handwritten messages. Felipe prays to *Juan el soldado* ("John the Soldier"), the secular patron saint whose weathered war photograph has attracted a devoted following. Later, they stop at a used car lot, and Jane buys a big American-made convertible.

Increasingly isolated, Liz spends more and more time watching the videos, particularly one that features performance artist Guillermo Gómez-Peña talking about the cultural fragmentation of borderlands. She barely notices that Paloma has taught Lupe to speak some Spanish, albeit a string of obscenities. In a photo shoot for the exhibit, Liz and Margarita Luna recreate Frida Kahlo's *The Two Fridas* painting.

After a farewell party in her hotel room, Jane prepares to cross the border with Felipe, who has also decided that Julián should come along as well. With the two men concealed in the trunk of the convertible, Jane nervously talks her way through the checkpoint, affirming that she is not bringing in anything special from Mexico. Successfully on the other side, they check into a cheap motel near San Diego called the Garden of Eden.

Meanwhile, during a conversation in which Juana tells Liz about the disappearance of Serena's son, Liz recognizes a photo of Felipe and Julián together. She and Serena first visit Jane's hotel, where they learn she has checked out, and then Frank's house. In his typically detached manner, Frank says that Jane can take care of herself and that "there is no point in going on with this." Disgusted by his refusal to get involved, Liz replies, "You're just a selfish person." While they are arguing, Serena wanders around the living room and notices the shark drawings that Sergio has given to Frank. Later that evening, Serena returns by herself and she and Frank sit together outside listening to the ocean. She tells him in Spanish about her family and asks for his help in finding Julián.

Across the border in the United States, Julián, who has grown tired of Felipe's bossiness and the cramped living conditions, leaves the motel and strikes out on his own. When Jane learns that Julián not only has disappeared but also is not Felipe's real brother, she demands that they immediately depart. Back on the road, they drive around the countryside and happen upon a makeshift migrant camp. A funeral for an infant child is taking place, and Jane intrudes to give some money to the grieving relatives. Insulted by the gesture, Felipe criticizes Jane for her privileged charity-giving, and they quarrel. That night they sleep outside in the convertible, and in the morning Felipe wakes, silently kisses Jane, and slips away into the hills.

Julián is later detained at the immigration services office in Tijuana. Serena arrives, and when she sits down next to him, he falls into her arms for a comforting embrace. Safely returned home, he joins his mother, Liz, Juana and all the children for a baseball game played in the dirt yard between their houses. Serena calls Frank and leaves a message explaining Julián's reappearance; he listens silently to the answering machine and watches the waves crash against the shore.

Picking crops in Oxnard, California, Felipe is caught in an immigration raid and deported back to Mexico. Jane, who has also crossed back across the border, says goodbye to Liz at the bus station in Tijuana. She has decided to travel on to Oaxaca, and as she leaves, is captivated by the sight of another beautiful young indigenous woman carrying a stack of caged birds. As night falls at the seawall border, Felipe surveys the activity and explains the territory to the actual younger brother who has joined him there. Out in the ocean a pod of whales swims freely northward.

Themes

The border looms over *El jardín del Edén* like an *idée fixe*, appearing in shot after shot and dominating the lives of the characters. It defines public activity, encloses private space, and influences personal identity. It exists as both tangible reality and imagined construct. Few scenes occur that are not physically or thematically related to that part of Tijuana situated on the boundary between Mexico and the United States.

In fact, the film opens with a binocular-framed shot of the border at night. Felipe, long before we meet him strolling down the highway toward Jane and Liz, is standing on a hotel balcony and watching several migrants attempt to cross over to the other side. Intercepted by the arrival of a United States Border Patrol car, they shout, "Somos Mexicanos" ("We are Mexicans"), and the patrol officers reply, "And this is the United States. Adios, amigo, see you tomorrow." Scurrying back across the border, one of the migrants, a hefty, high-spirited woman, stumbles and slides down a sandy ravine. Amused by the episode and the woman's safe landing, Felipe and the other spectators cheer the failed attempt, momentarily diverted from their own misfortunes.

For Felipe, the border constitutes an economic barrier, a political contrivance that separates him from the financial opportunity he seeks on the other side ("el otro lado"). His life is circumscribed by the border. He lives in a cheap hotel overlooking *la frontera*, gathers at a beach divided by the border, and is robbed and nearly killed within sight of the border. Tijuana is a limbo from which he is briefly delivered and to which he is abruptly returned. Even his quick peek at the promised land brings nothing but ill-paid, back-breaking labor in the fields.

For Jane, on the other hand, the border exists as the threshold to a land of colorful wardrobe and unique scenery, an exotic world she creates through her own fantasies. She looks past the poverty to see only sun-splashed beaches and energetic street life. Margarita Luna, the natively-dressed, Zapotec-speaking Huave woman she befriends, represents in particular for her the allure of an unknown foreign culture. As Miriam Haddu notes in an article on *El jardín del Edén* for the *Journal of Romance Studies*, "Jane takes in the fabricated vision of the exotic and unreal Tijuana (and Mexico) and projects the imaginary (or utopian vision) on the real, so that all she sees is in fact her own illusionary construct."[1] Both Jane's fantasy-driven travel and her desire to rescue others, genuine though it is, derive from her white, American-born privilege. Unemployed yet financially stable, she has the resources to rent hotel rooms, buy a used car, and contribute money toward the migrant child's funeral expenses. That charitable gesture at the funeral particularly infuriates Felipe, who views it as an example of the haves giving a scrap of spare largesse to the have-nots, reminiscent of the mounds of used American clothes and consumer goods that have found their way to Juana's junk shop. Like his sister, Frank is a privileged sojourner in a strange land but less interested in reaching out to help other people. For him, the Tijuana border zone provides an inexpensive retreat by the ocean, a place to indulge his personal, quasi-scientific interests.

Jane (Renée Coleman), the well-meaning *norteamericana* of *El jardín del Edén* (1993), functions with equal parts naiveté and privilege.

Tijuana, writes journalist Alma Guillermoprieto, is "a scorching-hot border town that can be seen either as the hideous, seedy product of more than a century of cultural penetration or as the defiant, lively result of cultural resistance."[2] Of all the characters, Serena most clearly understands and experiences that dichotomy. Her son Julián wears T-shirts with English-language slogans, keeps a Walkman glued to his ear, and gives in to the false promise of the other side. When Serena goes looking for him at night, she drives past a menacing tableau of girlie bars, sleazy nightclubs, and drunken revelers. Yet at the same time she has taken a dilapidated graffiti-filled house and transformed it into inviting domestic space, opened a business, and provided security for her children. Her relationships with Liz and Juana are constructive, and the visits to Frank's house expose her to the natural beauty that still exists in Tijuana and to the renewed possibility of desire. Together, Serena and the other major characters inhibit what Haddu calls "a place in a continuous process of hybridity, of juxtapositions, a space of encuentros [encounters], of criss-crossing ventures, a space of openness and closures and above all . . . a place where . . . a culture emerges."[3] As liminal territory, the border promises both danger and possibility.

Politically, Novaro also grasps and conveys the disparity of the border. Wealthy Americans, she points out, can freely cross the border to purchase bargain-priced oceanfront property in Tijuana, but poor Mexicans cannot travel in the opposite direction to pick crops in the fields of central California. The hardships of the migrant camps and the dangers of the nighttime coyote crossing contrast sharply with the carefree leisure activities of Frank, Jane, and Frank's neighbors. "Fortunately for the whales," Frank tells Sergio, "no one has put any boundaries on their territory." One obvious yet bureaucratically complex answer to the human boundary problem is a more open border policy with fewer restrictions on seasonal labor. But even as the issue is endlessly debated and negotiated, Tijuana will continue to be, in Novaro's words, "un iman que atrae a los muchos Mexicos que forman Mexico" ("a magnet that attracts the many Mexicos that form Mexico").[4]

The question of *mexicanidad* (Mexican-ness), touched on in the earlier films, fuels the central inquiry here. It arises during preparation of the cultural exhibit that brings Liz to Tijuana in the first place. As she reviews the many videos for the show, often alone in the darkness, she identifies with the speakers who feel distanced from their Mexican heritage. A Chicana from the states who speaks little Spanish, she has given her daughter an old-fashioned Mexican name, moved to Tijuana, and inaugurated a major cultural exhibit. Her intention is to apprehend identity through art, an effort most dramatically illustrated by her video recreation of Frida Kahlo's *The Two Fridas* painting, the one in which a white formally dressed Frida on the left is linked through exposed hearts and severed artery to a multi-colored natively costumed Frida on the right. In the reenactment, white gowned Liz is connected aspirationally to the idealized Huave woman (Margarita Luna) on the right. Ironically, Liz's preoccupation with the contrast between *chicanismo* and *mexicanismo* holds little if any meaning for most Mexicans themselves. When she tells Felipe at the restaurant about the exhibit she is installing on Chicano art and video, he nods his head in bewilderment. Her class abated identity crisis is as foreign to him as is Jane's entitled meddling.

Images of indigenous female beauty float through the film like elusive phantoms. When Jane parts the curtains to the Pescado Mojado kitchen, she is enchanted by the sight of Margarita Luna and the other Huave women cheerfully preparing food together. Sensing she has found the real Mexico, Jane introduces herself, helps Margarita Luna find a better job, and returns later to the restaurant to ask about her well-being. Sitting at the oceanfront, Jane and Liz peruse the book *Juchitán la ciudad de las mujeres* (*Women of Juchitán*), a collection of black-and-white photos by photojournalist Graciela Iturbide. Asked to find herself within the pages, Liz selects the picture of a sturdy, plain-featured woman with live iguanas on her head. "Look at these women, Liz," says Jane. "Surely they must be in paradise." Jane's obsession with native culture leads her to think later about following the female bird-seller to Tabasco. In each encounter, however, Jane merely recirculates demeaning stereotypes. As media studies professor Amy Kaminsky has proposed, "Always on the lookout for new experience, Jane inserts pre-formed ideas of Mexico into her encounters and only reproduces tired old representations. She has little to bring to new experience but her sweet nature."[5] Her dangerously clumsy misreading of individual identity parallels a failure to learn anything substantial about the indigenous culture to which she is so superficially attracted. Once she has finished with the Margarita Luna episode, she moves on to a new fantasy-driven adventure.

Jane (Renée Coleman, left) and Liz (Rosario Sagrav, right) look at photographs of indigenous women in *El jardín del Edén* (1993).

Indigenousness (*indigenismo*) is just one aspect of *mexicanidad* that Novaro explores. There are also the *cholo* lowriders who come to Tijuana for classic car shows, the undereducated farm workers, the middle-class families, the small entrepreneurs like Juana, the artists, the intellectuals, and the young professionals, like Serena, struggling to make a decent living. As part of her cultural survey, Novaro references social rituals (weddings, funerals, *quinceañeras*) and the folk spirituality that imbues much of Kahlo's work. Before he crosses the border with Jane and Julián, Felipe visits a shrine to *Juan el soldado*, the venerated figure represented there by a vintage photo of a young man in military uniform. For some reason, prayers delivered to Juan have met with considerable success, and the walls are covered with pleas for help and statements of gratitude from scores of once and future migrants. More than just a cursory detail, Felipe's extended prayer scene is Novaro's acknowledgment of the variegated religious experience that contributes to national identity. Additionally, in the recreation of the 1939 Kahlo painting, the medallion containing Diego Rivera's likeness has been replaced by one holding a photo of *Juan el soldado*. In his book on Novaro's early career, Óscar Robles sees that switch as ideologically significant in multiple ways: "Como elemento de subversión, la foto de Juan Soldado sustituye a la de Diego Rivera del cuadro original de Frida Kahlo. De esta forma, se entremezclan la alta cultura y la cultura popular, el arte y la religión, la fotografía y la pintura, el arte mexicano y el arte chicano, el personaje chicano (Elizabeth) y el personaje indígena (Margarita Luna)" ("As an element of subversion, the photo of Juan Soldado substitues for that of Diego Rivera in the original painting by Frida Kahlo. In this manner there is an intermingling of high culture and popular culture, art and religion, photography and painting, Mexican art and Chicano art, a Chicano character (Elizabeth) and an indigenous character (Margarita Luna)" [author's translation]).[6] That intermingling is the essence of Tijuana.

It is also no coincidence that one of the videos Liz watches at home by herself is Guillermo Gómez-Peña's *Border Brujo* (*Border Wizard*). A performance artist who often costumes himself in hybrid social signifiers such as mariachi hats, luchador masks, black leather, and English-slogan badges, Gómez-Peña concerns himself with the ethnic and cultural cross-breeding (*mestizaje*) spawned by the border. Born in Mexico and transplanted at an early age to the United States, he urges his audiences to keep traversing boundaries until they become meaningless. His artistic discourse examines the influence of social upheaval on individual human lives. In the clip studied by Liz, Gómez-Peña, wearing a sombrero with earrings and speaking in a combination of Spanish, heavily accented redneck English, and Spanglish, describes a "fragmented Mexico" with "unemployed mariachis, malnourished Indian dancers, and *federales* who dance the mambo." That vision of a fractured yet dizzyingly dynamic mosaic is one reenforced by Novaro's film overall.

As much as Novaro rightly depicts Tijuana to be a microcosm of the entire nation, it also offers a transnational model of the future. The postmodern hybridization documented in Gómez-Peña's video reaches beyond political borders and cultural traditions. On a thematic level, writes Robles, "la idea de Gómez-Peña es un intertexto que sirve de soporte ideológico de las identidades posnacionales que se escenifican en la trama de *El jardín del Edén* ("the concept of Gómez-Peña is an intertextual reference that serves to ideologically support the post national identities portrayed in the plot of *The Garden of Eden*" [author's translation]).[7] The crossing and recrossing of lines and borders remap conceptions of both culture and country.

One final point about the border is that Novaro's attitude, considering both the human hardships in evidence and the cultural synergy at work, remains ambivalent. Comparing *El jardín del Edén* with John Sayles's *Lone Star* (1996), Amy Kaminsky cautions against a "triumphant view of the border," adding that "Novaro and Sayles, incidentally neither of them Chicanos, look at the border with a certain jaundiced eye."[8] There is creative energy at the border but also economic exclusion. There are opportunities for self-realization but also "social, political, and economic realities that impel Mexicans to come to the border for reasons of survival."[9] Novaro remains aware of both perspectives.

Like Gómez-Peña, nearly all of the major characters seek ways to express themselves creatively, to give artistic shape to their personal thoughts and feelings. Julián and Serena take photos, Frank sometimes writes professionally, Jane tries to write, Liz organizes cultural events, and Sergio draws pictures. "I think I have a voice," insists would-be author Jane while Liz's verbally delayed daughter Lupe struggles literally to find her voice. Language itself is often more of an obstacle than an aid to communication, a kind of linguistic border. Neither Jane nor Liz speak much Spanish, making their initial conversation with Felipe an exercise in misunderstanding. Talking about herself, Jane tells him, "Soy un escritorio" ("I am a writing desk"). She uses the same broken Spanish with Margarita Luna even though the Huave native speaks only Zapotec. Jane's unfamiliarity with idiomatic usage causes her to unfortunately misinterpret Felipe's reference to Julián as his "carnal" ("brother"). When Liz tries to communicate with her colleagues, she falls back on a tortured blend of English and Spanglish. Trying to be authentic, she calls her daughter "Guadelupe" instead of the accurately pronounced "Guadalupe." Neither Lupe nor Sergio speak much at all, and Frank shuns human communication to focus instead on the decoding of whale sounds. Despite the limits of language, however, the photos, paintings, and hastily scribbled diary entries are all attempts by their creators to make sense of the often confusing social environment in which they find themselves. Jane and Julián in particular use writing and photography respectively to document their wanderings through the back streets and border beaches of Tijuana. The inclusion of so many conflicted, aspirational artists within the narrative is also Novaro's personal acknowledgement of how social upheaval and economic constraints complicate her own efforts to make artistically viable movies.

The urge to create is part of the broader journey of self-discovery that Novaro renavigates in film after film. Each major character, except for the appropriately named Tia Juana, has come to

Tijuana from somewhere else. Serena arrives from Mexico City, Felipe from the interior, and Frank, Jane, and Liz from across the border in the United State. Each is also looking for something—Serena and Felipe for livelihoods, Frank for isolation, Liz for a sense of ethnic identity, and Jane for fulfillment as a traveler in an exotic foreign land. Their individual journeys converge, overlap, and then spin off again in different directions, resulting in varying levels of self actualization. As Novaro remarked not long after the film's release, "todos buscan algo, todos tienen una pérdida interna y buscan su paraíso" ("all of the characters are searching for something, all of them have an internal loss and are searching for their paradise" [author's translation]).[10]

There are many such allusions to paradise beyond just the title itself. One of the stores in Tijuana is called Eden, and the motel where Jane, Felipe, and Julián stop on the other side of the border is the Garden of Eden. Stacked on Jane's desk is a copy of Milton's *Paradise Lost* as well as a dictionary open to the entry for "paradise" which reads "heavenly, out of this world, unearthly, divine, celestial" and "transliteration of the old Persian word (par-dae's) referring to a walled garden." Miriam Haddu has pointed out the significance of the interconnected references. "Besides the thematic of a quest for paradise on either side of the border," she notes, "the title of the film . . . is amongst other things, symbolic of the city of Tijuana. Like the 'walled garden,' Tijuana is surrounded by a twenty-kilometer-long wall."[11] Each character's subjective journey in and around the walled "paradise" yields different outcomes. Felipe's liminal experience holds him in a perpetual state of expectation while Jane returns to the road to resume her unfinished journey. Frank settles back into seclusion, and Liz continues to grapple with identity issues. Only Serena seems to have achieved a kind of resolution, building her business and reuniting her family. Ultimately, just as Tijuana is encompassed by a wall so too is it edged by the ocean, an unimpeded reminder of the true freedom that Novaro characters are generally seeking. As Elissa Rashkin suggests, "The ocean reappears as a symbol of liberty in *El jardín del Edén*, this time even more sharply in contrast with the constraints of human existence."[12]

For the female characters, the "pérdida interna" that Novaro mentions has to do partly with the absence of male support. Serena is recently widowed, Liz is divorced, and Jane is virtually ignored by her self-centered brother Frank. They are each struggling on their own to build new lives and, in two cases, to be successful single mothers. "Although female solidarity is not the main theme of Novaro's *El jardín del Edén*," argues Traci Roberts-Camps, "it is still central to the development of the primary female characters. Novaro develops this solidarity against the backdrop of absent male partners—husbands, fathers, and brothers."[13] Serena's three children are all powerfully affected by the loss of their father. Paloma takes his picture off the wall because it is too painful for her to see while Sergio and Julián look to Frank and Felipe respectively as older brother/father figures. The fact that Frank is emotionally unavailable, and Felipe is barely able to take care of himself underscores the futility of those efforts. Often, as we have seen, Novaro's men, even the well-meaning ones, are either missing in action or ineffective. One of the film's most resonant images is that of Serena sitting alone at her desk late in the night overwhelmed by the review of accounts and by worry over Julián.

Roberts-Camps accurately identifies the gender dynamic at work in the film yet the concept of a female support system is more significant than she would otherwise allow. Each woman, in shifting combinations, turns to another for sympathetic understanding and for advice. Liz tells Jane about her anxiety over her cultural identity, and Jane confides her desire to contribute something valuable to others. Early in the film, Liz and Serena sit in their adjoining front yards, watching their daughters play and sharing details about their past marriages. When Serena goes looking for Julián, it is Liz who accompanies her to Frank's house for information just as she had previously helped Jane bring new clothes back to the hotel for Felipe. As a crusty mother figure, Juana watches over both Liz's and Serena's children, encouraging each to lighten up and relax into their new lives in Tijuana. At the end of the film, she joins Liz, Serena, and all of the children in a baseball game that illustrates the special, extended family bonds they have managed to create. Leading each team, in place of their absent husbands, are the two single mothers, baseball caps lowered over their foreheads and eyes focused on the action. What surfaces through Novaro's frequent revisiting of the solidarity theme is how she gives new ideological context to each iteration. Here the female support network operates as a counterbalance to the instability of the border zone.

Style and Structure

With its overlapping multiple storylines, *El jardín del Edén* is perhaps Novaro's structurally most ambitious film. In addition to the main narratives that belong to Jane, Serena, and Liz, there are subplots involving Felipe, Frank, and Margarita Luna. Within the opening few moments, each of the three major characters is adroitly introduced along with the motivational force that drives her. Jane breezes into town in search of exotic adventure, Serena arrives with her three children to earn a living, and newly transplanted Liz prepares for the opening of her cultural exhibit. The overlaps between them come as credible character developments. Liz and Jane are old friends reuniting at Liz's suggestion in Tijuana while Liz and Serena rent adjacent houses from Serena's aunt Juana. Liz, in fact, becomes the script's first degree of separation, the only person to establish a connection with each of the other characters. She is with Jane when they first meet Felipe on the road, she accompanies Jane to the restaurant for news of Margarita Luna (whom she later uses in her Frida Kahlo video), and she takes Serena to Frank's house for information about Julián's disappearance. There are several other such narrative junctions, moments where two or more characters cross paths. Jane presents Margarita Luna to Frank for possible employment, Julián meets Felipe while taking photos at the border, Frank appears along with Juana and Serena as a spectator at Sergio's baseball game, and Liz crucially recognizes a photo of Felipe among the prints at Serena's house. Carefully plotted and developed, individual narratives dramatically converge before separating again into divergent directions.

Some commentaries on Novaro's work have complained that the multiple plotlines are not each sufficiently realized. "Although interesting and ambitious," writes Elissa Rashkin, the film's narrative strategy "impedes the development of strong characters with whom viewers can identify, falling instead into overly broad generalizations."[14] While it is true that the secondary figures fall into types (Frank as aloof observer, Margarita Luna as mysterious native), the three main female characters are all dynamic rather than static agents. Jane continues on her fantasy-driven journey but has also learned about the harsh realities of the border. Even though Liz has not resolved her identity issues, she has made herself available as a support for both Serena and Jane. Through the extended search for Julián, Serena has become a more tolerant, less tightly wound parent. Significantly, the baseball game at the film's conclusion shows how Liz and Serena, the two single mothers, have strengthened the bonds within and between their families. Certain questions, however, do remain unanswered. Will Frank start to write again or begin a relationship with Serena? Will Jane take the bus to Tabasco instead of Oaxaca? Will Liz remain in Tijuana after her exhibit opens? But rather than being structural deficiencies, these are simply some of the lingering options of a realistically open-ended narrative.

To reduce confusion between the various plotlines, Novaro keeps viewers firmly anchored in regard to place. Unlike *Danzón* with its minimal use of establishing shots, it is always apparent here exactly where the characters are located, from Jane's and Liz's arrivals in Tijuana at the beginning to Jane's departure from the bus station at the end. Restaurants, bars, and hotels within the city are clearly and repeatedly identified. The border itself tellingly dominates multiple shots including the views from Serena's window, Julian's nighttime photo taking, and Jane's crossing of the frontier in her convertible. Like Jane's endless bus journey, Felipe's steady surveillance of the border opens and closes the film, giving it a kind of formal symmetry.

The camera consistently identifies, collects, and catalogues information. Novaro often introduces a scene by panning or tilting onto the character(s) from a marked reference point. Jane's entrance, for example, comes by way of a slow pan across an arched "Welcome to Tijuana" sign onto a shot of her walking through a busy street with her travel bags. Most of the border scenes begin with an establishing shot of the fence followed by an extended pan across the many would-be migrants waiting for a chance to cross. As in a nonfiction film, the aim is to document a particular social milieu and the many different individuals who inhabit it. When Serena goes searching for Julián, the camera pans off of a building called El Eden onto her car threading through traffic just as it also pans left from the checkpoint sign onto Jane's convertible waiting in a long line at border control. Once on the other side, a tilt down from a neon Garden of Eden motel sign identifies her new location. The effect is always twofold—to place a character in a specifically identified geographical place and to suggest participation in a broader social context.

Novaro's use of the moving camera, on elaborate display in *Danzón*, is less apparent here but equally effective. The lateral tracking shots, like the pans, catalogue cultural detail while the forward and reverse tracks emphasize emotion. When Julián visits the car club rally, the camera tracks laterally with him as he walks along a line of vintage vehicles including one flamboyantly painted lowrider bouncing up and down on its suspension springs. Tracks to the left follow Jane and Liz's stroll along the beach embankment as well as Jane's inspection of the used cars. A series of linked tracking shots is used for Serena's nighttime drive through downtown Tijuana in search of Julián, and while Felipe prays at the *Juan el soldado* shrine, the camera tracks away from him past all the photos and messages on the walls. Most intricately choreographed of all is the sustained circular track along the edges of the infant funeral as the camera documents the faces of the weary, grieving migrants. It is a nearly 360-degree sweep which captures both the solemnity and the size of the outdoor gathering.

For set-ups with fewer characters, Novaro often uses a slow reverse track to place an emotional "cap" on a scene. After Frank dismisses Jane's announced intention to become a writer, the camera pulls back gradually from their two-shot, registering her visible disappointment. As Felipe lies injured in Jane's hotel room, another reverse track draws attention to his heavy, labored breathing. Slowly tracking forward at the end of the film, the camera moves in for a medium close-up of Felipe and his brother staring out once again at the border zone. In each case, the movement through space generates expectation while the final framing of the character announces the emotional or thematic significance.

As mentioned, the tracking shots of Tijuana at night are from Serena's perspective ensconced behind the wheel of her station wagon, one of several point of view scenes that occur throughout the film. Jane and Felipe, the two characters involved in the film's most dramatic physical action, are also the ones from whose perspective we most intensely perceive selected narrative events. The opening binocular-framed observation of the border, for example, is from Felipe's point of view, an early indication of how focused he will remain on crossing to the other side. Another, more visceral, instance is when he is ambushed attempting to slip over the border at night. A subjective handheld camera crowds along the trail with Felipe and El Maleno, halting abruptly before being jostled violently during the confusion of the attack. Followed by a shadowy long shot of Felipe being beaten and kicked, the point of view footage is a tangible reminder of just how dangerous the migrant journeys can be.

Different in tone are the gauzy interludes where Jane catches sight of the fantasy-embellished indigenous women who interest her so much. When she draws back the curtain of the restaurant kitchen, the subsequent subjective shot reveals the nature of that fantasy. Margarita Luna is bent over pots of simmering food, laughing and chatting with two other women in a language that Jane will never decipher. Her long black hair tumbles down in the back over a colorfully printed native dress. In slow motion, she turns to meet Jane's gaze, her beautiful face held for several seconds in soft focus. An almost identical subjective shot is used at the bus station as Jane is distracted by the presence of the bird vendor. Dressed similarly to Margarita Luna, the young woman drifts in slow motion among the passengers, seemingly unaware of the mystical effect she is creating.

Both episodes have Jane appropriating the traditional male gaze, the steady scrutiny of an attractive younger woman, for her own purposes. Beyond whatever sexual overtones may pertain, she is reclaiming the pleasure of looking from the exclusive domain of male privilege, one of the most innovative features of the film. Julia Solórzano's return of Carmelo Benitez's gaze in *Danzón* is matched and exceeded here by Jane's sustained appraisal of another woman's physical allure. Hispanic studies scholar Carla Olson Buck agrees that Jane clearly redirects the traditional male gaze but also correctly argues that the gesture still implies power and domination, based in this case on culture and class rather than gender. "Jane's gaze objectifies Margarita Luna," she writes, "so that she becomes the representation of the exotic Mexican woman. In Novaro's film, the power displayed in the fetishizing gaze is not the male over female so often exhibited in film, but the ethnic power differential in the North American fetishizing of the indigenous exotic other."[15]

Subjectivity and slow motion also combine for Julián's recollection of his dying father in the first example of a flashback in a Novaro feature film. As he keeps watch at the bedside of injured Felipe, he remembers a similar vigil for his father. There is a cut to a hospital room where his comatose father lies connected to tubes and monitors. The camera pans across the bed sheets to a medium close-up of Julián sitting next to him and crying. When the monitors signal that he has slipped away, Serena turns in slow motion from over on the other side of the bed and looks directly at her son. Swathed in billowing curtains, she holds her expression of sadness until the scene gradually fades to black. Because it is used only once and because it is executed so eloquently, the flashback communicates the lasting impact that the otherwise unseen father has on Julián.

Time is similarly manipulated in a fanciful flash forward where Felipe imagines how his family might react to modern technology. After he meets Julián and admires his Walkman, there is a cut to an old woman hanging clothes to dry in a barren field. The camera pans from her onto a group of cows, each listening to a Walkman, and comes to rest on a young boy, presumably Felipe's brother, with the same device strapped to his own head. Although only a brief comic insert, the shot is packed with detail—the desert-like setting, the carefully arranged animals, the oversized props, the choreographed pan.

Visual density is common to most of the frame compositions in *El jardín del Edén*. The need to identify characters and read the *mise-en-scène* heightens the level of viewer engagement, as evident from the opening scenes. Felipe is one of several spectators watching a chaotic cat-and-mouse border crossing attempt from the balcony of a crowded hotel. Next, Jane appears in the middle of a busy downtown street, and Serena arrives with three children at her new house in a unfamiliar neighborhood. Finally, we see Liz directing a swirl of activity at the gallery housing her art exhibit. There is a kind of information overload involved in sorting out the geography and the relationships, a need for focused concentration that continues throughout the film.

Often in those fully occupied frames, Novaro will plant a detail that only later becomes significant to the narrative. Felipe is just one of the unnamed balcony onlookers until we later realize he is the same guy who helps Liz and Jane change their flat tire. In her introductory scene, Liz struggles with the controls of a video recorder that gives her sound but no picture; we briefly hear the voice of Guillermo Gómez-Peña in an excerpt from his *Border Brujo* performance piece. Much later in the film, Liz sits in the living room of her house watching an extended version that shows us Gómez-Peña clothed in one of his eclectic outfits and delivering a full-throttled rant on cultural fragmentation. Similarly, two early shots at the cultural center and in Liz's house reveal paintings of Frida Kahlo in the background, a personal interest that is more fully clarified when Liz recreates Kahlo's *The Two Fridas* painting.

The feminized space inhabited by Liz and Serena is carefully organized around domestic priorities. Faced with a slightly run-down vacant house, Serena efficiently furnishes it with items from Juana's secondhand shop, providing rooms for the children and working space for herself. The kitchen, with its well-stocked shelves and wall portrait of the recently deceased father, quickly becomes the center of family activity. Liz's house next door is also richly layered with cultural artifacts, child possessions, comfortable furniture, and work-related materials. The scene where Liz and Serena chat together outside visually links the two single-mother households. They are seated in lawn chairs that angle toward each other and that focus on a point in the background where Paloma and Lupe are playing together. Their conversation begins as a frontal two-shot followed by over-the-shoulder cross-cutting, but in each shot both women are always in the same frame at the same time. Without interrupting each other and listening attentively, they talk about their absent husbands, one by divorce and one by death. It is the beginning of a friendship that will find Liz helping Serena look for Julián and that will bring them back to this same space for the inter-family baseball game at the end of the film. As Roberts-Camps explains, "It is in these 'feminine spaces'—such as the patio outside their houses, their living rooms, and their cars—that the female characters bond and support each other."[16] The intimate cohesion of domestic space points out the fragmentation of the larger urban environment just as the cutaways to the free-swimming whales contrast with the man-made constraints of the border.

Also adding to the discourse are the substantial number of intertextual references that Novaro includes throughout the film. Once again, as in *Danzón*, she uses signs and slogans to emphasize thematic concepts. Spray-painted messages such as "If the Berlin Wall fell, why not this one?" and official postings that read "Caution, Danger, Think of your family, Government of the United States" identify the political tensions of the border. Signs in Spanglish announce "Telephonos" and 'El illegal diner,'" Julián wears a T-shirt that proclaims, "Fight the Youth with Poisoned Minds," and Liz and Jane drive past a small billboard advertising "Casablanca" vacation property for sale. Each is a subtle indication of the cultural and economic penetration of Mexico by the United States.

Other examples of intertextuality include Graciela Iturbide's book of photographs depicting women from Juchitán, the performance piece by Gómez-Peña, and the many video interviews that Liz watches for her installation. As Miriam Haddu notes, "The women in the videos are coming to terms with the notion of Chicana identity as being separate from their Mexican ancestors."[17] They are also fulfilling a need to record and memorialize personal experience, the same need that drives Jane's use of her Polaroid, Julián's photo documentation of the border, and the decision of Serena's clients, Felipe, and a heavily tattooed *cholo* on the beach to have formal portraits taken with friends and family. The *Juan el soldado* shrine is also a repository for the print and picture memorabilia left behind by hundreds of hopeful travelers.

In her often tearful preoccupation with the question of identity, Liz pursues the most elaborate intertextual citation, the reenactment of Kahlo's *The Two Fridas*. In the original painting, two seated images of Frida Kahlo hold hands against a background of scudding white clouds while their exposed hearts are connected by a single, free-floating artery. The Frida on the right, dressed in a fringed green skirt and blue blouse, holds a medallion of young Diego Rivera that is attached to the lower end of the artery leading to her heart; the Frida on the left, clothed in a high-collared white linen and lace dress, has cut the bleeding end of the artery that dangles across her lap. In the video recreation, Margarita Luna sits on the right and clutches a medallion of *Juan el soldado*. Dressed in one of her colorful native outfits, she holds hands with Liz, who is in the white dress and seated on the left. A rear projection screen of clouds streams in accelerated motion across the background while "La Zandunga," a traditional song about a man's painful love for a woman who ignores him, plays on the soundtrack. Where the original painting expressed Kahlo's pain over her recent divorce from Rivera, the filmed update conveys Liz's ongoing desire to connect with a more authentic ancestry, an aspiration played out here within the broader context of feminist expression and artistic tradition.

A final stylistically inventive scene is Felipe's departure from Jane. It is morning, and the camera slowly tracks down the length of the parked convertible. Felipe wakens, quietly gathers his belongings, gently kisses the still-sleeping Jane, and disappears from the frame. And then the single take, 90 second shot is repeated in its entirety with no changes or interruptions. This somewhat startling foregrounding of the cinematic apparatus serves several simultaneous purposes. It emphasizes the finality of the parting, the essential innocence of the characters, and the solitude of the moment. More importantly, by calling attention to camera movement, editing, and real versus screen time, it reminds us that we are experiencing an art form with its own unique conventions and structural devices.

Felipe (Bruno Bichir) takes repeated leave of Jane (Renée Coleman) in *El jardín del Edén* (1993).

Cast and Crew

Film historian Norma Iglesias has identified more than 300 Mexican "border films" made between 1936 and 1992.[18] The label, she writes, "alludes to types of characters, a production form, a specific geographic space, a question of limits, and a confrontation between 'us' in relation to the 'other,'" before adding that "the genre in general is distinguished by being a cinema of poor technical and narrative quality."[19] Again, as they did with the *cabaretera* format in *Danzón*, Novaro and her sister Beatriz have collaborated on a script that takes a traditional lesser genre and reshapes it into a dynamic personal vision. In the last feature film they would write together, they have broadened the single character studies of *Lola* and *Danzón* to focus on multiple characters connected through interwoven narratives. Their most ambitious collaboration, the script fully develops each individual storyline while keeping the connections organically credible.

The large cast chosen to fill the multiple roles includes mostly young performers early in their careers. Thirty-two-year-old Canadian actress Renée Coleman, who had appeared in the films *Who's Harry Crumb?* (1988) and *A League of Their Own* (1992) and as Alia the "Evil Jumper" on the television series *Quantum Leap* (1992-93), was selected by Novaro to play Jane for her embodiment of the character's naiveté and idealism. In an interview conducted for this book, she further explained that "María did not want me to think about Jane's privilege and exotification of indigenous life but only about her openness to different people and cultures."[20] Unlike the extensive cast preparations for *Danzón*, Coleman recalls little rehearsal and none of the warm-up video exercises. According to her, the shoot was relaxed and amiable, a "completely sociable and civilized process" far different from her less than positive experience on *A League of Their Own*. Cast and crew members stayed together in the same Tijuana hotel, adding to the cooperative team atmosphere. "It was the best professional experience I ever had," she affirmed. "If every production had been like that one, I never would have left movies."[21] A year after *El jardín del Edén*, Renée Coleman retired from Hollywood to pursue a doctorate in mythological studies and a career as a certified Dream Tender.

Prior to playing Serena, Gabriela Roel had done film and television work in both Mexico and the United States. Along with small parts in the movie *Old Gringo* (1989) and the popular detective show *Miami Vice* (1988), she had appeared in three *telenovelas* and about a dozen Spanish-language feature films. For two of those pictures, *Amor a la vuelta de la esquina* (1986) and *Pueblo de madera* (1990), she was nominated for a Silver Ariel Best Actress award. Well known to Mexican audiences, she has continued to work steadily, appearing primarily in various television dramas.

Newest to the film business was Rosario Sagrav as Elizabeth. Since *El jardín del Edén*, she has acted only in the short film *Sensitive* (2002) and the feature length picture *Semblance* (2008). Her performance is sometimes tentative, but that hesitancy is in keeping with Liz's uncertainty about her own ethnic identity. She shifts back and forth between English and Spanish for her scenes with Coleman and Roel, and the broken Spanish is also indicative of the cultural dislocation she feels. Together, all three actresses give credible interpretations, underplaying the drama and emphasizing each character's essential resilience.

At the opposite end from Rosario Sagrav's inexperience is veteran actress Ana Ofelia Murguía as Tia Juana. Born in 1933, she began her decades-long career in the late 1960s first with television appearances and then a string of feature film roles. She has acted in over 60 movies, 18 short films, and 16 television series. Nominated for a total of 16 Ariel Awards, she has won three Best Supporting Actress trophies (*Cadena Perpetua*-1979; *Los motivos de Luz*-1985; *La reina de la noche*-1994) and a Special Golden Ariel in 2011. She is best known to English-speaking audiences as the voice of Mamá Coco in Disney's 2017 animated hit *Coco*. Olson Buck sees Tia Juana as a metaphor for the city as faded, mercenary harlot. "Wearing large earrings and a lot of makeup," she writes, "Tia Juana may be seen as a caricature of the 'decadent and grotesque prostitute,' a colorful character with a past, but who treats the children well, never putting them in real danger."[22] Murguía balances the duality convincingly—sternly calculating as the businesswoman who keeps track of everything, quick-witted and spry as the tolerant baby sitter who loves to play baseball. She received a ninth Ariel Best Supporting Actress nomination for the part and would work again with Novaro sixteen years later in *Las buenas hierbas*.

Bruno Bichir, a member of the Bichir acting family and younger brother of Demián Bichir, plays Felipe. Although still in the early years of his career, he already had been nominated for three Silver Ariels, winning the Best Actor award for his performance the year before in *Principio y fin* (1993). He has worked continuously in film, television, and theater in both Mexico and the United States. As the mercurial Felipe, he moves back and forth between amusement, anger, and despair. Talkative and energetic, he allows us to understand the perseverance that keeps Felipe searching for a better life.

Nominated as Best Actor for the role, he watched the Silver Ariel go instead to brother Demián for *Hasta morir* (1994).

Joseph Culp, son of Robert Culp and another cast member with acting in the family, plays Jane's brother Frank. It is a small part, but he effectively projects the sullen cynicism that isolates Frank from others. Equally well cast in their secondary roles are Alan Ciangherotti and Ángeles Cruz as Julián and Margarita Luna, each of whom has continued to appear widely in Mexican film and television. Novaro's young daughter Lucero Sánchez, who would later become a director and screenwriter herself, plays Serena's daughter Paloma.

In a significant change from the first two features, Portland, Oregon-born cinematographer Eric Alan Edwards replaced Rodrigo García behind the camera. Known at the time primarily for a series of music videos and the Gus Van Sant films *My Own Private Idaho* (1991) and *Even Cowgirls Get the Blues* (1993), he was making his first and only foray into Mexican filmmaking. Familiar with the vagaries of independent productions, he successfully met the assorted technical challenges—the multiple locations, the nighttime border shoots, the complicated camera set-ups. His tight-quartered tracking shots are remarkable, as is his ability to maneuver the camera within rocky terrain. In his review for *Variety*, Emanuel Levy called Edwards's cinematography "magnificent."[23] Subsequent credits have included director of photography on over 30 feature films and made-for-television movies.

Brigitte Broch, Novaro's set designer, was born in 1943 in a part of Germany that now belongs to Poland and had been working in art direction/production design since 1991. Her first major assignment, set design for Guillermo del Toro's *Cronos* (1993), earned her a Silver Ariel Award, followed the next year by another Ariel nomination for her work on Luis Estrada's *Ámbar* (1994). She was equally adept at fantasy and realism, collaborating not only with del Toro but also with Alejandro Iñárritu (*Amores perros* in 2000 and *Babel* in 2006). Her design for *El jardín del Edén*, as was always Novaro's preference, made use of actual locations and authentic details. A good example is the California migrant camp where Jane and Felipe witness the baby's funeral. "It existed just as it does in the film," remembers Renée Coleman. "We shot there for three days, and I couldn't believe there was this whole different world just miles from San Diego."[24] Another narratively important set borrowed for the film is the *Juan el soldado* shrine with its photos, notes, and memorabilia. "There were people lined up all around," according to Coleman. "I thought they were there for Bruno the celebrity but they were there for Juan."[25] Felipe praying for a safe crossing is exactly what people do when they visit the shrine. Among the other atmospheric locations used by Broch are the Pescado Mojado restaurant, the Garden of Eden hotel, the Tijuana Cultural Center, Frank's beach house, and the various border encampments. Ariel-nominated again for her set design on the film, she would win once more in 2000 for *Sexo, pudor y lagrimas* (1999) and would take home an Academy Award in Art Direction-Set Decoration for Baz Luhrmann's *Moulin Rouge!* (2001).

Diegetic music emanates from many of the locations, further evoking time and place. There are guitarists in the restaurant, dance music in the bars, radios at the border, and street music all over the city. Julián is always listening to a Walkman and Jane frequently plays music in her hotel room. The *norteño* music that Felipe enjoys speaks to his origins in Zacatecas while traditional ballads such as "La Zandunga," "Mujer Paseada," and "La Juanita" echo the tropes of popular melodrama. Among the composers selected for the soundtrack are Manuel Eduardo, Esteban Jordan, and Manuel Gonzalez; performers include El Dueto Rio Bravo, Los Errantes de Durango, and El Trio Montealbán. As always, getting the right music was critically important to Novaro, and she worked in close collaboration with composer José Stephens and credited music supervisor Annette Fradera. The end result is a soundtrack that functions like the other textual references to anchor the narrative in cultural tradition and to emphasize specific thematic correspondences.

Joining Novaro for a third time were her then husband Jorge Sánchez and good friend Dulce Kuri as producers and Sigfrido Barjau as co-editor. Despite what Coleman believes were obvious tensions in the marriage, both Sánchez and Kuri gave Novaro complete creative control. The problem was not executive interference but rather what the director feared was an imbalance in character development. Called to Mexico City for post-production looping, Coleman saw a frustrated Novaro "worried that audiences would only be interested in what happens to Jane and Felipe."[26] The concern seems misplaced, however, since although Jane and Felipe share the sole dramatic romance, just as interesting are Serena's family issues and Liz's cultural confusion. To keep the overlapping storylines clear, Novaro and co-editor Barjau rely on strict chronological sequencing, seamless continuity, master shots for most locales, and cross-cutting for dialogue.

Novaro received Silver Ariel nominations for Best Director and Best Original Story Written Directly for the Screen (shared with sister Beatriz). Although Jorge Fons was named Best Director for *El callejon de los milagros*, Novaro's work is impressive on several levels: the crowd wrangling, the location shooting, the ensemble staging, the dialogue direction in both English and Spanish. Layered and complex, the film was considered meandering yet compelling by the English-language critics who managed to see it. "Novaro throws out many ideas and indulges in pointed visual comments," wrote David Hunter in the *Hollywood Reporter*, "but comes to few definite conclusions, which is mildly frustrating."[27] Emanuel Levy, who praised the visuals, had a similar reaction: "Narrative is loosely structured, and it takes some time for this leisurely paced pic to build its power through the accumulation of details."[28] In a review for the *L.A. Weekly*, Hazel-Dawn Dumpert noted, "Novaro sets her characters... adrift in a dreamy stream of natural dialogue and random occurrence that inexorably pulls the viewer along."[29] Writing in the *International Herald Tribune*, Al Goodman was not enthralled, calling the film "a mishmash of directionless, badly acted scenes, filmed with a dizzying amount of camera movement."[30]

Since its initial release, *El jardín del Edén* has continued to attract a great deal of academic attention for its treatment of issues related to border politics, gender ideology, cultural identity, and indigenous representation. It is a major work whose thematic and structural virtues become more and more apparent on each repeated viewing.

Sin dejar huella (Without a Trace; also, Leaving No Trace)

Reaching out to Spain for help with financing, Novaro shot her fourth feature film as a co-production between Altavista Films, Televisión Española, Tabasco Films, Vía Digital, Tornasol Films, and Fondo para la Producción Cinematográfica de Calidad (FOPROCINE). Filming took place between October and December, 1999, in the Mexican states of Quintana Roo, Chihuahua, Veracruz, Tabasco, and Yucatán.

Sin dejar huella premiered on September 23, 2000, at the San Sebastián Film Festival where it received a Golden Shell nomination for Best Film. Four months later it screened at the Sundance Film Festival, sharing the Jury Prize in Latin American Cinema with Sandra Werneck's *Possible Loves*. In addition to well-received appearances at festivals in Sweden, Argentina, Poland, Colombia, and Greece, it was distributed commercially in both Mexico and Spain. The widest audience for the film was in Mexico, where it won two Ariel Awards and was nominated for two others.

Sin dejar huella is a fascinating and successful hybrid, an action-oriented road movie laced with Novaro's frequent themes of community, self-discovery, and national identity.

Story

An attractive young woman pulling a piece of carry-on luggage crosses from Arizona into Mexico through a hole in the wire-fenced border. She watches expectantly as a car approaches from a distance but is distressed to see that it is a federal agent named Mendizábal and his assistant El Chaparro. "How are you, Marilú?" asks the cop as he rolls down a tinted window and takes her into custody. A trafficker in real and fake Mayan antiquities, she has dealt with Mendizábal before, and his interest in her goes well beyond the professional. While she is detained, he sexually harasses her and threatens extensive jail time. Unintimidated, Marilú smashes a piece of would-be evidence to show that it is not an authentic relic and demands to be released.

Ana/Marilú (Aitana Sánchez-Gijón) crosses the border with fake relics in *Sin dejar huella* (2000).

Meanwhile, far away in Juárez, single mother Aurelia packs a lunch for her six-year-old son Juan and loads him and baby brother Billy into her paneled white station wagon. While Juan is at school, Aurelia parks by the Rio Grande, breastfeeding the baby and watching a man try to cross the border. That night her boyfriend Saúl, a low-level drug dealer, visits her at home and stashes some dope there. When he leaves, she and Juan share a pizza in front of the television, but their enjoyment is cut short by a news story about the approximately 250 young women, most of them sweat shop workers like Aurelia, who have been murdered in Juárez over the past few years. Fearing that she will not be safe when she returns to her job from maternity leave, Aurelia sells the drugs, loads a few belongings into the station wagon, and flees with the two boys. Their first stop is Torreón, where Aurelia asks her sister Lolis to take care of Juan until she can get settled with a new job in Cancún. Before saying good-bye, she gives Juan a plane ticket and promises that she will meet him on July 3rd at the Cancún airport with a mariachi band along as a welcome. Having discovered that the drugs are missing, Saúl and his cousin vow to find Aurelia before their boss Don Arnulfo has everyone killed.

Back at the border, Mendizábal finally has released Marilú. Obsessed with charging her for some kind of crime, he orders two henchmen, Trigger Happy and Niko, to follow her. In a clever bit of evasion, she tricks Niko into thinking he is following her out of town on one long-distance bus while she stows away in the restroom of another. When the bus stops for food in Tulacingo, Marilú overhears Aurelia, who coincidentally has happened into the same roadside restaurant, ask the cashier for directions to Cancún. Desperate to make a clean escape, Marilú convinces Aurelia to let her hitch a ride, and the two women leave together. Although she is not as good a driver as she claims, Marilú takes over behind the wheel to give Aurelia a rest, but things do not go smoothly. Marilú is surprised to find baby Billy aboard, and Aurelia is resentful of her companion's superior education and Spanish-bred accent. They bicker over little things until jolted by a greater common threat—a mysterious car that starts to follow behind them with blinking lights and blaring horn. After a brief chase, they pull into a gas station/motel area and spend the night in a shared room that Aurelia pays for. When asked her name, Marilú pauses a moment before replying, "Ana".

Early the next morning they get back on the road only to find that the mystery vehicle, seen in daylight as a red sedan with tinted windows, has begun once again to tail them. Unable to see through the dark glass, each woman privately believes that she is the target of the pursuit and fears what will happen if they are caught. As the red car holds steady behind them, Aurelia pulls off the highway in front of a police car to ask for help with the mechanical trouble she has faked by removing the distributor rotor. By this point, Aurelia has shared only that the pursuers might be her jealous ex-boyfriend Saúl and his cousin, but Ana still has not mentioned Mendizábal. After the station wagon is towed to a service garage, Aurelia replaces the engine part, and they make a briefly successful escape which ends when the red car once again appears in their rearview mirror. Ignoring a work crew barrier and a drug checkpoint, they buy enough time to reassess the situation. Relying on her professional knowledge of the area, Ana suggests taking a backroad through the oilfields to Campeche. On the way there, Aurelia asks how she plans to pay for all the expenses she has incurred, and Ana hands over her expensive sunglasses. They spend the night in an open-air motel cum camp where they begin to loosen up over playing with Billy and drinking a few beers together.

That newly forged friendship is strained the following afternoon when a damaged axle forces them to wait in a small town for a two-day repair job. They argue over whose fault it is, and Aurelia asks for Ana's watch as payment for a phone card. She calls Heraclio Chuc, a Yucatán-based pottery maker who is her partner in the fake relic business, to warn him that Mendizábal is wise to the operation. Aurelia calls Juan to let him know that she is still on the road.

With the station wagon fixed, they proceed along the coast, stopping for a break at deserted Bañanitas Beach. Holding hands and running into the water, they splash around like schoolgirls who have decided to be best friends again. As night falls, Saúl and his cousin coincidentally visit the same nearby cantina where Trigger Happy and Niko are drinking. Neither pair is familiar with the other nor aware that they all are looking for the same white station wagon. The pursuit heats up the next day when the red car tries to force the women off the highway. Ana instinctively climbs into the backseat to protect Billy while Aurelia runs the mystery vehicle into a sandpit. Knowing exactly where she is, Ana guides them down a dirt road to a huge old hacienda hidden away in the jungle.

Owned by an elderly Maya couple, Don Pascual and his wife, the hacienda is a paradise. Lush, airy, and full of children, it brings Ana and Aurelia even closer. They do laundry and go swimming in a large cavernous cenote. Ana confesses to the antiquities scam, explaining that it may be Mendizábal who is following them and apologizing for putting Billy in danger. Well aware of her own drug money guilt, Aurelia says it could be either of them who is being pursued. As protection, they use shovels to reroute the dirt entry road so that it leads directly to the cenote. Also, unknown to Ana, Mendizábal and Chaparro have arrived in Yucatán in search of both her and Heraclio.

Alerted by the children that a red car is in the area, Ana and Aurelia wait out on the road in the station wagon. When they hear the sound of an approaching vehicle, Aurelia shocks Ana by pulling out a gun which she claims will only be for protection. To their surprise, the red car fails to stop and plunges directly into the cenote. By the time they climb down into the cavern, the car is already sinking below the surface. Since there are no survivors, they still do not know who was inside.

Aurelia is so upset the next morning that she cannot produce any milk for Billy, and Ana goes into town to buy some formula. While there, she makes contact with associates for Heraclio, who inform her that Mendizábal has been to his village, roughing up a neighbor lady and discovering the kiln. Upon her return to the hacienda, Ana reveals that it must be Saúl and his cousin who have drowned in the cenote since Mendizábal has been spotted elsewhere. Aurelia reacts tearfully, recounting her bad luck with boyfriends and telling Ana about the planned July 3rd reunion with her other son Juan. The women pack up the station wagon, thank Don Pascual, who refuses to accept any money for their time at the hacienda, and drive away.

That evening they check in to separate rooms at a hotel in Ticul, Yucatán; the desk calendar indicates that it is the second day of June. Over drinks in the restaurant, they argue about the rolled-up peso notes that Aurelia keeps hidden in her makeup bag, a closely guarded supply of cash that Ana discovered at the hacienda and now cites as evidence of drug dealing. Aurelia explains the one-time theft of Saúl's stash and calls Ana an art swindler with a phony social conscience. When it is left behind at the table, Ana takes the bag, packs her few belongings, and checks out of the hotel. Back at the cenote, Chaparro, who is supervising the removal of the red car from the water, recovers the bodies of Trigger Happy and Niko.

Returning to her room, Aurelia finds Saúl there holding the baby. Wounded in the shoulder, he explains that he was betrayed by his cousin and killed him in self-defense. A noise in the corridor turns out to be Mendizábal, who believes he has found Ana. With Aurelia and Billy hiding in the bathroom, Saúl shoots and kills Mendizábal. Together, he and Aurelia wrap the body in a bedspread and drop it through a window to the back alley, where Saúl loads it into the station wagon and drives away. After cleaning up all the blood, Aurelia packs her luggage and discovers that the makeup bag is missing. Assuming that Saúl has taken the money, she rushes to tell Ana only to learn that she too has left the hotel. As dawn breaks, she walks through the town carrying Billy and boards a bus to Cancún.

It is a month later, and Ana finishes her job as bartender in a tourist resort. She returns to a barely furnished apartment to spend the evening drinking a beer and talking to Billy. The next day, July 3rd, she and the baby go to the airport to meet Juan. As the three of them exit the terminal, they find a group of musicians playing for them outside. Ana steps forward to greet them, take the baby's stroller, and return the makeup bag, indicating that most of the money is still there. At the seaside cottage that Ana has found for all of them, Juan plays in the water, Ana reads in a hammock with Billy, and Aurelia enjoys the view from an outdoor table.

A pre-credits sequence reveals that bullied El Chaparro has taken over Mendizábal's job, Saúl has become his bodyguard, and Heraclio has been elected to government office.

Themes

In most Novaro films, female solidarity is a given; in *Sin dejar huella* it is hard earned. The two women seem at first to be marked more by their differences than their similarities. Having never finished high school, Aurelia is a blue-collar single mother with sons from two separate fathers. She works long hours making diving apparel for Paradise Sports Incorporated, a border sweatshop. A highly educated specialist in pre-hispanic art of the classic period, Ana speaks Mayan, dresses stylishly, and steers clear of long-term romantic entanglements. Her accent sounds like it comes from Spain, where she spent some time as a child, while Aurelia has the less embellished accent of northern Mexico.

The contrasts lead initially to antagonism. Already suspicious of the way she hitches a ride with no luggage and no money, Aurelia is annoyed by Ana's inability to identify the type of vehicle that is following them. "I don't know about car models," she says nonchalantly. "What do you know about?" demands Aurelia. Ana responds by listing details of her superior education. Ana's Castilian accent also rankles as a reminder of her patrician pedigree. "Do you also lisp when you speak English?" asks Aurelia sarcastically.

Early in *Sin dejar huella* (2000), Ana (Aitana Sánchez-Gijón, behind the wheel) and Aurelia (Tiaré Scanda) regard each other with animosity.

In a reversal of position, Ana, who has been released from Mendizábal's custody with no carry-on and no money, must rely on Aurelia for all of her material needs. Carefully doling out each bit of cash, Aurelia pays for the food, beer, gas, lodging, and car repairs. As payment, she appropriates Ana's privileged accessories, taking first her Gucci sunglasses and then her Longines wristwatch. Even though she does not recognize the brand names, Aurelia realizes that the items carry both personal and economic value. Conversations between the two often deteriorate into arguments over everything from Ana's driving to Aurelia's drinking.

What slowly brings them together is the danger posed by the red car. Since both have reason to believe the threat is directed at them, they take responsibility for imperiling the other. Aurelia shares some of her Saúl backstory, and when the red car tries to overtake them, Ana immediately climbs into the backseat to protect Billy. As the pursuit stretches over several days, they also begin to appreciate the skills that each brings to the challenge: Aurelia's steadiness behind the wheel and Ana's knowledge of Yucatán. Their survival, they realize, is dependent on each other.

More importantly, they look beyond the surface differences and come to understand how similar they are. Both have long fended for themselves, and both have older sisters from whom they feel somewhat estranged. Ultimately, Ana becomes trusting enough to explain how she slipped into antiquities trafficking by seeing the example of the successful art dealers for whom she worked. When she says, "It can be hard not to take the money when they put it in front of you," Aurelia recognizes that the same rationale applies to her own theft of Saúl's drug stash. Flawed yet resilient, they are both trying to escape the past.

The growing friendship is mirrored in Ana's evolving attitude toward Billy. At first, she is surprised to learn that he is tucked away in the back of the station wagon; the need to feed him regularly seems almost like an imposition. When the red car begins to chase them, however, she reflexively makes sure he is safe and protected. As she and Aurelia spend more time together, they bond over such domestic tasks as caring for the baby and washing clothes. It is Ana who drives into town to buy formula after the cenote car crash leaves Aurelia too frightened to produce milk, and it is Ana who gives the bottle to Billy. Outside the Cancún airport, she takes over behind the stroller, and in the final scene she is lying in the hammock and reading with Billy. Just as she and Aurelia have become the sisters they have both been missing, so too has Ana become Billy's second mother.

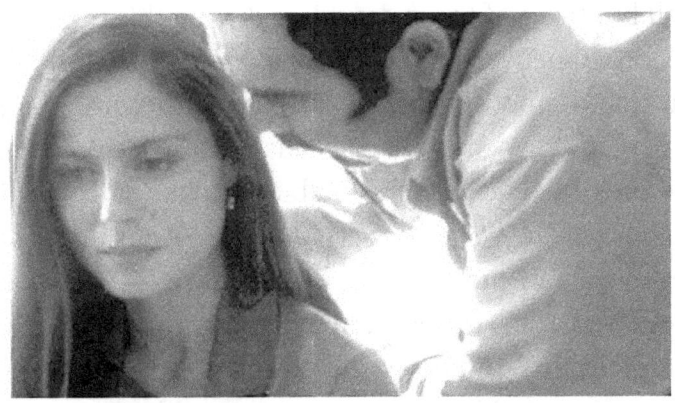

Mendizábal (Jesús Ochoa) threatens Ana (Aitana Sánchez-Gijón) in *Sin dejar huella* (2000).

By contrast, the women, individually and collectively, are menaced by violently unstable men in pursuit of them. Saúl's cousin, Trigger Happy, and Niko are particularly psychotic in their desire to find and punish their intended victims. Moreover, both pairs of henchmen work for patriarchal bosses with massive institutional power—Don Arnulfo the drug lord and Mendizábal the compromised federal police officer. As Traci Roberts-Camps observes, Mendizábal "represents the corruption of an institution that should be there to protect women such as Ana and Aurelia but, in fact, threatens them."[1] The omnipresent red car comes to represent the faceless social oppression that still confronts many women in Mexico. Given the overwhelming forces arrayed against them, then, Aurelia and Ana's feminist-themed victory is a hopeful message of resistance and solidarity. Other reasons for optimism are the supportive male characters Don Pascual and Heraclio as well as the fact that Juan and Billy, despite the typically absent fathers of a Novaro film, will be raised by two strong-willed, unconventional women.

Aurelia and Ana's road trip, the transformative journey of every Novaro film, functions very differently here. More time is spent on the travel than on the destination. Nearly two weeks pass from when Aurelia leaves Juárez until she arrives in Cancún; Ana is with her for all but three of those days. It is during this time together on the road, outmaneuvering their pursuers, that they forge the bonds of physical and emotional support that will become the mainstay of their new lives. Each challenge calls for a strategic response that neither woman would have been able to make solely on her own. "In *Sin dejar huella*," writes Roberts-Camps, "Ana and Aurelia progress from a state of individualism to solidarity—with a few lapses in between—as they travel from northern to southern Mexico."[2] During this excursion across the country, Novaro showcases the regional customs and landscapes that inform her sense of national identity and her conviction that cultural life extends far beyond Mexico City.

The closer the women get to the ocean, the more they begin to physically relax. "I like it here," declares Aurelia, breathing in great gulps of fresh air, as they float along on a barge in Yucatán. When they stop at Playa Bañanitas, they strip down to their underclothes, hold hands, and jump into the water. With much of the tension between themselves dissolved, they play like little girls, Aurelia sharing her simple dream of owning a tiny three-roomed hotel and Ana describing the remote magical beaches that lie south of Cancún. The same kind of emotional cleanse occurs at the hacienda when they go swimming in the cenote and Ana belatedly explains the antiquities scam in a way that makes Aurelia associate it with her own act of larceny. It is fitting that their reunion and escape from danger should find Aurelia and Ana settled happily next to the sea, here as always for Novaro a symbol of unrestrained freedom. In a final Edenic image, they lounge undisturbed on the beach, both boys safe within their care.

Having grown closer, Ana (Aitana Sánchez-Gijón in white) and Aurelia (Tiaré Scanda) frolic in the ocean during a stop along the way in *Sin dejar huella* (2000).

Six-year-old Juan, under the constant shadow of violence in Juárez, is thoroughly liberated by his nearness to the ocean, where barred windows give way to open horizons and where he romps contentedly by himself in the surf. He is one of Novaro's mature-for-their-age children, innocent yet hyper-aware at the same time. We first see him bundling his brother into a baby carrier and loading him into the station wagon. Acting more like his mother's chaperon than her son, he opens the door to Saúl, announces him as Aurelia's "novio" (boyfriend), and casts a disapproving glance at the showy new snakeskin boots he is quick to display. Alone in his bedroom, Juan solemnly watches the news of the Juárez murders and reacts skeptically when Aurelia makes up a story about where she got her bag of cash. "You're just like me," he tells her. "It's easy to tell when you lie." He is not happy about staying behind with his Aunt Lolis in Torreón but goes along with his mother's relocation plan. During her one phone call from the road, he questions her closely about her slow progress and tells Lolis that he thinks she is just driving around aimlessly with Billy. So apprehensive is Juan that he does not once smile until he sees the musicians outside the airport in Cancún, and his full return to the joys of childhood comes only after Ana has taken everyone to their new home by the sea. Even when he is absent from the narrative, Juan is a reminder to Aurelia of why she is so desperate to start over again. Like the children who befriend the two women at the hacienda, he represents a guileless personal world far removed from the violence and intrigue of the adults. His example is meant to be instructive. Also, considering his solicitude toward his baby brother and respect for his single mother, it is certain that Juan will not ever become one of the director's habitually absent, irresponsible fathers.

The personal is always political for Novaro. In each of her films, and *Sin dejar huella* is no exception, there is a free-floating unease about the way in which government works against the interests of the individual. Law enforcement is either corrupt or ineffective, its presence on the street a cause for alarm not comfort. "When did the country become so full of soldiers and *federales*?" asks Ana as she and Aurelia confront one of the highway checkpoints. In addition to the trappings of a police state, official graft exists as a condition of everyday life. Mendizábal may be investigating Ana's antiquities trade because she is no longer paying him off with a share of the profits, and Saúl's cousin is probably working for both Don Arnulfo and the feds. The physical mayhem is equally real; to flush out Heraclio's whereabouts, Mendizábal orders the beating of the elderly woman who lives next door to him.

In the last of the pre-credit updates, a worker at one of the pollution-spewing oil refineries takes down a sign for Pemex, the state-owned Mexican Petroleum company, and replaces it with one for "Exell," a fictive portmanteau of Exxon and Shell. The implication is that the new Mexico with its restructured NAFTA agreements and roadside convenience stores awash with imported consumer goods is manipulated by economic forces beyond its borders, that behind the drug traffic king and corrupt politicians lie the power structures of Wall Street. Against this institutional theft, Ana and Aurelia's larceny is insignificant.

Novaro's response is to flirt with the radical left. "Long Live the EZLN," a reference to the Zapatista Army of National Liberation, reads some spray-painted wall graffiti that the women pass on their way to Ticul, Yucatán. A militant anarcho-socialist group advocating indigenous ownership of local resources, the EZLA by 2000, the year of *Sin dejar huella's* release, already controlled major portions of territory in the southernmost state of Chiapas, Mexico. When Aurelia insists that "the ideal man does not exist," Ana jokingly responds, "Mine does, but he's deep in the Lacandon Jungle and he's not coming out." To clarify the point, she adds, "He's Subcomandante Marcos," a respectful name-checking of the Zapatistas' charismatic leader. Peripherally topical, the references never go further into any kind of sustained political analysis or advocacy. There is admittedly a touch of fairy tale to Aurelia and Ana's isolated seaside haven but the search for personal autonomy is a legitimate response to what Elissa Rashkin has called "the fragmentation and confusion of a nation undergoing crisis and uneven change."[3] Personal resistance, coupled with alternative public forms of organization (as suggested by Heraclio's electoral victory), continue to be Novaro's answer to the institutional corruption of Mexican politics. As Rashkin writes, "Given the choice between a sterile nationalism . . . and an uncritical embrace of the mass culture that now bombards Mexican cities and countryside . . . many artists have chosen a third path: a vindication of popular culture that embraces modernity and syncretism but remains on the side of ordinary people, whose creativity is recognized as an act of survival."[4] Aurelia and Ana's journey is one such act of self-preservation.

Style and Structure

Famously declaring her opposition to conventional, action-oriented filmmaking, María Novaro once told an interviewer, "That 'proper' way of narrating bores me. I studied 'proper' narration in school, I could do it, but I didn't see any point to it," adding, "The truth is that I am not concerned about things happening . . . ."[5] This is the film which verifies that traditional film school technical savvy. On the surface, it looks like a tautly directed road trip/buddy film complete with high-speed chases, multiple murders, and a spectacular car crash. Following a traditional narrative arc, two causal events generate two overlapping pursuits which proceed through advances and setbacks to a final resolution of conflict. What subverts the straightforward storytelling, however, is how Novaro rations out critical information.

In his historical analysis of Hollywood screenwriting conventions, film scholar David Bordwell notes, "Every narrative presents a flow of information about the ongoing action. But typically that information is distributed unequally. What economists call information asymmetry is central to storytelling in all media. Some characters know more, some know less."[6] It is precisely that dynamic between restricted and complete knowledge of the events that Novaro plays with in *Sin dejar huella*, whose title itself references informational limits. Both Aurelia and Ana withhold crucial backstory from each other. Not until their time at the hacienda does Ana explain about the antiquities trafficking, and only later still in Ticul does Aurelia confess to stealing Saúl's drug stash. They also delay the exchange of details about how each has compromised the safety of Heraclio and Juan respectively. As viewers, we seem to have a more omniscient point of view. We are aware of both women's initial misdeeds and we know there are two separate red cars—the one that Mendizábal and Chaparro use to pick up Ana at the border and another one that Saúl's cousin parks in front of Aurelia's house. We know that Mendizábal has followed Ana to Yucatán, and we see that Trigger Happy and Niko are the victims of the cenote crash. But even we are cut off from key pieces of information. We have no idea how Saúl shot his cousin nor how he disposed of Mendizábal's body. At the end of the film, despite the credit update sequences, there still remain multiple unanswered questions. What did Ana do with the money she "borrowed" from Aurelia? How did Saúl and Chaparro connect with each other? What new position has Heraclio attained?

One result of this tight control on information is to shift focus to the way characters process the knowledge that they do possess, how, for example, Saúl handles his betrayal, the women respond to the car crash, and Aurelia reacts to her stolen money bag. On an equally significant level Novaro's strategy is subtextual commentary on narrative conventions and expectations. Having confounded us with gaps in exposition, she teases us with the possibility of an unresolved ending and then jokingly delivers an audience-friendly resolution as improbable as it is satisfying. "Look, this really would not happen this way," she seems to be saying, "but since it is what we all want, here you go." It is like the ending of *Gloria* (1980), where a tongue-in-cheek John Cassavetes allows Gena Rowlands to outmaneuver an army of gangsters against all odds and reunite with the young boy she has promised to protect.

Novaro's lightness of touch is also evident in the way she adds dark comedy to the mix of genres. Mendizábal and Chaparro are clownish villains in the manner of Captain Hook and Smee. Each time Chaparro thinks he has pleased his boss, he is rudely insulted, his unctuous grin collapsing into a grimace of humiliation. No matter how hard he tries, he can never be evil enough. Saúl is similarly dismissed by both his cousin and Juan as a vain screw-up more interested in flashy clothes than good decisions. He haplessly kills Mendizábal and his cousin in what is arguably self-defense and then rises to power alongside El Chaparro in an ironic triumph of losers, a successful revenge of the incompetent.

More traditionally comic, reminiscent of nearly every buddy film ever made, is the bickering relationship between Aurelia and Ana. Much of the humor derives from their personality differences—Aurelia the beer-drinking *norteña* and Ana the sophisticated cosmopolitan. When Aurelia balks at taking her sunglasses as payment for her share of the travel expenses, Ana insists, "But they're Gucci." Trying them on, Aurelia gauchely remarks, "They may be *fuchi* ('ugly'), but they look good on me." Stopping the station wagon to feed Billy, Aurelia announces, "Ten minutes on each tit and off we go." As she tosses down a few beers herself, Ana watches Aurelia change the baby's diaper and laughingly recalls the crooked genitalia of an ex-boyfriend. "You should drink more often," says Aurelia approvingly. "I might even get to like you." While the mismatched friends wait at the edge of the cenote for the red car, they entertain each other with actual jokes. Aurelia tells one in which a "dumb Spaniard" is sent to check whether some highway flashers are working and reports back, "Now yes, now no. Now yes, now no." Ana asks, "What do women do while waiting for the ideal man?" Answer: "They get married." The airport scene itself ends with a kind of punchline. As they stroll along with the musicians, Ana says, "I have something to tell you. My name's not Ana," and Aurelia says, "You bitch," before adding, "Wait 'til you hear what happened to me."

The beer drinking is one of several recurrent gestural motifs Novaro uses to structure and develop the narrative. Among the others are loading and unloading the station wagon, packing clothes, attending to Billy, and stringing up hammocks for sleep. Each activity brings the women closer together, often signaling a shift in attitude. For example, Ana moves from casual disregard of Billy to active protection and nursing in a progression that mirrors her growing identification with Aurelia. Once the women reach

Yucatán, starting with the open-air lodging and continuing through the hacienda, they set up the bedrooms with hammocks, physical expressions of the looser, more relaxed lifestyles they are encountering. At one point Aurelia says she will only use hammocks in the future, a pledge born out by the blue one hanging inside her otherwise bare apartment in Cancún. The final oceanside image of Ana, holding Billy while relaxing outside in a hammock, weds two of the most important motifs in a reassuring statement of reunion and tranquility.

Textual commentary also inevitably surfaces in a Novaro film through signs and slogans embedded within the settings. Soon after she sets out on the highway, Aurelia passes signs which read "Sifting Sands" and "No Return," foreshadowing the unavoidable dangers of her journey. A posted hand-painted message at Bañanitas Beach promises "Here we find only friends." Upon seeing it, Aurelia asks, "Are you my friend, Ana?" In response, Ana takes her hand and they run into the water together. The imminent hostility of the cantina where the red sedan stops is reflected in a sign over the bar which warns, "No minors, men in uniform or mentally ill." Unsurprisingly, a random confrontation almost erupts there between the two unrelated pairs of pursuers.

To visually underscore the role of chance and coincidence in the story Novaro pulls off some intricately engineered shots in which unknowing subjects are placed in the same space at the same time. In one such set-up, the bus Ana has boarded pulls into the left edge of a ground-level shot while an old woman gets on and Aurelia's station wagon crosses left to right in the distant background. Not much later, after the bus has stopped for a lunch break, Ana discusses departure times with the drivers in the foreground while over her shoulder Aurelia pays her check at the counter. The anticipated meeting between the two then occurs when Ana overhears Aurelia asking for directions to Cancún and hitches a ride. The unshakable presence of the red car following them is ominously stressed in a single shot where the camera pans right across a bridge with the station wagon to reveal the red sedan waiting underneath and then exiting the left frame in quick pursuit. At the roadside cantina, as our confusion over the car chase continues, Saúl and his cousin argue about Aurelia in the foreground as Trigger Happy and Niko get progressively drunker at a table just behind them. The fact that neither duo is aware of the other's identity adds to the slightly absurd nature of the entire situation.

Once Novaro has introduced Aurelia and Ana, she tends to link them together in two-shots, visual affirmations of their growing solidarity. These shots function metonymically to represent the film's central dynamic—that is, the coming together of two women for mutual support and defense. Conversations at the gas station snack table, the motel bedroom, the open-air camp, the ferry barge, and the car repair shop, scenes where Aurelia and Ana plan strategy, are primarily two-shots with the camera positioned at mid-range. The characters can be seen in relation to their surroundings, but visual importance is given to the centrally framed intimacy between them. In other scenes, movement within the two-shot frame calls attention to an actual physical bond. After Aurelia forces the red car into a sand pit, Ana reaches across the front seat to pat her reassuringly on the shoulder. Later, thinking that it was Saúl who crashed into the cenote, Aurelia frets by herself in the hacienda bedroom. She is in the foreground, lying in a hammock that stretches across the width of the frame. "What did you expect?" says Ana offscreen before entering the shot to gently console Aurelia. In both instances, as with the beach scene where she takes Aurelia's hand to jump into the waves, Ana initiates a gesture that bridges the physical and emotional distance separating the two women.

Novaro uses two-shots like this one of Ana (Aitana Sánchez-Gijón, left) and Aurelia (Tiaré Scanda) on the ferry barge to suggest the women's developing solidarity in *Sin dejar huella* (2000).

For some of the more intense bickering, Novaro cross-cuts back and forth between one-shots. Strained by a series of damaging revelations and suspicions, the friendship threatens to completely unravel at the hotel in Ticul. Ana sits alone at a table in the restaurant, coldly regarding Aurelia as she enters the frame and sits down across from her. Noticing the frosty reception, Aurelia asks, "Do you have a toothache or something?" Ana's answer, when it finally comes, is to question, "Aurelia are you into drug trafficking?" As the conversation heatedly expands to cover the money bag, the car crash, the relics trade, and the trip itself, they angrily exchange accusations of blame and betrayal. Seen primarily in alternating one-shots, their reactions emphasize temporary discord rather than unity. Instead of making a gesture of consolation, Aurelia snaps, "Let's settle this tomorrow" and exits the left edge of the frame, leaving Ana alone in the same one-shot that opened the scene. It is at this point that Ana takes the money bag which Aurelia has left behind, a rupture which is not repaired until Ana walks into the frame outside the Cancún airport and returns the money to Aurelia. Film professor Susan Hayward explains the shot variation at work here in the simplest of terms: "Compare a two-shot MS and a series of separate one-shots in MS of two people. The former suggests intimacy, the latter distance."[7]

Novaro introduces the restaurant scene with one of her elegant trademark tracking shots. As Aurelia leaves her second floor hotel room and walks down the corridor to the restaurant, the camera tracks laterally along with her from across the open courtyard. In the beginning of the film, the camera tracks in on Aurelia sitting in the hills above Juárez and breastfeeding Billy and then later makes a nearly 360 degree circuit around the station wagon at the cenote as Ana and Aurelia wait inside for the red car to appear. Prowling and exploratory, the camera in each instance seems to be anticipating a significant shift in the action. For the comprehensive visual coverage of the actual road trip, the camera is crouched inside the station wagon, mounted atop the hood, or placed on an escort vehicle. Once the chase begins, Novaro plays adroitly with the familiar imagery of an action film. The red car flashes its lights in the darkness, materializes ominously in the rearview mirror, screeches its tires in pursuit, and threatens to crowd the station wagon off the highway. The cenote crash, shot from multiple angles and edited in slightly extended time, reveals a flair for spectacular, large-scale stunt work not usually evident in Novaro's typically more intimate filmmaking.

Despite the far-reaching influence of the past on the lives of Ana and Aurelia, there are no flashbacks anywhere within the film. Scenes are arranged sequentially in strict chronological order, with cuts between simultaneous actions. As Ana and Aurelia argue at the hotel restaurant, for example, Novaro cuts away to the red car being craned from the cenote. She also uses cuts as exclamatory markers throughout the narrative. "Can you drive?" Aurelia asks Ana, and there is a cut to the station wagon bumping into the curb outside the restaurant in Tulacingo where the two women meet. Further along in the trip they float peacefully on a ferry barge as Ana draws a map of the route they will take; the next scene finds them sitting on a couch outside a repair shop and arguing over who is to blame for the station wagon's broken axle. "Are you my friend, Ana?" asks Aurelia in that critical Bañanitas Beach scene and the next shot has them running hand-in-hand to the water. Temporarily safe at the hacienda, Ana and Aurelia prepare their bedroom for the night, and Novaro cuts to a shot of Mendizábal getting his boots polished in a town not too far away. After the red car has crashed and the women try futilely to see who is inside, there is a revelatory cut to Mendizábal and Chaparro walking down the corridor of a nearby police station. While Aurelia and Saúl reconnect in her Ticul hotel room, cuts to the lobby and hallway show Mendizábal about to intrude. In each instance, the direct cut presents new information that either confirms or contradicts the assumptions of one of the characters.

Novaro gets similar dramatic effect through her use of color. Once again, as in *Danzón*, the key colors are red, green, and blue, but this time around with slightly different connotations. The reds begin simply enough as highlighted compositional details within the frame. There are the red thermos bottle that Aurelia packs, the red bedspread in Juan's room, and the red table at the gas station. With the inescapable appearance of the red car on the road behind Ana and Aurelia, however, the color takes on more sinister implications. Each glimpse of the vehicle—waiting under the bridge, blocking the service station entrance, parked outside the roadside cantina—confirms the danger closing in on them. The coded association of red with impending violence reaches a climax with the blood seeping under the hotel doorway and gathering in the great puddles that Aurelia works frantically to mop up with the hotel towels and bedsheets. "You're lucky to be a boy, son," she mutters to Billy. "Women always do the cleaning."

By contrast, the green of the jungle and the blue of the ocean are soothing to the eye and to the soul. As soon as the landscape shifts from the barren north to the verdant south, Aurelia releases much of the tension that has been gripping her. Point of view shots from the station wagon document pristine beaches and dense green foliage. The salty blue ocean water comes as a revelation to Aurelia as does the first panning shot of the endless lawn of the hacienda. It is significant that all traces of red have been scrubbed from the seaside haven that ends the film, a blue green refuge that also cleanses away the lingering smudge of the oil refinery smokestacks that frequently have blotted the skyline throughout the journey.

Cast and Crew

In their respective roles of Ana and Aurelia, Aitana Sánchez-Gijón and Tiaré Scanda, demonstrate the same appealing screen chemistry shown by such memorable buddy film partners as Brigitte Bardot and Jeanne Moreau (*Viva Maria*, 1965), Geena Davis and Susan Sarandon (*Thelma & Louise*, 1991), and Salma Hayek and Penélope Cruz (*Bandidas*, 2006). Like those other female duos, they react to each other with resentment, bemusement, and ultimately, protective empathy. Their scenes together vibrate with a tension that is balanced by growing affection. Difficult though it is to pull off parts that freely mix danger and dark humor, neither actress ever stumbles out of character. As they share wardrobe and transform physically into mirror images of each other, the rapport between them becomes increasingly more trenchant.

Aurelia (Tiaré Scanda with gun) and Ana (Aitana Sánchez-Gijón) brace for trouble at the cenote in *Sin dejar huella* (2000).

Having already starred with Keanu Reeves in *A Walk in the Clouds* (1995) and Javier Bardem in *Mouth to Mouth* (1995), Aitana

Sánchez-Gijón arrived on Novaro's set with a lengthy résumé in theater, television, and film. Born in Italy to a Spanish father and Italian mother, she had been working professionally since her teens. In addition to roles on several popular Spanish-language TV series and parts in over twenty feature films, she had appeared on stage in plays by Jacinto Benavente, Jean-Paul Sartre, and Tennessee Williams. Named Best Actress by the Spanish Cinema Writers Circle (*Havanero 1820*, 1994), the Spanish Actors Union (*La regenta*, 1995), the Association of Latin Entertainment Critics of New York (*Boca a boca*, 1998), the San Sebastián International Film Festival (*Volavérun*, 1999), and other award groups, she would go on to a long career that includes being elected President of the Spanish Academy of Motion Picture Arts and Sciences (1998-2000), serving as a Cannes Film Festival jury member (2000), and co-starring with Christian Bale in *The Machinist* (2004). Her European parentage and cultural bona fides are perfectly suited to Ana's well-educated, cosmopolitan-centered backstory.

Five years younger than co-star Sánchez-Gijón, Tiaré Scanda already was well known to Mexican audiences from her many recurrent roles on such popular *telenovelas* as *Muchachitas* (1991-92), *Buscando el paraíso* (1993), *La culpa* (1996), *Azul* (1996), and *Laberintos de pasión* (1999-2000). She had also appeared in several feature films including *Un año perdido* (1993), *El callejón de los milagros* (1995), and a remake of the 1940s classic *Salón México* (1996), the latter two of which also co-starred *Danzón* actress María Rojo. For her role of Maru in *El callejón de los milagros*, she received an Ariel Award nomination as Best Supporting Actress. She also had worked with Salma Hayek, the Bichir brothers (Demián and Bruno), and Jorge Sanz. A native of Mexico City like Novaro herself, Tiaré Scanda has maintained an extensive career in film and television up to the present. Always an excellent ensemble player, she also enlivens her portrayal of Aurelia with an unexpected flair for low-key comedy.

Another familiar actor joining the cast was Jesús Ochoa as the corrupt federal police official Mendizábal. A versatile character actor known in the business as "Choby," he had previously won Best Supporting Actor Ariel Awards for *Entre Pancho Villa y una mujer desnuda* (1996) and *Bajo California: El límite del tiempo* (1998). Equally adept at comedy and drama, he uses his deep voice, expressive face, and sizable girth to make Mendizábal equal parts threatening and ridiculous. Subsequent career highlights include playing a bad guy in the James Bond film *Quantum of Solace* (2008) and dubbing the Spanish language voice of "Manny" in all installments of the *Ice Age* franchise.

Just twenty-three years old at the time of production and already a past Ariel Award nominee for Best Actor (*Libre de culpas*, 1997), Argentinian-born Martín Altomaro adds a sympathetic shading to Aurelia's handsome, none-too-bright boyfriend Saúl. Well cast as the various thugs are Juan Manuel Bernal (Saúl's cousin), Roberto Rios (Trigger Happy), and Gerardo Taracena (Niko). José Sefami, who appeared the same year in Alejandro Iñárritu's *Amores perros*, plays El Chaparro as a resentful, slow-smoldering flunky to Mendizábal. Despite the relatively large cast, there are few crowd scenes, and Novaro concentrates as usual on the dramatic interactions between two or three characters at a time. Her special skill in directing children is evident in the winsome, totally believable performance of Edmundo Sotelo as levelheaded Juan.

For the first time in her feature film career, Novaro was flying solo as screenwriter, minus the collaboration of sister Beatriz. Regardless of that change and the six-year gap since *El jardín del Edén*, Novaro's vision, themes, and style are remarkably consistent with her earlier work. She is operating on a grander scale here but still in full control of the process. Her script received an Ariel Award nomination for Best Original Screenplay.

The director of photography is Serguei Saldívar Tanaka, and the editor is Ángel Hernández Zoido. Both had been working professionally since the early 90s, having begun their careers, like so many Novaro crew members, in shorts and documentaries. Saldívar won the second of his four career Ariel Awards for Best Cinematography; he and Hernández would work together again on Pablo Perelman's *A Painting Lesson* (2011). As an indication of the film's rich production values, Novaro also enlisted the participation of special effects master Alejandro Vazquez, who received the fourth of what to date have been ten Ariel Awards for Best Special Effects. His most notable win is for his work on Alfonso Cuarón's widely acclaimed *Roma* (2018).

Carefully chosen from a variety of traditional and contemporary sources, music is used here as in *Danzón* to reflect characters and settings. From the drug and lost love themed *norteño* ballads of Juárez to the Caribbean influenced rhythms of Cancún, the selections track the geographic sweep of Aurelia and Ana's journey. Among the soundtrack contributors are Daniel Tierra Negra, Ana Gabriel, Grupo Mono Blanco, and Mexican music legend Juan Gabriel. The film's overall sound design garnered Ariel nominations for Nerio Barberis and Juan Borrel Soldevila.

"When you are sitting at your desk alone, thinking, listening to your music, it is easy to get in touch with yourself, but when you are filming, it is very, very difficult," Novaro once revealed in an interview. "People don't imagine the work required to make a movie. It is a titanic, almost military, and even hellish job, because it is extraordinarily expensive and involves a large amount of stress and demands made by the technology used in filming a movie."[8] With one of her largest production budgets to date, she successfully handled the "stress and demands," shooting in multiple locations across the country and commanding a small army of cast and crew.

Ten years would pass before the release of her next feature film, a more intimate project and one with the most controversial subject matter yet.

Las buenas hierbas (The Good Herbs)

María Novaro wrote *Las buenas hierbas* in 2000 and filmed it ten years later. Funding came from a Guggenheim fellowship, Axolote Cine, IMCINE, FOPROCINE, and various other private and public sources. After the bloated production that was *Sin dejar huella*, this was a happily scaled-down personal project with a handful of young crew members and a condensed cast that included Ofelia Medina and Ana Ofelia Murguía. Intimate and candid, the story touched on such topics as Alzheimer's, herbal medicine, euthanasia, family relationships, and spiritualism. Ironically, it was a film that featured one of the smallest crews and two of the biggest stars with whom Novaro had ever worked.

The company shot entirely on location in Mexico City and Oaxaca. The total budget, including all postproduction costs, was less than a million dollars. Following its premiere at the Guadalajara Film Festival in March of 2010, the movie was screened at festivals in Italy, France, Cuba, Poland, and China. In a review posted from Guadalajara, *Variety* called it "Novaro's most visually accomplished film,"[1] and *The Hollywood Reporter's* account from the Rome Film Festival praised the "sure-footed direction by leading Mexican filmmaker María Novaro."[2] Commercial distribution, despite the picture's critical success, was limited.

Although consequently it was barely seen in either the United States or in Mexico, *Las buenas hierbas* played, curiously enough, for over a year in theaters all throughout Japan.

Story

Dalia lives in Mexico City with her two-year-old son Cosmo, works occasionally at an independent radio station, and subsists mainly on the regular checks sent by her father, with whom she speaks often on the phone but whose voice and image never appear on screen. She is, however, very close to her mother Lala, a divorced ethnobotanist who specializes in collecting and processing healthful herbs. Located in one of the city's leafy old neighborhoods, Lala's house is filled with plant specimens and surrounded by a lush garden. During one of Dalia's frequent visits, Lala casually mentions that a man broke into her house and stole her keys. Dalia discovers the keys in a glass cookie jar, but Lala brushes off the whole affair, concentrating instead on the small nose piercing that her daughter has gotten.

Arriving late at the radio station, Dalia is warmly greeted by the other staff members, especially by el Rot, a scruffy on-air commentator who is romantically interested in her. She takes a seat next to him as he tells a rambling story about how a naked poet is like a snail and welcomes his listeners to Radio Cactus, a free "communitarian" station that is the "slimiest on the dial." Acting as bemused co-host, Dalia seems to enjoy his eccentric performance and personality. After work, Dalia takes Cosmo for a walk; they linger on a pedestrian overpass to watch the cars below and the little boy becomes preoccupied with his mother's nose piercing. Later they visit Dalia's ex-husband Luis and while Cosmo plays in the yard, Dalia tells him about the keys incident. Luis sympathizes with her concern but offers no suggestions.

An older woman, who turns out later to be Dalia's neighbor Blanquita, listens to Pedro Infante singing on the radio. In what seems to be an unrelated cutaway, a teenage girl in a dirty pink formal dress crosses another pedestrian overpass, bumping into a young man who takes no notice of her. She stops to watch a metro train passing underneath. As if prompted, Dalia and Cosmo board a train at the Estadio Azteca station on the Xochimilco line. Also on board is a twenty-something guy who stares at all the pretty female passengers.

On a different afternoon, Dalia, Lala, and Cosmo walk through Mexico City's Botanical Garden. Dalia agrees to help her mother organize her papers, articles, herbal instructions, and scraps of information. The work is slow and challenging, but she resolves to keep at it. Taking a break, Dalia goes to the movies and finds herself seated just in front of the lovelorn guy from the metro train. His name is Gabo, and he is telling a friend all about his inability to pick up the various girls he likes. Touched by his despair, Dalia hands him her name and number on a piece of paper and tells him to give her a call.

Dalia, Blanquita, and another neighbor named Ana are hanging clothes to dry on the roof of their apartment building. Blanquita asks for a "funny cigarette," and she and Dalia smoke a joint. "I made a mess of my men," says Blanquita as she talks about her three ex-husbands. Declaring that all women have secrets, she laughs when Dalia says that her mother kept marijuana plants for medicinal purposes only and tells the younger woman that she doesn't know her mother as well as she thinks she does. Ana claims that she is an "open book," a comment that not even she can process with a straight face.

Confirming the notion of secrets, Gabo wakes from a night spent with Dalia and rides off into the early morning streets on his bicycle. When Dalia arrives later at the radio station, Rot's co-workers are kidding him about his unrequited love for her, but he proceeds calmly with his broadcast criticism of the government's decision to remove the prickly pear from the national emblem. Taking the randomness in stride, Dalia leaves early to visit her mother, who has locked herself inside the house and frantically insists that the place has been invaded by a horde of strange men.

A doctor's exam and brain scan indicate that Lala has early onset Alzheimer's disease. After sharing the news with Dalia, Lala confides, "I don't want to be a dependent person who cannot live by herself" and makes her daughter promise to not ever let her "be treated as an old sack." Aware of Lala's condition, Ana and Blanquita have a serious rooftop conversation about life and death. When Ana wonders what people with Alzheimer's die from, Blanquita replies, "I don't know, everything and nothing." Asked about the brutal murder of her only granddaughter, Blanquita explains that the killer was let go after less than a year in prison. "Six months for the life of my child," she says bitterly.

Along with the neighbors, Dalia also reveals the diagnosis to her father, who agrees to pay all the medical bills. During their phone conversation, she begins to cry, and Cosmo reacts by sadly touching the side of his check. Home alone that night, Lala mixes up a special herbal potion, chanting about a spirit woman who "can go in and out from the kingdom of death." The face of a weathered old woman in a *rebozo* materializes and then disappears outside her window. In an equally eerie incident, Blanquita seems to witness a second appearance of the girl in the pink dress. As the young woman dances against a black background, a large red stain spreads slowly across her midsection.

Lala, meanwhile, continues to deteriorate rapidly. Even getting dressed becomes an ordeal. Prompted by Dalia to select a skirt, she instead pulls one blouse after another out of the closet while obsessing over her inability to find a specific plant reference in the *Aztec Herbal Codex* of 1552. Clothes pile up on the bed, Dalia begins to cry, and the episode ends with Lala dressed in a slip, two sweaters, and no skirt. A search for specimens in the botanical garden ends prematurely when Lala focuses instead on telling Dalia about a man who keeps touching her in her dreams. An attempt to introduce a new home caregiver fails when Lala decides she doesn't like the woman's clothes. Wandering around a park by herself at night, Lala randomly asks visitors, "What time does the concert start?" Blanquita and Dalia grow exhausted in their efforts to provide around-the-clock attention.

Both women also deal with personal issues. Dalia continues to sleep with Gabo despite the lack of any meaningful communication between the two of them. When Gabo visits the radio station, Rot takes an immediate dislike to him. Similarly jealous, Luis pumps Cosmo for information on the special men friends who visit his mother. On her own accord, Dalia loses interest, and Gabo fades from her life as quietly as he entered. Blanquita once again sees the girl in the pink dress sitting in a jacaranda tree outside her window and experiences an extended flashback in which it becomes clear that the mysterious figure is the granddaughter who was murdered on the day of her *quinceañera*. Unable to pass gently into the afterlife, she roams unseen (except by the film viewers) through the familiar places of her childhood.

With their mother-daughter roles completely reversed, Dalia cares for Lala as best she can. She prepares aloe vera gel to soften her skin and aromatherapy to jog her memory. For help in navigating the house, she prints hand-lettered signs for the furniture and other no-longer-familiar objects. Seating Cosmo and Lala at the kitchen table, Dalia tries to feed her older "child" a quesadilla, but Lala begins to rave that Dalia's real biological father is a South American guerrilla fighter who also sings and plays the guitar. Even though a visibly disturbed Dalia asks her to stop, Lala spins the tale more furiously, picking up Cosmo and announcing that he too will grow up to be a handsome *guerrillero*. Some days later, Lala wakes in the middle of the night, slips past a drowsing Blanquita, and wanders out into the garden. Losing her way and breaking some pottery, she wets herself and begins to scream. When Dalia arrives to relieve Blanquita the next morning, the house is trashed, and Lala is still howling. Dalia packs a bag for Cosmo to stay with his father and stops going to the radio station.

During a calm period, Dalia and Lala play with a set of paper cut-out dolls. Looking directly at her daughter, Lala asks, "Who are you?" Frustrated by the unfamiliar face, she becomes hysterical and rushes fearfully from the room. Afterwards, Dalia smokes a joint on the roof while quoting from *Alice in Wonderland*. In a flashback, she recalls gathering plants in the woods with Lala when she was a little girl. Attempting to help her mother access those same memories, Dalia shows Lala a card game involving plant illustrations, but the older woman remains unresponsive.

After a swift downward slide, Lala can no longer leave her bed. When Blanquita finishes sponging and changing her, she whispers, "I think you will leave this world before me . . . you have to take care of my granddaughter Citlali . . . I want you to find her." As if in acknowledgment of this concern, Citlali appears more often, even following Blanquita onto the metro and resting an unseen hand on her shoulder. In need of more support, Dalia summons a home nurse who shows her how to treat the bed sores stretching across Lala's back. Dalia asks whether her mother is aware and if she is suffering, and the nurse replies that it is hard to know. What she does say, however, is that Lala's condition "can go on for a very long time" and that "this illness is worse for younger people . . . the process is more violent."

Worried by Lala's descent into a semi-comatose state, Dalia takes her to the hospital, where indifferent staff members exclude Dalia from the examination room and begin to handle Lala like the "old sack" she envisioned. Remembering her promise, Dalia interrupts the proceedings and takes Lala back home. Curled up next to her mother on the bed, Dalia strokes her hair and asks unanswered questions about her travels, boyfriends, and mystical experiences. Flashbacks of mother and daughter making semolina soup alternate with shots of the chanting spirit woman and clouds gathering against a mountain top. "How can fear be cured, mama?" asks Dalia. Holding a pillow embroidered with the words "I give my heart to you" against Lala's face, Dalia peacefully ends her mother's life. The two of them lie next to each other in bed for the rest of the night. In the morning, Dalia calls her father and tells him that Lala has died. "Can you come?" she asks. An image of a single flowering herb fills the screen.

Themes

Not surprisingly, men have little impact on the action and issues of *Las buenas hierbas*. Dalia's father is an unnamed, unseen presence on the other end of a telephone line. He provides money but very little emotional support as she copes with Lala's illness. They speak on three separate occasions, each phone conversation brief and devoted to practical details. When she calls her father with the news of Lala's death, she asks poignantly for a physical connection that so far has been absent.

Dalia's actual father may literally be missing from her life as well. Although she is probably lost in a delusion, Lala insists that Dalia is the daughter of a dashing South American revolutionary with multiple musical talents. Resisting the idea as ridiculous, Dalia pleads with Lala to stop talking but is rattled enough to share the story with her friends, who rather than dismissing the possibility outright suggest instead that Dalia bears a strong resemblance to the famous Uruguayan singer/songwriter Eduardo Mateo. The reassurance she had hoped to find collapses into the vague but not impossible chance that she has never known her biological father at all.

Her romantic relationships with men seem to be similarly unfulfilling. It is again a question of emotional availability. While she and ex-husband Luis share custody of Cosmo on very amicable terms, he fails to help Dalia process her grief. He downplays the lost keys incident and responds to her confusion in sending Cosmo away by stating that she is overpacking. Rather than inquire about her state of mind, he pumps Cosmo for information about Dalia's male visitors. Immature, sex-starved Gabo is even less helpful. With nothing between them but casual hook-ups, they stumble through awkward conversations where he pretends to be interested in her habit of pinning random words and phrases on the wall and she does not even attempt to tell him about Lala. Before his fickleness sends him chasing after another radio station employee, Dalia has lost interest anyway. Rot, the witty on-air commentor, has a loyal romantic crush on Dalia, but as with Lola and Duende's relationship in Novaro's first feature film, Dalia does not feel any sexual attraction toward him.

Blanquita has had three husbands and by her own description has made a "mess" of each one. Whether she is widowed, divorced, or separated is left unexplained. Living by herself, she thinks continuously about the murder of her granddaughter, and it is through the example of Citlali that Novaro focuses once more on the issue of violence against women. Mario and Mendizábal, the inept sexual predators of *Lola* and *Sin dejar huella*, have morphed here into a psychopath who murders fifteen-ear-old girls on their birthdays. Citlali is uniquely tragic but also representative of a broader national crisis. "According to a recent report by Amnesty International," writes Haydn Welch in a Council on Foreign Relations blog, "at least ten women and girls are killed every day in Mexico. The report says that all too often, law enforcement fails to investigate the murders properly, leaving the families of the murdered women and girls to seek justice themselves . . . and while women's rights activists have advocated against femicides, both Mexican law enforcement and the Mexican government have tended to diminish the severity of the problem."[3] Rather than show the grisly details of Citlali's murder, Novaro concentrates on its aftermath—the effect on Blanquita and the lax punishment handed out to the killer. She lets Blanquita's bitter comment about "six months for the life of my child" stand as a stark indictment of official indifference.

Minus meaningful male engagement in their lives, the women support and sustain each other. In a pattern reminiscent of all previous Novaro films, they bond over shared confidences and household tasks. As Dalia, Blanquita, and Ana hang clothes to dry on the roof of their apartment building, they laugh about old boyfriends and about their hidden pasts. Reviewing the movie for *The Hollywood Reporter*, critic Deborah Young declared, "Feminists will appreciate Novaro's sly description of the secret life of women, from bonding over laundry and smoking pot in the back yard, to the secret lovers who course through their lives."[4] When institutions fail them, the women rely on these personal ties. The best practical support that Dalia receives in dealing with Lala's illness comes not from the medical professionals but from Blanquita. The domestic space the female characters inhabit encompasses salutary, family-based labor (such as Blanquita's custodial care of Lala) that is usually underappreciated by society. As Joanne Hershfield and David Maciel have pointed out, Novaro's films restore value to "the spaces in which women's lives take place (bathrooms, kitchens, places of work, children's rooms and playgrounds) and the relations that define their lives (divorced husbands, faithless lovers, their young children and teenagers moving into independence and adulthood)."[5]

From left, Ana (Miriam Balderas), Blanquita (Ana Ofelia Murguía), and Dalia (Úrsula Pruneda) bond over household chores in *Las buenas hierbas* (2010).

Blanquita, Lala, and Dalia are all strong, unpartnered women charged with raising an only child. Each in her own way explodes the bifurcated *buena madre/mala madre* (good mother/bad mother) stereotypes of Mexican melodrama, so entrenched, writes film scholar Óscar Robles, that "en ambos casos, la dicotomía asfixiante y excesiva no permite que la experiencia real de la madre aflore" ("in both cases, the suffocating and excessive dichotomy does not allow the authentic experiences of motherhood to surface" [author's translation]).⁶ Blanquita's maternal history is sketchy; she has suffered the loss of her daughter through estrangement and of her granddaughter through a shocking murder. Accepting responsibility for three failed marriages, she lives alone, haunted by memories of happier times. Still, as the emotional linchpin in the intergenerational support network, she unhesitantly steps forward to help Dalia care for Lala and Cosmo. Lala is equally complex, a well-educated professional whose career sometimes has kept her away from family. Her interest in alternative medicine and spiritualism have tended on occasion to make her seem remote and self-absorbed. Distorted by the ravages of Alzheimer's, her erotic fantasies nevertheless indicate a secret inner life of passion. Likewise, Dalia is a devoted mother yet also a sexual being who casually beds a younger man she has picked up in a movie theater. Free-thinking and unconventional, she is also financially dependent on the regular checks sent by her father.

The point Novaro is making is that all three women are uniquely perceptive, gifted, and flawed. Each one possesses a personal agency that has been tested by fate and circumstance. Citing Novaro's rejection of generic stereotypes, film scholar Romy Sutherland has written, "A consistent feature of her work is her acknowledgment of the many complex sociological forces that influence women's lives, while simultaneously emphasizing the role free will and individual psychology have played in the unfolding of her protagonists' stories."⁷

Variously mothered and protected by all three women, Dalia's son Cosmo is the quintessential Novaro child of nature (his name intentionally references *el cosmos*). Serenely innocent, he connects with the adults in ways that mitigate their anxiety and sorrow. Engaging many of them in play, he gathers fruit with his father, sorts colored beans with Lala, and makes "music" with the neighbors. His fascination with nature ranges from the bottled insects in his father's laboratory to the exotic plants in the Botanical Garden. Witness to moments of emotional turmoil, he tries but fails to understand the grown-ups' distress. When Dalia cries while telling her father about Lala's illness, he touches a make-believe tear on his own cheek. Off to the side, he watches in bewilderment as Lala raves on at length about her South American lover and as Dalia packs his bag for an unexpected stay at his father's house. Starting with *Lola*, Novaro has always taken the English Romantics' view of childhood, the notion that children embody the joy, curiosity, and empathy that most adults have lost. Having forfeited the state of grace themselves, Novaro's troubled adult characters still find consolation in recognizing and protecting it in the young and innocent. It is the same dynamic that literary critic Alex King has found at work in Wordsworth's evocation of the universal child: "Only when we have taken on ourselves the yoke of common human existence do we know how to name the radiant vision of childhood."[8] The thematic hope of every Novaro film is that some of that natural radiance adheres as the child characters grow into adulthood.

In *Las buenas hierbas* (2010), angelic little Cosmo (Cosmo González Muñoz) exerts a soothing influence on both his mother Dalia (Úrsula Pruneda, center) and his grandmother Lala (Ofelia Medina).

The study of nature professionally undertaken by Lala is related to Novaro's continuing exploration of Mexican identity. Lala's occupational reverence for the *Aztec Codex* establishes an important link to the country's indigenous part. A compendium of ancient Mesoamerican wisdom assembled prior to the Spanish Conquest, the *Codex* explains how to unlock the medicinal value of native plants and herbs. As a trained ethnobotanist, Lala not only has kept the knowledge alive but also has helped to advance its scientific legitimacy. In the best folk tradition, she has passed the secrets down to Dalia, who has used them to make a lotion for her mother's skin and a balm for her son's fever. The discourse of Novaro's earlier work has cautioned against exoticizing indigenous people and has called out ongoing government-sanctioned violence against them, but here she goes beyond exposé to extol the profound pre-Columbian world view of unity with nature rather than opposition to it. "That's the idea, plants heal the soul," she has explained. "If you know you are part of nature, your soul is at peace."[9] Documenting endangered cultural tradition is a creative role that Novaro has taken on before, most notably in *Danzón* and *El jardín del Edén*. In this case, the intention is to help reestablish respect for the natural world as part of the nation's collective cultural memory.

Individual memory is also a major issue examined in the film. "'The Good Herbs' plays on thematic variations of memory and recovering the past," noted critic Robert Koehler in his brief but perceptive review for *Variety*.[10] This was relatively new terrain for Novaro, the first time in a feature film that she would show characters struggling with questions of memory and loss. Mostly benign, Dalia's recollections of the past center on moments with Lala—searching in the woods for plant specimens or making soup together. Her enjoyment of those remembrances, however, is cut short by the bitter knowledge that the vibrant woman they depict is lost forever, unable to control her mind or body. Blanquita thinks constantly of her granddaughter, her reveries dominated by the day of Citlali's murder and her emergence from the afterlife as a restless, blood-stained phantom. Although sensing Citlali's presence brings some moments of comfort, Blanquita is unable to escape a memory loop that continually replays the events of the *quinceañera* itself. Her recollections are typically involuntary, triggered by the most unexpected detail. Lala's memory deteriorates over the course of the film, retaining in the end only a few shards of fantasy and delusion. She is ultimately unable to remember her family or the contours of her existence. Memory is dangerous, Novaro is saying, as unstable and transitory as one of Gabo's romantic infatuations. Unless, as in the *Codex*, its lessons are documented and preserved, memory lives and dies with each individual. Lala and Citlali take their uniquely remembered experiences with them. As Dalia lies next to her unresponsive mother, she asks a series of questions whose answers she will never know.

Dalia (Úrsula Pruneda) grooms an increasingly memory-ravaged Lala (Ofelia Medina) toward the end of *Las buenas hierbas* (2010).

At first glance, *Las buenas hierbas* would seem to be missing the personal journey that anchors every Novaro film, but Lala's passage through life is, in fact, that journey. "I wanted to say that life is a cycle and that it ends and that nothing happens," revealed Novaro in her interview with Lourdes Portillo. "There's nature, and nature goes on, and we are a little part of nature. Something you start understanding at a certain age."[11] Lala has traveled as far as she can on her own and needs assistance in moving on. Blanquita and Dalia are the helper guides of her archetypal quest, and it is in that context that the act of euthanasia must be viewed. It is Dalia's final gift, the fulfillment of her promise to not let Lala be treated like the "old sack" she feared. "I believe in euthanasia," Novaro has confirmed. "I think euthanasia is an act of love."[12] What might have been the sensationalistic climax of a melodrama is instead a serene release from prolonged suffering. Given her own mother's tragic battle with Alzheimer's, it is one of Novaro's most candid personal statements.

Style and Structure

María Novaro has never been a fan of direct exposition. The relationships between her characters take time to crystallize and develop. We meet Luis, Blanquita, and Gabo long before we learn how they figure in the narrative as Dalia's ex-husband, neighbor, and bedmate respectively. Blanquita looks out the window of her kitchen; Gabo stares at young women on the metro. Neither is connected visually or verbally to Dalia. Only later, when Dalia sits in front of Gabo at the movie theater and hangs clothes with Blanquita on the roof, does Novaro place them in the same space and introduce an association. Dalia and Luis initially are framed together in a three-shot as they watch Cosmo play outside under a fruit tree, but the family ties between them are revealed only gradually. Most mysterious of all is the presence of Citlali. She appears at first as a disheveled girl in an incongruously formal party dress crossing a pedestrian overpass in the middle of the day. A young man bumps into her and takes no notice. Not until after more unusual manifestations and a conversation about the murder between Blanquita and Ana do we put enough clues together to identify the girl as Citlali's afterlife spirt. An extended flashback in which Blanquita attends the *quinceañera* confirms the relationship.

Withholding immediate exposition involves viewers in the same search for diegetic clarity that confronts the major characters and also reenforces the inexplicability of Citlali's post-mortem existence. But beyond those considerations, Novaro's usual structural impulse has always been to make her audiences work harder than they do when watching a *telenovela* or action picture. "I don't like following formulas," she once told a reporter. "I love very original films, like the French make. I want to be surprised."[13] Part of the surprise of her own films is seeing which ostensibly random characters ultimately connect with one another. In fact, two of the characters in *Las buenas hierbas*, the musician couple who live in or near Dalia's apartment building, never surface in the narrative as more than background players. Not every casual acquaintance in real life or in a Novaro movie develops into a close friend.

The two songs performed on screen by the couple are part of a multi-layered assemblage of texts, extra-diegetic imagery, political commentary, and animated illustration. *Las buenas hierbas*, in fact, is the most collage-like of all Novaro's films. Peripheral to the main action, these inserts comment directly as well as associatively on theme and narrative. The song lyrics, for example, depict birds chirping outside a window, bright sunny mornings, and blue islands in the ocean—references to the world of nature catalogued throughout the film. An even more emblematic image is the extreme long shot of a mountain top encircled by clouds that Novaro cuts away to on several different occasions. Appearing first at the beginning of the film, it brackets two scenes where Dalia walks with Cosmo on the pedestrian bridge and then watches him play in his father's backyard. Later, as its clouds slowly fill the screen, the same shot punctuates the scenes where Dalia decides that the best way she can help Lala is to end her suffering. Never specifically identified, the recurrent image of the summit becomes a visual correlative for the serene permanence of nature, the cosmic stillness to which Lala ultimately returns.

There are dozens of similar cutaways—shots of flowers, bees, hummingbirds, moon-lit skies, dense forests, and running streams. They contextualize the characters' actions within a curative environment whose rediscovery promises a certain degree of solace. The intercutting is slow, leisurely, almost hypnotic. Several of the images are associated with the six animated chapter headings that divide the narrative. Deftly executed, these titles show plant illustrations from the *Aztec Codex* suddenly sprouting new tendrils and leaves. "Morning glory seeds: to heal fright and the loss of the spirit," reads one. "Hand-flower and magnolia: to strengthen the heart. Slowly sip the boiled water," instructs another. The descriptions roughly align with emotions and anxieties felt by the characters.

A reverence for nature unites mother and daughter (Ofelia Medina and Úrsula Pruneda) in *Las buenas hierbas* (2010).

Dalia is a textual collage artist herself. She writes down random phrases, pins them to the wall, and looks for oracle-like associations. "I collect words," she tells Gabo. "Why?" he asks. "I don't know yet," she replies. There are epigrams ("Unwritten words are forgotten"), maxims ("Dreams are real as long as they last. Can we say if life is any different?"), and half-formed messages ("Acapulco, travels, highway"). Along with the scraps of language, photographs and other memorabilia are also puzzled together on the walls. Dalia collects words, Lala collects plants, and Luis collects insects—each one searching for the essence of the things gathered and contained.

The radio station studio is also wallpapered with cultural artifacts such as posters and album covers. A banner reading "One world where many worlds fit in" hangs above the entrance. The broadcast sequences are incidental to the main narrative but give Novaro the opportunity to add political commentary to her intertextual collage. During one extended on-air editorial, three reporters call out such government-sanctioned acts of aggression as the massacres of Acteal, Aguas Blancas, and El Charco, the killing of eleven Mixtec Indians, and the assault on the entire town of Atenco. No authorities have been sanctioned, they continue, for their involvement in two murders and over twenty rapes. "What crime has been punished?" one of the reporters asks bitterly. As always, Novaro comes at the politics from the side but with a distinctively leftist viewpoint.

When Blanquita listens to the radio it is not for the news but for popular music. In particular she listens on two different occasions to Pedro Infante singing "Club verde," a romantic ballad extremely popular in the 50s. "If you ever doubt me or the love I've given you," go the lyrics, "just remember the hours we had together." The nostalgically themed music accompanies Blanquita's reveries and serves as an aural bridge into the *quinceañera* flashbacks.

Only once before in a feature film has Novaro utilized a flashback—Julian's remembrance of his dying father in *El jardín del Edén*. However, for a movie like this one, in which memory plays such a critical role, it is a highly appropriate narrative device. Blanquita's flashback begins with Citlali and four young escorts coming down the steps of a ballroom. Her father greets her at the bottom, and they share the first dance. Two cross-cuts reveal Blanquita watching contentedly along with the other guests, the last time she will see her granddaughter happy and beautiful in her unstained party dress. Dalia's two flashbacks involve similarly pleasant moments with Lala. In one sequence, they are gathering plants together in a heavily wooded area next to a stream. Dalia holds a basket and calls out to her mother, who moves through the foliage in slow motion. The second flashback has them making semolina soup together; in a close-up, they hold hands while rolling the dough. For both

Blanquita and Dalia, the flashbacks are attempts to reverse time and return to a more idyllic past. Focusing only on Citlali's murder and Lala's disease are untenable psychological options.

"There is an assumption of temporality and order in the flashback," explains film theorist Susan Hayward, "but simultaneously—by its very nature—it is patently calling into question our assumptions about chronological time. Time is carved up and layered."[14] In an example of this segmented temporality, the opening scenes seem to exist outside of time. As the camera pans across a table filled with plants, there is a cut to a two-shot of Dalia sitting next to Cosmo's bed and applying a compress to his forehead. Another cut takes us to a tracking shot along a row of trees at night. It is raining and thundering. Dalia enters the left edge of the frame and runs to a phone booth at the end of a tunnel-like canopy. In a medium close-up, she dials and reaches Lala. "I didn't think you would answer," she says, "since you are not alive." Slowly, in a single extended take, the camera tracks around her while she holds the line. "I put the red flower of myrtle under his pillow, but he won't sleep," she continues. The conversation is completely one-sided; we never hear her mother's voice on the other end. "I thought I would never talk to you again. I am happy you answered me," she concludes, turning away from the camera just as the screen goes suddenly dark.

An introduction placed before the title credits, this sequence can be read as either a real event or as a dream occurring in any of three different time frames. After some days without seeing each other, it may simply be Dalia's present or recent past tense request to Lala for help in treating Cosmo's night fever. Given the somewhat surreal placement of a fully functional public telephone in the middle of a forest, it could also be a dream. Why else would Dalia need to leave her house on a rainy night for a phone we soon learn she already possesses? More likely, given the examples of magical realism throughout the film (inspired perhaps by friend and mentor Gabriel García Márquez), it is a flashforward to a moment in the future when Dalia communicates with her deceased mother to obtain advice. We are meant to take Dalia's reaction literally when she expresses surprise at talking to someone who is "not alive." Additional confirmation of Lala's supple otherworldliness comes later in the film during the incantation scene in which she refers to herself as a "soulful woman" who can "get in and out from the kingdom of death."

The other magical apparitions include not only Citlali but also the aged spirit guide who first materializes as a hazy figure outside Lala's window. She reappears via two separate cutaways when Dalia is preparing to end Lala's suffering. Existing simultaneously within and apart from the narrative, she has no physical interaction with other characters but rather inhabits an indeterminate space associated with the mountain top and a misty cornfield. Framed in profile against the sky, she is the welcoming gatekeeper to Lala's new existence and contributes as such to the film's mystical ambiance. The pastoral imagery, minimal action, and muted colors of *Las buenas hierbas* give it a trance-like essence, a feeling that the characters are moving quietly through a different dimension.

That special pace also derives from the predominant use of slow fades to transition between scenes—a device hitherto seen as infrequently in a Novaro film as the flashback. In the closing moments alone there are five different fades linking Lala's death to the world of nature. Elsewhere in the film, Novaro fades from the animated chapter headings to images of the depicted plants. A throwback to an earlier style of filmmaking, the fade slows down forward momentum and suggests the gradual passage of time. The briefly darkened screen also evokes that "nothingness" to which Novaro has claimed all corporeal things return.[15]

As expected in any film by María Novaro, there is also the familiar use of long takes, moving camera, and composite framing. The most dramatic example of the single extended take comes in the scene where Dalia tries to help Lala get dressed. Positioned in the foreground, Dalia keeps directing her mother to choose a skirt while Lala instead frets over her inability to locate a specific reference in the *Aztec Codex*. For two minutes, the camera holds on a medium long shot of Lala pacing to and from her closet before the effort fails and the scene cuts to black. Dalia appears alone in an uninterrupted long take when she retreats to the roof of her apartment building to smoke a joint. Quoting Alice responding to the caterpillar, she remarks, "I can't remember things as they were" as she stares steadily into the darkness.

Although often confined to interiors, the camera moves whenever possible to explore the settings. Slow tracking shots accompany Dalia's entrance into the radio station and her walk through the Botanical Garden with Lala and Cosmo. During the *quinceañera* flashback, the camera tracks laterally through the ballroom as Citlali dances past the admiring guests with her father. Similarly, Dalia's memory of gathering plants with her mother is visualized as a subjective forward tracking shot through the dense undergrowth of a forest.

Novaro's continuing preference for handling dialogue is to sustain it within a two-shot or three-shot rather than to cross-cut for individual lines. Those composite group shots visually reenforce the characters' solidarity as in the rooftop laundry conversation between Dalia, Blanquita, and Ana and the scene where Dalia drinks *mate* and discusses her possible South American heritage with two women friends from the radio station. The majority of Dalia's scenes with Lala are two-shots, most touchingly those where they play with Cosmo, discuss Lala's Alzheimer's, and lie next to each other in bed. One-shots are reserved for temporary moments of fracture and isolation, like the scene where Lala pulls away from the dinner table to insist that Dalia's real father is a guitar-playing guerrilla fighter. Cosmo is also framed alone on screen at those moments when he tries to understand the adult behavior he is observing—for example, Dalia's tearful phone call to her father and the bag-packing scene where she and Luis talk about one of Lala's severe anxiety attacks.

Compared to *El jardín del Edén* and *Sin dejar huella*, *Las buenas hierbas* is an intimate chamber piece. Essentially a three character drama, it plays out in a limited number of locations. It is, however, neither stagy nor claustrophobic. Opened up through its intertextual references and impressionistic cutaways, *Las buenas hierbas* is as engaging in its own minimalistic way as any of Novaro's other films.

Cast and Crew

Casting Úrsula Pruneda, Ofelia Medina, and Ana Ofelia Murguía as Dalia, Lala, and Blanquita respectively was one of the best production decisions that María Novaro ever made. Alone and together, they deliver the emotional impact of the film. Their performances are intense but never cloying or melodramatic. In a break with tradition, the official jury of the 2010 Rome Film Festival honored all three women collectively with the award for Best Actress.

Having worked mostly in short films and television, Pruneda was the least experienced of the trio but easily holds her own on screen. As the central figure Dalia, she interacts with every one of the other characters (except Citlali) and brings something unique to each of those encounters. With her radio station colleagues she is playful, with Gabo she is sensual, and with Luis she is relaxed and direct. She is Cosmo's easy-going but solicitous mom and Blanquita's affectionate, respectful neighbor. Her most sustained relationship is with Ofelia Medina's Lala, and their chemistry together is a marvel to watch. The wardrobe dilemma scene shows why. Medina rambles around her bedroom railing about the *Codex* reference and pulling blouses from the closet rather than the skirt she actually needs. She is like an inattentive child and Pruneda, the indulgent parent, watches patiently at first and then grows increasingly exasperated as her suggestions are ignored. Unable to control the situation, she begins to cry, and Medina, frightened at the breakdown, instinctively reverts to adult mode. By the end, both women are on their knees, Medina in two sweaters and a slip and Pruneda unable to stop crying. It is a bravura piece of acting by two performers at the top of their games.

Dalia (Úrsula Pruneda, left) tries to help Lala (Ofelia Medina) get dressed in one of *Las buenas hierbas's* most emotional scenes (2010).

Ofelia Medina, like María Rojo, already had built a highly successful career prior to working with Novaro. Active in Mexican cinema since her debut in 1968, she was well known for the films *El cambio* (1971), *Diplomatic Immunity* (1992), and *Frida, naturaleza viva* (1983), in which she played artist Frida Kahlo. A dancer, singer, political activist, and screenwriter as well, she had starred in several popular television series and had made pictures in the Philippines, France, and the United States. As Lala, she traces the whole devastating arc of early onset dementia from initial confusion and forgetfulness to more serious panic and delusion. In a series of wrenching scenes—wandering a city park in search of a nonexistent concert, rejecting a prospective caretaker, failing to recognize Dalia, wetting herself at night in the garden—she captures Lala's steady deterioration. They are big emotional moments, but she underplays the theatrics. It is her eyes that tell the story of an intelligence slowly dimmed and extinguished.

Ana Ofelia Murguía, who had played Juana sixteen years earlier in *El jardín del Edén*, has the least demonstrative but most relatable of the parts. She is the helpful neighbor whose cheerful exterior masks a deep personal tragedy. The joking with Ana and Dalia or the asking for a joint at the radio station can shift unexpectedly to the sadness of recounting her granddaughter's death or seeing her image outside the kitchen window. The wordless metro scene, where she registers Citlali's presence solely through facial expressions, is a fine example of how subtly Murguía's technique plays out on the screen.

In addition to the honors in Rome, Pruneda and Medina were named Best Actress and Best Supporting Actress by the Mexican Cinema Journalists. Both were also recognized at the Ariel Awards, Pruneda nominated for Best Actress and Medina winning for Best Supporting Actress. Chosen Best Actress at the Amazonas Film Festival, Pruneda would collect her own Ariel Award as Best Actress two years later for her performance in *El sueno de Lu*.

The male characters, as often the case with Novaro, are less well drawn. Alberto Estrella is Dalia's cordial but distant ex-husband Luis, and Rodrigo Solis is her equally impassive admirer Rot. They are practically interchangeable in their bearded appearance and laconic inability to meet Dalia's real needs. Gabino Rodríguez plays the transient younger boyfriend, giving him just the right combination of cluelessness and self-absorption. Another one of Novaro's perfectly cast child actors, Cosmo González Muñoz is Dalia's young son Cosmo. His naturalness comes from Novaro having learned through plenty of experience that the best way to film children is to catch them at play or observing the adults. Little González Muñoz went on to make two additional films—*Camelia la Texana* in 2014 and *Eres mi pasión* in 2018.

The small cast was matched by an equally limited number of crew members. "The crew was made exclusively of my former students, some from CUEC and some from CCC," revealed Novaro, and the total number of people behind the camera never exceeded fifteen.[16] With the help of digital technology, they became a lean, streamlined production unit. Novaro used her own house and garden for locations and also shot at the nearby Botanical Garden and at the national university. Gerardo Barroso, who had been urging his former teacher to make the kind of film that she was advocating in class, came aboard as cinematographer and wife Lisa Tillinger as his assistant. Sebastián Garza co-edited the film with Novaro. Together, Novaro, Barroso, and Garza are responsible for the distinctive look of the film—the long takes, graceful tracking shots, exploratory pans, slow fades, and stately pace.

This was very much a personally important project for María. In addition to sharing the editing work, she wrote, directed, and co-produced the film. Elements of the story mirrored her own mother's terminal battle with Alzheimer's, a struggle which she has recalled tearfully as "brutal."[17] Like late-career Orson Welles, she personally hustled for the funding, shooting only as often as cash on hand permitted. Along with her own intense involvement, María recruited the participation of her adult children. Daughter Lucero Sánchez Novaro worked as a set dresser and appeared in one of the metro scenes. Santiago Chávez and Judith de León, her son and daughter-in-law, contributed seven original songs and portrayed Dalia's musician neighbors. The end credits included thank-yous to various friends and to María's brothers Luis, Gabriel, and Octavio. (Adding to the family feel was the casting of Úrsula Pruneda's real-life daughter, Emilia Sama Pruneda, as young Dalia in the flashback.)

Las buenas hierbas collected its share of critical honors. Apart from the acting awards, María won Best Screenplay at the Amazonas Film Festival and one of the Best Film prizes at the Havana Film Festival. Alejandro Valle received a Best Visual Effects Silver Ariel for his chapter animations and Lorenza Manrique was nominated for Best Art Direction. More importantly, María herself was pleased with the film. "It's the movie I wanted to make," she has affirmed.[18] Her only regret is that *Las buenas hierbas* was not more widely screened in her own country.

Tesoros (Treasures)

Novaro's sixth feature film comes as a radical departure from the dramatic intensity and topical controversy of *Las buenas hierbas*. In the tradition of Jean Vigo, Francois Truffaut, and Louis Malle, it is a buoyant celebration of childhood. Working closely with friends and family and on location in an idyllic seaside setting, Novaro uses a simple adventure story to explore deeper issues of community, ecology, and culture.

Collectively financed through several independent production companies and institutional grants, *Tesoros* was released simultaneously on February 13, 2017, in Mexico and at the Berlin International Film Festival, where it was nominated for a Crystal Bear Award. Despite limited commercial distribution, it circulated widely through global film festivals, winning best picture awards at the Seattle, San Diego, and Valencia festivals, an award for best editing in Havana, and the best direction prize at China's Film for Children Festival. Critic Ana Morgenstern called it "a true gem in the Miami International Film Festival."[1]

Acquired for distribution by Amazon Prime, *Tesoros* has currently begun to reach a much wider audience in the United States.

Story

A light blue green van makes its way along the Pacific coast of Guerrero, Mexico. Inside are six-year-old Dylan, his unhappy older sister Andrea, and their sweet-natured toddler brother Lucas. Driving the van is their mother, who is from Mexico, and asleep in the passenger seat is their English-born father. To keep himself occupied, Dylan plays a video game featuring Sir Francis

Drake ("El Draque") and other pirates of the Pacific. Eventually the family reaches its new home by the ocean in the tiny coastal village of Barra de Potosí.

Explaining the journey and arrival is a local first-grade girl named Jacinta ("Jaci"), who wears big blue glasses and will be the voice-over narrator of the film. Jaci lives at a wildlife shelter with her biologist parents and her small terrier dog Toto. Hurrying to finish breakfast, she catches a ride to school in a jeep driven by the mother of a classmate. Waiting at her elementary school, which is also located next to the beach, are a friendly young teacher and his two daughters Fabiana and Mati. Best friends, Jaci and Mati greet each other with big hugs and happily walk arm-in-arm to the first grade classroom taught by Mati's dad. Jaci also introduces some of the other children, including Aranza and Michel, who have no parents but whose older sister Zindu takes loving care of them and brings lunch to them every day at school. They live with Zindu and their Uncle Owen, a fisherman, in an open-air house near the ocean. Julio, a quiet, curly-haired classmate with no apparent family of his own, is also looked after by Zindu and Owen.

Meanwhile, Dylan and his siblings are settling into their new home, which is called Casa de la Luna (House of the Moon). Adopting easily to the new surroundings, Lucas splashes around in the wading pool while Dylan keeps busy with his tablet computer. After telling her father how angry she remains at being separated from her friends, Andrea wanders down to the ocean for a solitary swim. Awakened that night by a rainstorm, Dylan sees El Draque outside his window, and the phantom pirate tells him he has been waiting four hundred years for Dylan to discover his buried treasure.

The next day Dylan and Andrea arrive apprehensively at their new school. As *"güeritos"* or "little blondies" with pale skin and light-colored hair, they look physically different from the others but are warmly welcomed. Several little boys immediately introduce themselves to Dylan and excitedly accompany him to Mati and Jaci's first grade class. Aranza takes Andrea's hand and leads her to the combined fifth/sixth grade classroom. "Don't be so sad. You'll love this school," says Aranza. "Everyone is very nice." Mati's father teaches the students about the rich natural resources and abundant sea life of Barra de Potosí, and the following day his class visits a turtle preserve at the wildlife center run by Jaci's parents. The children release baby turtles into the ocean and everyone, including Dylan, is delighted. Jaci ends the day by feeding snacks to her favorite animal at the shelter (a porcupine named Lala) and reading a story about a bottle top crab to Toto.

More new experiences and new friends await. Jaci finds a real crab using a broken bottle for a shell and lectures the others on how to care for it. Andrea makes friends with sisters Julieta and Jazmin, who swim as often as they can at the local seaside hotel where their mother works, and accepts the overtures of a tall, handsome boy named Juan Carlos who stands wordlessly next to her at school one day. Lucas's father warns him about the dangers of scorpions, and Dylan learns how to net and eat crabs with his new pals David and Michel.

Slowly, Dylan comes to realize that the bay of Barra de Potosí looks very much like the one in his video pirate game. He convinces the others that if they find the right maps, they will discover El Draque's hidden treasure. After failing to locate what they need on the internet, they ask Jaci's father to print them a satellite map of the rocky outcroppings (Los Morros) that lie offshore. Calling their project "Cangrejos" ("Crabs"), they embark on a search for the x-shaped sign that will mark the treasure.

During a field trip to the beach with Zindu, they all scan the surroundings for clues. Even though Julio sees x-marks in the crossed palm tree trunks and in the saltworks beds, nothing comes of their efforts. Days pass and life continues. Lucas explores the beach with wonder and joy, and Andrea learns to deep sea dive. On another trip to the nature preserve to see a whale exhibit under construction, the children climb to the top of an observation tower. Using a toy telescope, Jaci sees a large x-shape carved into the rocks of Los Morros. After much pleading, the treasure seekers convince Uncle Owen to take them out to the islands in his small fishing boat. Drawing straws to see which five can go, they nose around the rocky inlets only to find lots of x-carvings and a current that Uncle Owen says is too treacherous for them to swim in. Julio gets seasick but Dylan assures everyone that they can still find treasure if they keep looking.

Jaci (Jacinta Chávez de León, left) and Andrea (Andrea Sutton Chávez, right) scan the offshore rock formations for signs of treasure in *Tesoros* (2017).

Inspired by another of her books and by a song that has been sung throughout the film, Jaci decides they need a mermaid to lead them to the right spot. They set out again, only this time with two boats so that everyone can go and with Andrea the diver as their mermaid guide. Once underwater, Andrea follows a feathery little fish to a fluorescent "x" etched into the sea cliff and to a well-preserved chest. Full of excitement, they raise the treasure chest to the surface but later discover that it is empty. Undeterred and only slightly disappointed, they sell the antique chest for a profit that allows them to throw a party for all their friends. As they dance and share Zindu's delicious cooking, Jaci concludes, "My grandma says the true treasures are us, the children and the planet we live in."

Themes

The children who have hovered at the periphery of each of Novaro's previous films step forward here and take thematic prominence. The movie is solely about them—their lives, friendships, adventures, and insights. The adults are marginal at most. Some, like Dylan's mother, remain essentially unseen, speaking offscreen and only partially entering the frame. Others, such as Jaci's parents and Dylan's father, appear briefly to give advice or support. Uncle Owen and Zindu, the adults with the most fully developed characters and the most screen time, function as allies of the children, keeping them fed and facilitating their various excursions. The schoolmates refer to the adults as "the papa of Dylan" or "the mama of Jaci" and never call them by their own full names. In each instance, the grown-ups are distinguished by their connection to a specific son or daughter rather than the other way around.

The children themselves, like the characters in Jaci's storybooks, model how to live in harmony with each other and with nature. When new students come to school, they are instinctively embraced as friends. There is no social hierarchy, only the single cohesive group where members share their resources, information, and affection. Best friends Jaci and Mati hug each other tightly to start the day, Dylan intends to share the buried treasure with his new friends, Michel and David teach Dylan about netting crabs, and everyone looks after little Lucas. Surrounded by natural beauty, they are also protective of the wildlife they encounter. With the same sensitivity shown by the children in releasing the baby turtles into the ocean, Jaci protects the bottle top crab she has found and tends to the animals in her parents' preserve. (Compare these moments to the opening title sequence of the 1969 film *The Wild Bunch* in which director Sam Peckinpah has a group of children enjoy a death struggle between a scorpion and hundreds of red ants.)

Jaci (Jacinta Chávez de León) shows her friends the proper way to handle a bottle shell crab in *Tesoros* (2017).

Children are frequently portrayed in movies as stand-ins for adult hopes or fears, their true lives circumscribed by a limited set of narrative conventions. They are either separated from families and menaced by villains or endowed with skills that allow them to achieve seemingly unattainable triumphs. Even top-tier directors appropriate childhood for personal ontological reasons. Vittorio de Sica's child protagonists are emblematically tragic as are those of Satyajit Ray. In an article for the book *Lost and Othered Children in Contemporary Cinema*, film historian Debbie Olson similarly argues that the typical child in an Alfred Hitchcock movie is a hyper-precocious observer who "functions as a significant criticism of adult illusions about the state of guilt or innocence."[2] Dismissing Francois Truffaut's examination of childhood in *Small Change* (1976) as "horribly cute," David Thomson goes on to call the film "a facile collage about the vitality and preciousness of childhood, but spoiled by its creeping sense of adult nostalgia and sentimentality."[3] Novaro largely avoids such tonal spoilage by rejecting shopworn narrative formulas. There are no life-threatening scorpion bites, no boat lost in a storm, no juvenile misfit saved by the attentions of a cantankerous old recluse.

For the most part, Novaro allows the children to simply be. Their behavior seems authentic rather than performative. Jaci plays with her animals, Julieta and Jazmin swim in the hotel pool, Julio helps Uncle Owen untangle the fish nets. The group scenes, in the classroom or during the outdoor excursion, emphasize everyday tasks rather than dramatic complications. The students take notes on local resources and conduct marine fieldwork, intently engaged in the routine details. Climbing trees or steering a boat through a tree-covered inlet, they fully if unspectacularly inhabit the space around them. The conversations are as straightforward as the activities. "How does it feel that your dad is our teacher?" Jaci asks Mati. "It feels nice," replies her friend. "Why is Andrea so angry?" wonders Lucas, and Dylan tells him simply, "I don't know."

Lucas is the closest Novaro comes to creating a strictly symbolic character, but his unsullied innocence is never used as a plot device to counter some act of social intolerance or aggression. Instead, he wanders freely through the narrative as an ideal observer, interested in each new activity and natural phenomenon. Curious and sensitive, he is as ready to climb into a sibling's lap as to watch the fishermen push out to sea. His example is instructive without being didactic, projecting a way of being that is marked by joy, spontaneity, and companionship.

As suggested earlier, the adults of Barra de Potosí, although peripheral to the action, represent Novaro's best take on parenting, advice gleaned from personal experience and the lessons of previous films. Each role model offers gentle mentoring. Jaci's dad and Uncle Owen provide maps and transportation for the treasure hunt, Mati's father teaches about the gifts of nature, and Andrea's diving instructor introduces her to underwater exploration. Aranza's sister Zindu is a key ally who cooks for everyone and keeps the local heritage alive. Especially significant is the fact that all the adults come together to see that lonely little Julio is cared for and fed. Seems, after all, that it really does take a village to raise a child. Succinctly stated, the message to adults is this: point out where the scorpions and riptides lurk, give food and guidance, then get out of the way and allow children to have their own special adventures.

Most of Novaro's other frequent themes are also focused here through the lens of childhood. The transformative coastal journey is the one that takes Andrea and Dylan from their old home to Barra de Potosí. Initially resentful at being uprooted from her comfort zone, Andrea makes new friends and learns to love her life by the sea. Despite being only casually interested at first in the buried treasure project, she is the group member who learns how to use the diving equipment. It is through her newly acquired skills that the chest is found and brought to the surface, a feat which earns her shouts of admiration from the other children. Along the way, with no obvious effort on her part, she also takes on a devoted boyfriend in the person of handsome, upper-grade student Juan Carlos. Fittingly, after realizing how happy she has become, Andrea reconciles with her father, whom she had consistently blamed for all of her troubles. At the celebratory party, she prepares a plate of food for him and helps him interact with the other guests.

Dylan experiences a similar although slightly less dramatic transformation himself. He goes from being an easily bored little kid with his eyes glued to the computer screen to a fearless adventurer alive to all the natural treasures that surround him. He learns to net crabs, navigate the water, and organize expeditions. Sharing his technology, he motivates the other children and values the different skills each of them brings to the Cangrejos project. During the opening van ride along the coast, he pesters his parents by continually asking, "how much longer until we get there?" Once immersed in the treasure hunt, he learns to patiently accept setbacks, regroup, and start again. A likable young man has stepped out from behind the video games.

The bonds of solidarity that link all Novaro heroines are present here as well albeit at a junior level. Each little girl is usually presented in relation to a friend or sister. Jaci and Mati go everywhere together, delighting in each other's company and protective of each other's emotional welfare. Julieta and Jazmin are so inseparable in and out of the water that they seem like the same person. Most supportively, with a grace way beyond her years, Aranza welcomes Andrea to the new school and assures her that all the students will be friendly. What Novaro does differently in *Tesoros* is to broaden the gender-defined parameters of the support system. Dylan, Michel, and David are equally important partners in the various friendships, and there are multiple scenes where the boys and girls come together to share meals, make plans, and pursue the treasure. In true collaboration, everyone participates in the decision-making, everyone contributes a skill. Dylan shows how to use the technology, Jaci secures the satellite maps, Andrea learns to dive, Michel and Aranza recruit Uncle Owen. Protean in nature, the overall team circulates members as time and circumstances demand.

Without forcing the point, Novaro delivers a behavioral model, beyond the adult efforts of her previous films, where relations between the sexes are based on respect and shared labor. The focus is on the children, but the parental co-operation is also exemplary. Unlike the earlier films, men are not absent or inadequate fathers here but rather are directly involved in the raising of their families. Jaci's mother and father both operate the wildlife shelter just as Dylan's parents both oversee the care of him and his two siblings. In the extended family they have established, Zindu and Uncle Owen also equitably divide the household chores. Across the generations, the male and female characters come together, undramatically but convincingly, as mutually supportive partners and caregivers.

That progressive vision would seem to definitively address Novaro's persistent "question about what it is to be a woman and what it is to be a man."[4] As evidenced, the ideal gender roles are interchangeable, based on consensus rather than convention. In a humorous coda to her frequent unmasking of women's sexual objectification, Novaro includes a scene where Dylan and Aranza inspect an exotic miniature doll. She is a scantily clad dancer whose top falls down when you push a button below her base. Neither impressed nor shocked by the exposed breasts, they question whether the doll is meant to be "voluptuous" or "chubby." The intended titillation seems absurd even to the children, given how far removed the likeness is from the truly remarkable women they see around them.

Child-centered fantasy and masquerade, on the other hand, is very much a part of everyday life in Barra de Potosí. The search for buried treasure is initiated when Dylan wakes during a storm to see El Draque speaking to him from outside his window. It is a visit presented matter-of-factly like the *quinceañera* apparition in *Las buenas hierbas* rather than as an episode framed by a dream. Once inspired, the children look for secretly carved messages in a landscape that even normally is filled with wonder. "Although there is fantasy in the children's lives, I wanted to find a way for that fantasy to be completely linked to a real world, a world as experienced by the children in my country," Novaro revealed in an interview for *Variety* at the time of *Tesoros*'s release.[5] So, Jaci talks to her animals, the boys pilot boats through mysterious lagoons, and Lucas discovers different natural wonders with each new day. There are songs of mermaids and adventures under the sea. During a visit to the Casa de la Luna, the children all dress up in discarded finery and parade à la Fellini along the shore. The trees and ocean shimmer under bright tropical skies.

Multiple scenes involve the children in the preparation, serving, and enjoyment of food. Zindu lovingly delivers lunches and makes seafood dinners for her many siblings, Andrea's mother offers tortilla wrapped snacks to her daughter's friends, and Jaci's parents give the treasure hunters milk and sweets. The final celebration, an outdoor feast brimming with local produce and ocean specialties, echoes several earlier scenes where children and adults gather together for meals. "As a Mexican, I love my culture, our food, the taste of life, the joy we find in life . . . I wanted children to share this, live it," explained Novaro. "My film talks about that joy of living."⁶ The Cangrejos don't find buried treasure but do realize how lucky they are to live harmoniously in an unspoiled natural enclave.

The children and natural wonders of *Tesoros* (2017) are the real treasures.

The ethnic culture that Novaro references and whose transmission is highlighted in *Danzón* and *Las buenas hierbas* also surfaces characteristically here through music and dance. Along with instruction in local natural resources, the children practice *folklórico* dancing as part of their schooling. Early in the film, two elegant young teachers give a performance outside near the beach as both boys and girls watch in rapt appreciation. The music, much of it diegetic, speaks of mermaids, sharks, and other sea creatures. During one of the children's field trips and at the closing party, Zindu sings ethereal melodies that capture the tranquility of Barra de Potosí. Traditional folk songs heard throughout the film include "El pato" ("The Duck"), "Pajarillo jilguero" ("Linnet Songbird"), and "El cangrejo" ("The Crab")—additional references to the natural world through which the children move so respectfully. Traditional instruments accompanying the songs include guitar, guacharaca, bajo, and teclado. With her love for both the unique food and music of her country, Zindu is exactly the kind of cultural preservationist that Novaro feels is so important to a society which is growing increasingly more deracinated all the time.

Ironically, given its children's adventure story line, *Tesoros* is also one of Novaro's most political films. During her voice-over introduction to Barra de Potosí, Jaci gives a brief Eduardo Galeano-like history of European colonization. "The American continent wasn't that new," she explains, "but the Europeans had only just discovered it. So they arrived with their ships and started stealing everything they could." Over a colorful antique map of the area, she continues, "The Spaniards stole the gold and other riches from the peoples of the Americas. And the pirates stole those same riches from the Spanish ships. Robbery upon robbery!" Adding a personal touch, she tells how deliriously happy Queen Elizabeth was with the looted treasure brought to her by Francis Drake. As interpreted by an intelligent little first-grader, the story of colonial avarice seems not only unfair but shamefully absurd.

Dylan and his siblings are also pale-skinned, half-English strangers who show up unexpectedly in the community, but they have not come to plunder. Their classmates refer to them as "*güeritos*" but with affection not malice. For the children, skin color is no big deal. "Some of us got our father's color and some of us got our mother's," says one little girl nonchalantly. The most repeated physical gesture among the children, boys and girls alike, is a welcoming embrace.

The serenity of life in Novaro's idyllically imagined fishing village is intended as a thematic antidote to the violence that has long ravished the rest of Guerrero. "So I wrote the story to happen in this place," she has acknowledged, "a paradise, though part of one of the most violent states in all Mexico, the state of Guerrero."[7] Since the 1960s marijuana and opium cultivation proliferated in the area, controlled for many years by a single powerful cartel. When then-President Felipe Calderón ordered the military in 2006 to take on the major syndicates, bloody conflict broke out between rival factions vying for a piece of the drug trade. According to reporting done by *The Guardian*, "In Guerrero, the larger groups splintered into local gangs, which branched out into kidnapping and extortion.

They also found additional profits in illegal mining and clandestine logging. Instead of moving drugs, these gangs needed control over territory and they subjected villages to waves of terror when their armed men descended to lay claim to power."[8] Compounding the problem is the complicit control of local government by a powerful white elite and by party bosses who have ruthlessly suppressed every social movement that has attempted to challenge their political dominance. "All of those moving parts," writes *The Guardian's* Elisabeth Malkin, "came together in the kidnapping and disappearance of 43 students from a rural teachers' college in September 2014. They are believed to have been handed over by local police to a local gang, Guerreros Unidos, which killed them. Federal officials have also been implicated in covering up the investigation."[9]

Directly addressing this incident in one of the end credits, Novaro declares, "This film is dedicated to all rural schoolteachers in Mexico, especially those who studied in Ayotzinapa, Guerrero. We are still missing 43 of them. And we do not forget." Appearing over the image of an ocean sunset, it is one of the most explicit political statements to be found in any of her films, an expression of solidarity encapsulated as well in the character of Ari, the children's gentle, devoted first-grade teacher. Novaro also includes an additional postscript in which she concludes simply, "Barra de Potosí should be declared a Protected Natural Area in Mexico."

As always, the ocean is everything. "I always find an excuse to film by the sea," Novaro admitted early in her career.[10] In *Tesoros*, it is essentially the main character, the source of sustenance, wonder, and spirituality. Nearly every scene takes place on or in sight of the ocean. "I need an ocean to teach me," writes Pablo Neruda in *Memorial de isla negra (Black Island Memorial)*, "whatever it is that I learn,"[11] and so it is for Novaro. Wrapping the village and its residents in a great creative force, the ocean is beyond human constraint of any kind. Its message is one of personal fulfillment in conscious accord with nature.

Style and Structure

María Novaro has frequently expressed her disinterest in making films that are heavy with action and suspense, preferring instead "to put pieces of life on film."[12] For Novaro, "the way in which events affect us is more important than the action itself, because the action distracts; when there is no action, your attention focuses on something else."[13] *Tesoros* is her most uncompromising expression of that artistic preference. Not much, in terms of conventional drama, actually happens. The children attend school, take trips to the beach, visit each other's houses, and interact continuously with the ocean. Even the treasure hunt, which weaves intermittently throughout the other daily events, is anticlimactic by action film standards; the children discover a submerged chest which turns out to be empty, so they sell it and throw a party. Absent any deep sea thrills, we are left with what has always interested Novaro more—"the characters, their experiences, and their feelings."[14]

The film is structured like a mosaic of interconnected, loosely plotted vignettes. There are around fifty such sequences, and they look like typical moments in a child's experience of Barra de Potosí. Novaro achieves the realism not by writing detailed scenes with extended dialogue but by designing situations (releasing turtles, climbing trees, netting crabs) and letting the children react naturally. Whether the activity involves a single child (Jaci feeding her porcupine, Dylan playing the video pirate game) or several (the children arriving at school, Dylan eating crabs with Aranza's family), the pacing is slow and deliberate with the monologue/dialogue commenting directly on what we are watching on screen.

Except for the opening, where Jaci's narration introduces us to a prior event (Dylan's family traveling to the village in their van) that she could not possibly have experienced, the sequences are arranged in chronological order minus any flashbacks or projections into the future. Essentially, the vignettes accumulate additional characters as they proceed and, given the large number of adults and children so presented, Jaci's voice-over narration helps to clarify information and to offer skittish viewers a conventional story-telling device. What is not always clear is how much time passes between the various sequences, an intentional structural element which keeps the children bathed in a kind of eternal present.

The shooting style is similar to that of a travel film or documentary. Gone are the carefully staged blocking and complicated tracking shots of the earlier films and in their place a more pared-down visual style. The camera still moves, but it is a handheld one working to keep up with the children. Also missing are the director's signature long extended takes, technically unfeasible options for so many untrained actors. Getting the reactions she wants in bits and pieces, Novaro relies primarily on extensive cutting to stitch together the "performances." With more of a need here than a film like *Danzón* to keep audiences spatially oriented, she also makes regular use of establishing shots to open the scenes.

The initial school sequence is typical of Novaro's overall stylistic approach. In the establishing shot, a mother rides up to the school entrance and helps her daughter dismount from the rear seat. As the girl enters the gate, there is a cut to Jaci arriving from the opposite direction in a jeep driven by Julieta's mother. A handheld camera follows Jaci as she gets out, hugs Mati, and walks hand-in-hand with her into school. There is a cut to a slow pan across the feet of several children who are perched on steps outside near the playground. A montage of shots shows the children at recess, playing soccer and hopscotch, followed by a cut back inside to shots of the same students sitting around a worktable. The sequence ends when Zindu arrives with wrapped lunches for Aranza and her siblings. With a running time of just over three minutes, the sequence cuts on action every ten seconds or so, a pace that is fluid without being frenetic. Looking as if they were discovered rather than staged, the children's activities dictate what gets filmed and how each shot is framed (children in center mid-ground).

Novaro's handheld camera goes everywhere with the characters—wading into the water, climbing the observation tower, diving for treasure. Though not quite as technically challenging, coverage of the van and boat sequences is equally agile. As Dylan's family drives along the coast to Barra de Potosí, the camera is edged closely into the backseats with the children. Multiple low-angle shots combined with tight pans show the boys shifting around uneasily and pestering their mostly offscreen mother with questions. Cutaways alternate between point-of-view glimpses of the passing scenery and long shots taken from an escort vehicle of the van advancing along the curved coastal highway. The three boat sequences are handled similarly. The camera is either on board with the children or shooting alongside from a support vessel. For dialogue, there are cuts between various medium close-ups, and for atmosphere, there are subjective shots of what the children see as they glide through the canopied inlets. Despite the confined shooting space in these sequences, the overall effect is continuous forward movement through nature.

As the camera adroitly follows along, the children of *Tesoros* (2017) search Barra de Potosí's inlets for buried pirate treasure.

In addition to following the children wherever they go, the camera is also consistently at their own eye-level, never shooting down at them from above. Dylan's father must bend down into the frame to be seen in the conversations with his children, and Jaci's parents are often partially cropped out of the scenes at their house. Some of the most visually dynamic shots are those where a handheld camera follows at Lucas's height as he scrambles across the terrace and into the pool or where it accompanies Jaci and Mati as they walk to class. Even Toto the dog is photographed peering into a camera positioned at ground level. The child-level camera height is maintained consistently throughout the film; essentially every scene plays out from this non-adult perspective. Like the tatami mat camera height in the films of Yasujiro Ozu, the practice is a distinctive stylistic feature but also one more indication of Novaro's respect for the children. To film them from any other level would be to diminish their uniquely authentic experiences.

The fullness of the children's imaginative lives is also emphasized through Novaro's custom of incorporating related pieces of media into her films. Illustrations and text from Jaci's story books reflect her love of animals and the connections she makes between what she reads about and what she sees around her. The satellite images provided by her father link with the man-made antique maps and further convey the children's curiosity about everything from history and legend to modern technology and marine biology. Most inventive of the collaged inserts are the bits of animation from Dylan's video game. Colorful depictions of Francis Drake's voyages and battles at sea, they are what fuel the children's belief in buried treasure and what prepared Dylan for the nocturnal appearance of El Draque himself, an embrace of fantasy also common to most of Novaro's films.

Given the setting, there are also many vignettes that simply celebrate the beauty of the land and sea. Nearly a dozen shots, absent either adults or children, catalogue postcard-like images: multi-colored parrots against green palm fronds, iguanas basking in the sun, a pelican at rest in the water, a flock of birds crossing the horizon, an iridescent school of fish, the beach at sunset. A leisurely pan across the fluttering streamers of an outdoor restaurant proves Novaro's ability to find beauty in even the most commonplace locations. The village's vibrant greens, blues, and yellows, colors that often suffuse the seaside sanctuaries of any Novaro film, are ultimately much more alluring than the gold-toned seaweed stains that the children briefly mistake as signs of hidden treasure.

Cast and Crew

The production of *Tesoros* was a large, interconnected family affair. Most of the young, untrained actors who appear as siblings are in fact siblings in real life. Novaro also uses the children's real first names for the names of their characters. Dylan and Andrea are played by Dylan and Andrea Sutton Chávez, Julieta and Jazmin by Julieta and Jazmin Bárcenas Nava, and Mati and Fabiana by Mati and Fabiana Hernández Guinea.

Parents of the main characters are also portrayed by their real-life fathers and mothers. Dylan and Andrea's parents, the papa and mama of "*los güeros*," are their actual parents, Martin Sutton and Mara Chávez. It is the same for Jacinta Chávez de León, the young actress who appears as Jaci. Her biologist parents are played by her own father and mother Santiago Chávez and Judith de León. Little Lucas (Lucas Barroso Tillinger) is not related to the cast members who play his siblings and parents but is the son of the directors of photography, Gerardo Barroso Alcalá and Lisa Tillinger. Similar extended family relationships link other members of the cast and crew.

Novaro herself is the true matriarch of the production, the most deeply and widely connected person of all. Her son Santiago is Jaci's father, and her daughter Mara is the mother of Dylan and Andrea, making Jaci and the two "*güeros*" her grandchildren. Family members have always been present in some capacity on the sets of each of her previous films, but this time around they contribute significantly to what is essentially a home movie with really professional production values. Santiago also designed the sound and visuals for the computer pirate game while daughter Lucero Sánchez Novaro, a screenwriter and director herself, not only wrote and illustrated the story Jaci reads about Alejo the hermit crab but also served as second unit director. Considering all the family input, the film's testament to children can be read even more closely as Novaro's personal tribute to her daughters, son, and grandchildren.

As with the children, the names of the other major adult characters come from their real first names. Zindu is played by Zindu Cano, Uncle Owen by Howin Albarrán Bañuelos and Avi the teacher by Avimael Cadena Bañuelos. Except for professional singer Zindu Cano, the adults were as inexperienced at performing as the children, and once again Novaro used video camera games and exercises before filming to get her cast members comfortable. For the film itself, as discussed previously, she devised play-like activities that allowed the children to react rather than to perform. Dialogue was altered or improvised according to the situation.

In an essay on the films of Vittorio de Sica, André Bazin argues that neorealism's use of nonprofessionals runs counter to the traditional view of movie acting. "According to the classic understanding of this function," he writes, "inherited from the theater, the actor expresses something: a feeling, a passion, a desire, an idea. From his attitude and his miming the spectator can read his face like an open book."[15] By contrast, the neorealist actor relies on natural presence rather than formal technique to build a screen character. Reflecting a similar approach, Novaro never directs her child performers to project some complicated emotion like fear or sadness or jealousy. More pointedly, she never asks them to pretend to be anyone other than themselves.

Solo credits for writing and editing also go to Novaro, further evidence of the project's intensely personal nature. The design and assemblage of the narrative work hand in hand to emphasize the children's everyday reality. Individual scenes are intended to show events rather than to comment or theorize on them. Again, Bazin's remarks on neorealism are instructive: "But it is perhaps especially the structure of the narrative which is most radically turned upside down. It must now respect the actual duration of the event. The cuts that logic demands can only be, at best, descriptive. The assemblage of the film must never add anything to the existing reality."[16] The editing of *Tesoros* is unobtrusive and seamless; there are no cuts designed for shock value or symbolic resonance.

Neither is the *mise-en-scène*, unlike earlier in *Danzón*, engineered for thematic effect. "Almost everything you see in the movie really exists," Novaro has confirmed. "I just chose the best places and the best colors. But it was already there: the wonderful mural outside the school; the designs of the man and woman outside the bathrooms; the seahorses on the balcony."[17] So too with Lucas's colorful bobble-head toys and the imaginative decor of the Casa de la Luna. Novaro and her art directors Alettia Molina Rivera and Angélica Vasquez found just the right settings to evoke a mood of timeless serenity.

The incidental music by Zindu Cano and Kevin Garcia, co-founders of the band Ampersan, adds to that same mood with a sound that *New York Music Daily* has called "lush, dreamy, slowly crescendoing" tropical anthems.[18] Garcia accompanies Zindu on guitar for the scenes where she sings during an evening trip to the beach and at the final party.

Over 80 children and 60 adults are also listed as credited extras in the film, one final acknowledgment by Novaro of the human chemistry that helps to make Barra de Potosí such a special place.

Conclusion

The auteur theory, as first espoused by the daring young critics at *Cahiers du cinéma* and later championed in the United States by Andrew Sarris, has always made the most sense when applied to directors who have also written or co-written most of their films. A consistent authorial identity is unmistakable, for example, in the work of Buster Keaton, Sergei Eisenstein, Orson Welles, Michelangelo Antonioni, Ingmar Bergman, Jean-Luc Godard, and Agnès Varda, all of whom involved themselves in the writing, producing, and often the editing of their uniquely personal pictures. Such is also the case with María Novaro, who wrote her first three feature films with sister Beatriz and the next three on her own. Besides working closely with the cinematographers, she co-edited three of her movies and took a solo screen credit as editor for *Tesoros*.

Referencing but never copying traditional genres, Novaro's films are distinguished by a clearly defined thematic and stylistic consistency. Central to each movie is the notion of a woman's journey, both physical and spiritual, toward a greater awareness of self. Lola travels to the beach, Julia Solórzano to Veracruz, Ana and Aurelia to Cancún, the women of *El jardín del Edén* to Tijuana, and the family of *Tesoros* to Barra de Potosí. Along the way, lessons are learned, knowledge is gained. Lola assumes responsibility for her daughter, Julia embraces life more fully, Ana and Aurelia overcome male aggression, *Edén*'s Serena secures her family's safety, and the children and adults of *Tesoros* reaffirm their respect for nature and each other. Awaiting the travelers at journey's end is the ocean, whether extending beyond the harbor of Veracruz, caressing the beaches of Yucatán, or sustaining the village of Barra de Potosí. It is the ocean, Elissa Rashkin has noted, that "reappears as a symbol of liberty" for

Novaro in film after film and represents the creatively potent independence that most of her characters are seeking.[1]

In *Danzón* (1991), Julia Solórzano (María Rojo) takes a trip to Veracruz and finds romance with a younger man (Victor Carpinteiro) and a new sense of empowerment.

The typical Novaro heroine is a young single woman whose agency has been compromised by circumstance or choice. Most often working-class, she labors within an economic system that neither values nor protects her. Lola is a street vendor, Julia is a telephone operator, Aurelia works in a *maquiladora*, and Serena takes wedding photographs. Even the highly educated women exist on the margins of society; in *Sin dejar huella*, Ana runs a fake artifact operation and in *Las buenas hierbas*, Dalia depends on the checks written by her father. Few of their jobs are rewarding and some, like those of the sex workers in *Danzón*, are dangerous. Despite their financial instability, Novaro's women consistently place more importance on romance, friendship, or family than on money.

In addition to earning a living, Novaro's female characters also struggle to raise families. As Traci Roberts-Camps writes, "Novaro's films focus solely on women's lives from a female voice and from a time in Mexican history when women work outside the home as single mothers supporting their families, and, at the same time, try to realize their potential as individuals."² Every Novaro movie features multiple mother-child relationships. Lola and Dalia, for example, are raising a very young daughter and son respectively while sorting out issues with their own mothers. In *El jardín del Edén*, Elizabeth copes with daughter Lupita's refusal to speak, and Serena confronts her teenage son Julián's hostility while both simultaneously attempt to establish livelihoods in the border city of Tijuana. When the mothers are away at work, Serena's aunt and surrogate parent Juana watches over their four school-age children. A similar dynamic exists in both *Danzón*, where Julia, the mother of a grown daughter, helps to care for the prostitutes' children and in *Sin dejar huella*, where Ana slowly becomes a second mother to Aurelia's infant son. The only female character with no maternal connections is Jane, the naïve, privileged American wanderer in *El jardín del Edén*.

With so many variations on a theme, Novaro has posited a multi-faceted view of *maternidad*. Although she plays with the binary stereotypes of domestic melodrama (suffering, self-sacrificing mother vs. neglectful, pleasure-seeking mother), motherhood is not, for her, an either/or proposition. "Times have changed," she told a *Village Voice* reporter, "and I'm not interested in mystifying women, but rather in exploring how we live. I want to deal with the contradictions we face in life and in ourselves."³ Deeply attached to her daughter Ana, Lola is also a sexually active young woman who occasionally ignores parental responsibilities to satisfy physical desire. When several bad decisions jeopardize Ana's safety, Lola temporarily relinquishes her to the guardianship of her own disapproving mother Chelo. Similarly, after she steals a valuable stash from her drug cartel boyfriend, Aurelia places one of her sons under the supervision of her older sister and flees on a cross-country journey with the other one, a still-nursing infant. Julia Solórzano leaves her daughter in Mexico City to follow a favorite dance partner to

Veracruz, and Dalia takes a break from caring for her son and ailing mother to embark on a romantic fling with a younger man she picks up in a movie theater. Even Serena, the closest Novaro comes to a traditionally "ideal" widowed mother, becomes exasperated with her children's behavior and quietly expresses a sexual interest in the expatriate American whale watcher Frank. A Novaro mother is neither impossibly pure nor hopelessly errant. She is a realistically drawn woman with virtues and flaws, a strong individual who ultimately accepts equally engaged responsibility for her family and herself. Her narratives, argues Óscar Robles, "privilegean la perspectiva de la mujer, y construyen sujetos independientes y diferentes a los estereotipos y arquetipos patriarcales: La *buena madre*, la *mala madre*, la santa, la prostituta y todas sus variantes"[4] ("favor the woman's perspective and build characters independent and different from the patriarchal stereotypes and archetypes: the good mother, the bad mother, the saint, the prostitute and all their variations" [author's translation]).

As mentioned, children play an important part in each of Novaro's feature films. Like Truffaut's children, they are precocious and untainted. Often they comment directly on the adult behavior they observe so closely. Aurelia's son Juan, for example, calls her out for lying about where she got her sudden infusion of cash, and Julián rebukes his mother Serena over how tense she has made the family since the death of their father. At other times, much younger children seem confused by the adult interactions they are watching. Cosmo is thoroughly puzzled by his grandmother Lala's erratic outbursts, and Ana listens guardedly as her mother and father argue in front of her. Always, however, the children are ready to reconcile and forgive, tolerance being one of their most exemplary qualities. In *Tesoros*, where adults have only minimal roles, Novaro uses the children to teach a variety of such lessons. Their curiosity, collaboration, generosity, and stewardship of nature are intended as behavioral models and as tokens of Novaro's respect for her own children and grandchildren, who appear as major characters in the film. That respect is also evident in the way she handles all of her child actors, filming them at appropriate camera height and capturing them in authentic moments of play.

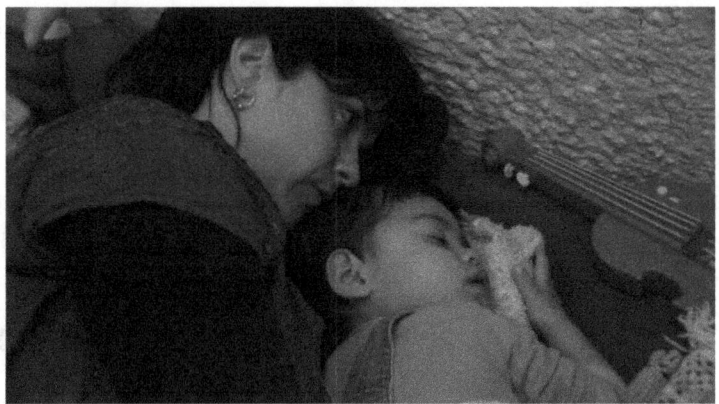

Cosmo (Cosmo González Muñoz), an innocent Novaro child of nature, offers comfort to his mother Dalia (Úrsula Pruneda) in *Las buenas hierbas* (2010).

Except for the attentive fathers of *Tesoros*, Novaro's male characters—the husbands, boyfriends, and fathers—are largely missing in action. Dalia and Elizabeth are divorced, and Serena is widowed. Lola's rock musician boyfriend abandons her, and Julia's love interest Carmelo suddenly disappears. Those men who remain on the scene, such as Jane's brother Frank and Dalia's bedmate Gabo, are oblivious to the female characters' emotional needs. Beyond the personal neglect, there are patriarchal social forces actively aligned against the women. "In fact," comments Traci Roberts-Camp, "in many instances, men and larger institutions—police, border patrol, and drug traffickers—are a menace to the female characters."[5] Lola is plagued by street patrols, Ana is sexually harassed by a federal sheriff, and Aurelia is pursued by cartel members.

In the absence of meaningful male support, Novaro's women build their own networks and alliances. It is a pattern set early on in *Danzón* when Julia Solórzano turns to the other telephone operators for companionship and advice in Mexico City and to Doña Tí and the prostitutes at her hotel for help in Veracruz. As Roberts-Camps again accurately notes, "Novaro's films are a celebration of the strength of female bonds to create a network capable of filling the spaces of absent male counterparts and the gaps in institutionalized assistance due to the economic crisis of the 1970s and 1980s in Mexico."[6] In addition to the social and psychological support, the associations also frequently involve shared custodial care. When Julia takes off in search of Carmelo, she asks her co-workers to look after her daughter. Both Serena and Elizabeth leave their children with Tia Juana, and Dalia relies on Blanquita for help in caring for her Alzheimer's-stricken mother. That assistance, marked by Blanquita's warmth and compassion, is conspicuously superior to the institutional indifference afforded by the hospital.

Establishing trust constitutes an important secondary plotline in many of the films. In *Danzón*, Julia gradually becomes accepted into the communal sisterhood at Doña Tí's hotel, helping to care for the babies and sharing meals. Serena and Elizabeth, the single mothers of *El jardín del Edén*, meet as neighbors and develop a friendship of traded backstories and combined family outings. When Serena's son Julián disappears, it is Elizabeth who helps search for him. The women of *Las buenas hierbas* meet regularly over laundry to smoke a little weed and share some confidences. Domestic spaces, such as kitchens, bathrooms, laundries, and children's rooms, reappear frequently as centers of female labor and multitasking camaraderie, places made important by the informal social power they contain. Every Novaro feature film also includes one and usually multiple scenes of food preparation, another example of critical work performed exclusively by women, either singly or in collaboration with one another.

In *Sin dejar huella*, the slow forging of bonds between Aurelia and Ana becomes a major focus of the narrative. Separated by class and education, they start out as reluctant travel companions and end as mutually supportive allies. Ana's transformation is revealed through her growing attachment to Aurelia's infant son Billy as she protects, feeds, soothes, and becomes his second mother. After a temporary rupture in their alliance, the two women are reunited at the film's conclusion in a seaside sanctuary free from the threatening men who have been pursuing them. Their bonded solidarity, as elsewhere in Novaro's films, represents what Óscar Robles has rightly termed "una nueva familia Mexicana, sin el control moral, económico y sexual del patriarcado"[7] ("a new Mexican family minus the moral, economic and sexual control of the patriarchy"[author's translation]).

Sin dejar huella is also a road movie, taking us from Juárez across Mexico's interior to the coast of Yucatán. A similar geographic sweep is reflected as well in the multiple locations of the other films. Stories are set in Mexico City, Veracruz, Tijuana, Guerrero, and Oaxaca. Every place is authentic; the *mise-en-scène* does not rely on green screens, rear projections, or soundstage fabrications. "I write for places," Novaro once disclosed in an interview, acknowledging the important role that geography plays in each of her films.[8] *El jardín del Edén*, with its interlocking stories of lives impacted by the border, is unimaginable anywhere else but Tijuana, and to capture its essence Novaro lived there for several months while researching and writing the script. The result is a film alive to the hybridized energy of a place that scholar Miriam Haddu has characterized as "almost unrecognizable in its complexity and beauty."[9] Having internalized the city's special culture, Novaro gets its visual details just right—the street art, the eclectic clothing, the Spanglish advertising. Equally well realized is the evocation of place in *Tesoros*, where Novaro's extended family and crew lived in the small Pacific coast community of Barra de Potosí while filming an intimate story about its natural treasures and its children. Once again, the beaches, nature preserves, and open-air restaurants are the real thing, catalogued with documentary-like clarity. And of course the command of space is unquestionably precise in *Las buenas hierbas*, which used Novaro's own house, garden, and neighborhood in Mexico City for its primary locations.

Miriam Haddu notes further that "Novaro attempts to rediscover her nation, and so her films find their locations within the contrasting terrain and vastness of Mexico. Equally, with each geographical journey, Novaro aims to revisit traditional cinematic sites within Mexican filmmaking."[10] Thus, Veracruz suggests the *cabaretera*, Mexico City the domestic melodrama, Tijuana the border films, and the itinerary of *Sin dejar huella* the road movie. In each of these examples, as we have seen, Novaro adjusts the generic tropes to fit her own artistic concerns. Through that discourse on genre and place, again according to Haddu, "Novaro projects . . . a vision of what she deems to be an acute interpretation of a specific sense of 'Mexicanness' on the screen."[11] The question of national identity connects and contextualizes all the other themes. "I want to always talk about my country," Novaro has remarked. "I don't want to talk about anything else."[12]

Each film sees Mexico through a slightly different lens. *Lola* documents a capital struggling with an economic crisis and still recovering from the catastrophic 1985 earthquake. In addition to revealing the failure of government agencies to support citizens, Novaro's first feature film also exposes what film professor Diane Sippl has called "deep rifts in the socioeconomic system that produce parallel but significantly stratified spheres of living," structural fissures that adversely affected the labor force and the family.[13] *Danzón*, on the other hand, argues for the preservation of Mexico's traditional popular culture and its celebration, in Novaro's words, of "a world of things as you would like them to be . . . a Mexico that shouldn't be allowed to get lost."[14] It is a world which references the Golden Age of Mexican cinema, Caribbean-influenced ballroom dancing, and the history of Mexican popular music. Along with that cultural legacy, *Danzón* also extols the fluid social norms that

Julia encounters in Veracruz. With its fusion of regional and international cultures, the Tijuana of *El jardín del Edén* embodies something quite different, namely a process of globalization destined to alter some traditional paradigms as it expands across the country. While Novaro shows the creative synergy of hybridization, she also takes note of its threat to erode Mexico's unique national character. "There are many American influences which are detrimental to my culture," she has warned.[15]

Beginning with *El jardín del Edén* and continuing through each of the subsequent films, Novaro has also stressed the importance of indigenous communities to national identity. *El jardín*, through the example of Jane, cautions against the fetishization of those communities whereas *Sin dejar huella* and *Las buenas hierbas* emphasize indigenous artistic and scientific contributions. In *Las buenas hierbas*, the *Aztec Codex*, with its detailed information on the healing power of plants, is offered as a legitimate alternative to institutionalized medicine. Folk art, folk medicine, and even folk religion are continually validated by Novaro. Nowhere in any of her films, for example, is there a scene involving a conventional Roman Catholic church service—no weddings, masses, christenings, or funerals. Instead she gives us the *Juan el Soldado* shrine and makeshift infant memorial of *El jardín del Edén* and the Tarot card reader of *Danzón*. The thematic movement of her work is away from the marginalization of underrepresented voices, whether they be poor, female, or indigenous, toward their full inclusion in a society connected to its historical traditions and, as modeled in *Tesoros*, its natural treasures.

Such advocacy begs the question of Novaro's politics. There are countless references, usually in the form of graffitied street messages, to official malfeasance and to revolutionary opposition groups such as the Zapatistas. Ana tells Aurelia about her admiration for Zapatista leader Subcomandante Marcos, the radio commentators in *Las buena hierbas* detail a series of government-sanctioned killings, and an end credit in *Tesoros* denounces the police-involved kidnapping and disappearance of 43 rural schoolteachers from Ayotzinapa, Guerrero. In a much more sustained way, *El jardín del Edén* documents the economic disparity between impoverished Mexican workers denied entry to the United States for backbreaking agricultural jobs and affluent American tourists crossing the border to take advantage of low housing and food prices in Tijuana. Similarly, both *Lola* and *Sin dejar huella* illustrate how inequities in class and education negatively affect the two single mothers trying to raise children on their own. Some Novaro critics have argued that her appropriation of leftist political rhetoric constitutes a kind of "magical Marxism" which pays lip service to revolutionary change but does not provide the rigorous investigation, historical research, and dialectical analysis needed to make it happen. There is a degree of truth in the observation that political commentary is not the driving force behind Novaro's artistic endeavors, but the casualness of her leftwing sympathies should not be confused with complacency. She is a secular humanist committed to social justice and economic equality. As Elissa Rashkin has written, "Novaro's perspective . . . can be best said to represent that of the Mexico City progressive intellectual sector, a perspective developed through the conflicts and idealism of 1968, the feminist and guerrilla movements of the 1970s, the disillusioning aftermath of the latter, and an emergence of an organized civil society after the 1985 earthquake."[16]

Novaro's handling of political context is indicative of her approach to composition. She is like a collage artist in the way she assemblies carefully selected pieces of image, text, and sound to create a unified whole. In *El jardín del Edén*, for example, she incorporates photos, signage, book excerpts, T-shirt slogans, drawings, Frida Kahlo paintings, *ranchero* music, video presentations, recorded whale sounds, and televised news reports as part of the overall discourse. Later films utilize animated segments, video game effects, and computer screen shots. More than just *au courant* stylistic flourishes, the intertextual references comment directly on character and theme. *El jardín's* cross-media texts broaden both the notion of *Mexicanidad* and the scope of the border's socioeconomic impact on specific populations. *Danzón's* pop culture intertextuality is the means by which Novaro reconfigures the structural elements of the *cabaretera* genre to construct a new model of female solidarity and empowerment.

Novaro is particularly sensitive to the way music contributes meaning. In each film, popular music, usually diegetic, firmly establishes time and place. The rock music performed by Lola's boyfriend immediately situates us in Mexico City's New Wave milieu of the 1980s just as *Danzón's* Caribbean ballroom music evokes a retro world of cabarets and dance salons. Lola lip syncs a rock song with Ana, and Julia explains a trumpet solo to Rubén, the young seaman she meets in Veracruz. The performative aspect of that music emphasizes the direct existential importance it plays in the women's lives and facilitates the viewers' apprehension of it. In other examples, the *norteño* music of *Sin dejar huella* denotes Juárez, the tropical strolling musicians of that same film signal that Juan has arrived in Cancún, and the mariachis of *El jardín* help to identify Tijuana.

The non-diegetic music is just as evocative. The use of Vivaldi's *Stabat Mater* in *Lola* provides one of the most dramatic examples. As Lola carries Ana through the damaged streets of Mexico City, the mournful baroque soundtrack music mirrors her pain in having to abandon her daughter. Knowing beforehand that the *Stabat Mater* was to be layered over the visual, actress Leticia Huijara as Ana orchestrated her movements to match the dirge-like rhythms of Vivaldi. In *Danzón*, the romantic ballads that Julia listens to contain such lyrics as "I kissed you and then I lost you . . . maybe I'll die without you" and "Love is an anguish, a question," sentiments that reflect her own passionate yearnings. Likewise, in *Las buenas hierbas*, Blanquita continually listens to a song that references the film's treatment of memory in the lines "If you ever doubt me or the love I've given you, just remember the hours we had together." Reflecting the rich history of Mexican popular music, Novaro's selections include works by everyone from Juan Gabriel and Pedro Infante to the folk singer Zindu Cano and her own son Santiago Chávez. Always, the words and music are intended to advance the narrative and broaden characterization.

A typical Novaro narrative unfolds gradually, taking its time to reveal information that a conventional film would deliver more rapidly. Relationships between characters emerge slowly, after they have been introduced in the middle of activities that appear to be unrelated to one another. There are no title cards to help with exposition and, except for little Jacinta in *Tesoros*, no voice-over narration. *Las buenas hierbas*, for instance, introduces us to about ten different characters before we realize the central story will revolve around Dalia's care for her Alzheimer's-stricken mother Lala. Similarly, in its opening scenes, *El jardín del Edén* presents seven major adult characters and four child characters, some of whom will have significant interconnecting narrative arcs and some of whom will never meet each other. Occasionally, as with Gabo and the musician neighbors in *La buenas hierbas*, characters are introduced and then disappear almost immediately from the plotline. In a Novaro film, as cinema studies professor Amy Kaminsky has noted, "the characters are not so much developed along traditional narrative lines as traced through a series of visual moments that the viewer must piece together."[17]

Once established, the narrative proceeds sequentially, with scenes following one another in strict chronological order. Except for one brief instance in *El jardín del Edén* and three more extended ones in *Las buenas hierbas*, there are no flashbacks. "For Novaro," writes Kaminsky, "there is no need to dig up the past to make sense of the present."[18] Although previous romantic relationships have significantly shaped the lives of Novaro's female characters, she includes no backstories that permit us to speculate on the exact psychological nature of that influence. Julia, Serena, Elizabeth, Aurelia,

Dalia, and Lala have all been married yet we learn almost nothing about their ex-spouses. "I made a mess of my men," Blanquita tells Dalia and Ana but then refrains from providing any more details. It is the present, with its immediate challenges to face and choices to make, that matters most to Novaro's female protagonists.

Not much by way of spectacle happens to those characters. Lola fights with her boyfriend, temporarily abandons her daughter, and seeks solace next to the ocean. Julia travels to Veracruz to find her missing dance partner, enjoys a romantic fling with a younger man, and returns to Mexico City. The children of *Tesoros* haphazardly search for buried treasure but discover natural wonders instead. "I don't like action films," Novaro has commented on more than one occasion, a preference clearly demonstrated in each of her films.[19] Even the car chases and stunt crash of *Sin dejar huella* are downplayed, almost immediately overshadowed by Aurelia and Ana's emotional reactions to the chaos. Other acts of violence in that same film, such as the beating of Heraclio's neighbor and the shooting of Mendizábal, occur offscreen. How events are impacting Aurelia and Ana's understanding of themselves and each other is more important to Novaro than the actual events. "In the manuals on how to write screenplays, by contrast, a different view is taken: spectacular events are set in place and then things are forcibly made to mesh," she has explained. "First you program what is going to take place and then, in the action, you fit in the characters, their experiences, and their feelings. I don't see life this way and I don't like to narrate like this. I don't impose a given action on the characters. I let them guide me to whatever might happen in their life."[20]

That refusal to provide her narratives with a conventional beginning, middle, and end entails a corresponding lack of closure concerning the characters' personal affairs. "Novaro's ease with ambiguity," writes historian Romy Sutherland, "is certainly evident in the endings of all of her feature length films. She manages to take the film to a point of plot resolution, while retaining open possibilities. None of her films end with a strictly determined conclusion."[21] Lola strolls happily along the beach with her daughter, but it remains to be seen if she can build a new life there. Although Ana and Aurelia have also taken refuge next to the ocean, they too may not be permanently safe from the corrupt federal police and the ruthless drug cartels. Julia's newly found *joie de vivre* may or may not survive the drudgery of her job at the telephone company. Almost nothing has been resolved in *El jardín del Edén*. Jane is still wandering, Serena is working to keep her family intact, Elizabeth is struggling with her cultural identity, and Felipe is waiting to cross the border again. At the conclusion of their narratives, most of Novaro's characters continue to inhabit what Sutherland calls the "gray areas of human involvement."[22]

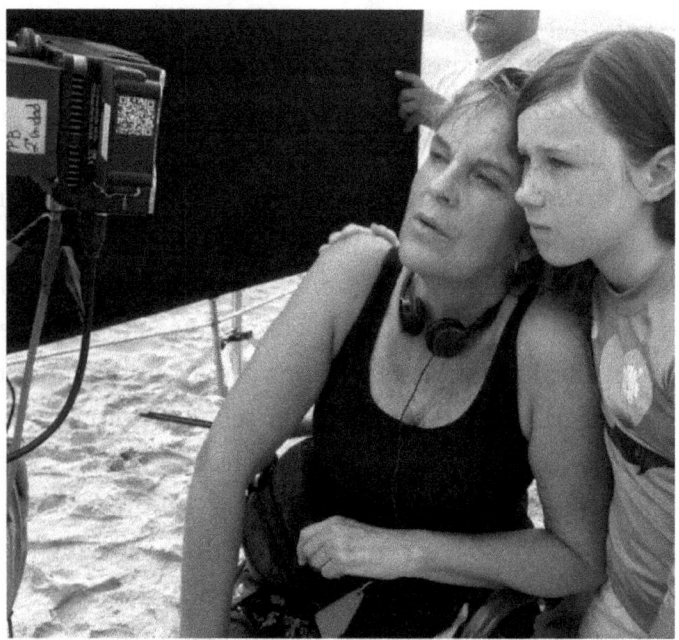

María Novaro, with granddaughter Andrea
Sutton Chávez, lines up a shot for *Tesoros* (2017).

In keeping with her dislike of action films, Novaro's visual style is elegant yet restrained. There are no swooping crane shots, no fast zooms, no jump cuts. The camera movements, however, are consistently well-orchestrated and expressive. The slow pans catalogue detail and document the physical settings in which characters navigate their options. Sweeping slowly across the abandoned toys and clothing items in Lola's apartment, the camera reveals the cluttered chaos of her life. In *Danzón*, to show context, the camera pans across the multiple switchboard stations, the faces of the cantina guests watching Julia, and the women doing chores at Doña Tí's hotel. Similar shots in *El jardín del Edén* and *Las buenas hierbas* "accumulate" cars waiting at the border and herbal specimens on Lala's worktable. Novaro also pans from one image to another for thematic comment. When Julia agrees to board Rubén's boat for the night, the camera slowly pans away from them to focus suggestively on the hull rocking gently against its moorage. In *Lola*, pans from Lola to the damaged buildings equate her struggles with the broader deterioration of Mexico City.

Novaro's tracking shots, which can be either brief or extended, linear or circular, are masterful. They follow the movements of the characters, explore narratively significant space, and collect visual detail in the same way that the pans do. Each one of the films makes effective use of the tracking camera. In *Lola*, to illustrate the main character's growing isolation, the camera tracks alongside as she walks behind an iron fence separating her from daughter Ana's schoolyard and then in a single long take later in the film tracks laterally across a deserted playground to discover Lola drinking by herself in the darkness. *Danzón* opens with a ground-level tracking shot of Julia's high heels gliding across the dance floor. Similar travelling shots elsewhere throughout the film capture the graceful elegance of the various ballrooms and dance salons where Julia feels most alive. A series of linked tracking shots in *El jardín del Edén* documents Serena's nighttime drive through Tijuana in search of Julián, and when Felipe prays at the *Juan el Soldado* shrine, the camera tracks away from him to show all the photos and messages of the migrants who have come before him. Despite the difficulty of the terrain in *El jardín*, Novaro tracks the camera in a nearly 360-degree sweep around the edges of the infant funeral and down along the side of the parked convertible as Felipe silently takes leave of Jane, an extended take that is then repeated in its entirety.

Equally supple are those travelling shots in *Sin dejar huella* where the camera tracks in on Aurelia and Billy sitting in the hills above Juarez and later makes another 360-degree circuit around the station wagon while Ana and Aurelia wait near the cenote for the red car to appear. For the road scenes, the camera is crouched inside the station wagon, mounted atop the hood, or placed on an escort vehicle. In *Las buenas hierbas*, slow tracking shots are used for Dalia's walk through the Botanical Garden with Lala and for Blanquita's remembrance of the *quinceañera*. Dalia's memory of gathering plants is visualized as a subjective forward tracking shot through a heavily canopied forest. The child-level tracking shots of *Tesoros* follow Jaci and her friends as they explore the beaches, inlets, and jungles of Barra de Potosí. Stunning though they may be, Novaro's tracking shots are not for the sake of ornamentation. She moves the camera because she has to move the camera. Anything less would restrict the open-ended journeying of her characters. As David Thomson has said of Max Ophüls, "His films are not decorated by movement, they consist of it."[23] The same holds true for Novaro. Her camera must move to keep up with characters who are in turn keeping pace with the passage of time.

The uninterrupted camera movements are matched by a preference for not breaking dialogue into a series of shot/reverse-angle shot exchanges. Rather than multiple alternating over-the-shoulder camera positions, Novaro likes instead to place her characters together in the same frame, especially for important conversations between friends. Some of the most dramatic moments, in fact, emerge from those bonded group shots. When Julia returns from Veracruz, she shares details of the trip with her friends and daughter in a sustained four-shot where they all stand around a table in her living room. In *Sin dejar huella*, Aurelia asks, "Are you my friend, Ana?" and the subsequent two-shots have them running hand-in-hand to the beach, splashing around in the water, and sharing confidences. The scenes in *Las buenas hierbas* that involve the laundry conversations about men and the mate-drinking discussion of Dalia's parentage are both three-shots. In all of these cases, the female solidarity is conveyed verbally and visually at the same time.

In general, Novaro limits cross-cutting to those few sequences such as Serena's search for Julián and Mendizábal's pursuit of Ana that are intended to generate either tension or suspense. Much more common are the cutaways that pause the narrative for lyrical effect. One of the first of these interludes comes in *Danzón* when Julia strolls along the docks and watches a gauzy progression of romantically named ships cross the harbor. As a contrast to the arbitrary barriers of the frontier in *El jardín del Edén*, Novaro cuts to some large gray whales swimming freely up the coast. Once Ana and Aurelia arrive in Yucatán, cuts to the verdant countryside signal a thawing in the frigid relations between the two of them. The uniquely hypnotic atmosphere of *Las buenas hierbas* stems largely from the dozens of cutaways to such serene natural images as wind-ruffled trees, flowering plants, chirping birds, and the mystical cloud-covered mountaintop. Cutaway images in *Tesoros* also focus on the world of nature: a pelican at rest in the water, a flock of birds crossing the horizon, iguanas soaking up the sun, an iridescent school of fish. Complementary rather than extraneous to the narratives, the pastoral cutaways slow the progression of events and link characters to a spiritual influence that can be both calming and instructive.

Novaro gets similar atmospheric effects from her adroit use of color. Barra de Potosí's paradisiacal beauty is revealed through the vibrant yellows and greens of its jungle and the dazzling blue of its ocean. The same palette greets Julia's arrival in Veracruz a well as Ana and Aurelia's journey toward Cancún. In *Danzón*, bursts of red signify female centered sexuality and in *Sin dejar huella*, they connote the threat of violence. The muted, rain-streaked colors of *Las buenas hierbas* help to create that film's somber, trance-like ambiance while the grayish hues of *Lola* capture the decay of post-earthquake Mexico City. Tijuana's cultural mosaic, as depicted in *El jardín del Edén*, is mirrored in the clashing colors of its street life, its natural landscape, and its folk art. Color always operates on multiple levels in Novaro's films, as the objective documentation of reality, the subjective evocation of mood, and the ideological expression of meaning.

For all the stylistic consistency, each film also has unique structural components. *Danzón* lessens the number of establishing shots to generate a sense of discovery while *El jardín del Edén* does the opposite in carefully anchoring its many overlapping narratives. For Felipe's chaotic ambush at the border, *El jardín* uses a jostled handheld camera, and for Julián's memory of his dying father, it relies on a slow-motion subjective camera to set the mood. Dreamlike flashbacks and slow fades, mostly absent from all the other films, differentiate the languid pace of *Las buenas hierbas*. More energetically, the constantly moving camera of *Tesoros* stays close to the ground as it captures the eye-level bustle of its young characters. With Novaro, form always adjusts to content.

María Rojo, pictured here with Victor Carpinteiro in a waterfront scene from *Danzón* (1991) is one of the many actresses who did some of their best work with María Novaro.

The long takes and two-shots maintain uninterrupted focus on performance and are indicative of Novaro's respect for her actresses. María Rojo, Carmen Salinas, Ofelia Medina, Ana Ofelia Murguía, Úrsula Pruneda, Tiaré Scanda, Aitana Sánchez-Gijón, Leticia Huijara, and Gabriela Roel have done some of their finest work in the films they made with Novaro, films that earned multiple Ariel Award acting nominations. Highly memorable are such moments as the mother-daughter dressing scene in *Las buenas hierbas*, the hotel restaurant argument in *Sin dejar huella*, and the meatloaf dinner debacle of *Lola*. Novaro has always taken great care with her casts, including extensive video rehearsals for the first couple of films to get everyone comfortable in front of the camera. Even when correcting the theatrical flourishes of stage-trained actors, she never dismissed them, like director Felipe Cazals famously did, as "footed props."[24] Open to suggestions, she always encouraged the actors to make the parts their own. "We all wanted to work with her," recalled Carmen Salinas.[25] "If what I see when we are doing a scene moves me," Novaro once explained, "I know how the camera should move. If the actor gives me goose bumps, if he makes me feel a knot in my throat, I immediately have the camera follow this character."[26] It is an intuitive, emotional process that also relies on careful preparation and broad collaboration.

"The collective is fundamental," Novaro has insisted. "I can't scream like Cazals. I can't mistreat people the way (Arturo) Ripstein does."[27] Her authority on set has always been a calm and self-assured one. Trained in all the technical aspects of filmmaking, she has selected equally qualified crew members and worked closely with them to realize everyone's best.

To date, Novaro has made six feature films and several shorts. It is not a huge body of work but one that is consistently rich, both stylistically and thematically. Rooted in a very specific cultural tradition, her films also carry universal meaning and significance. "What moves me is tenderness," María Novaro revealed in an interview. "I try to perceive that tenderness that means so much to me and organize my story around it."[28] The tenderness is surely there in the complex female characters she has created, timelessly relevant characters who remain flawed yet admirable in their struggles to sustain family, self, and community.

Filmography (Major Works)

Una isla rodeada de agua
(*An Island Surrounded by Water*)

Production of Centro Universitario de Estudios Universitarios and Universidad Nacional Autónoma de México. Released in 1985. Color, 16mm. Running time of 30 minutes. **Cast**: Mara Chávez, Silvia Otero, Conchis Arroyo, Carolina, Yolanda Ocampo, Chencha Marín, Alejandro Marín. **Crew**: María Novaro (director, writer, editor), Marie-Christine Camus (cinematographer).

Azul celeste (Sky Blue)

Production of Dirección de Actividades Cinematográficas de la Universidad Nacional Autónoma de México. Released in 1988. Color, 35mm. Running time of 28 minutes. Episode in anthology film *Historias de ciudad* (*Tales of the City*). **Cast**: Gabriela Roel (Laureana), Cheli Godínez (voceadora), Carlos Chávez (delivery man), Gerardo Martínez (señor del carro), Gina Morett (wife), Damián Alcázar (Edmundo Garza), José Antonio Estrada. **Crew**: María Novaro (director, co-writer), Beatriz Novaro (co-writer), Santiago Navarrete (cinematographer), Luis Manuel Rodríguez Bermúdez (editor).

Lola

Production of Macondo Cine Video, Conacite Dos, Cooperativa José Revueltas, Televisión Española (TVE). Released in 1989. Color, 35mm. Running time of 92 minutes. **Cast**: Leticia Huijara (Lola),

Alejandra Vargas (Ana), Martha Navarro (Chelo), Roberto Sosa (Duende), Mauricio Rivera (Omar), Javier Zaragoza (Mario), Cheli Godínez (Dora), Erando Gonzalez (manager), Gerardo Martínez (Mudo), Edmundo Mosqueira (Pedro). **Crew:** María Novaro (director, co-writer), Beatriz Novaro (co-writer), Rodrigo García (cinematographer), Sigfrido Barjau (editor), Dulce Kuri and Jorge Sánchez (producers), Gabriel Romo (music), Marisa Pecanins (art director), Rosy Duprat and Guadalupe Sánchez (makeup artists), Lucia Holguín (wardrobe), Carlos Aguilar (sound editor), Rebeca Becerril (assistant director).

Danzón

Production of Fondo de Fomento a la Calidad Cinematográfica, Gobierno del Estado de Veracruz, Instituto Mexicano de Cinematografía (IMCINE), Macondo Cine Video, Tabasco Films, Televisión Española (TVE). Released in 1991. Color, 35mm. Running time of 104 minutes. **Cast:** María Rojo (Julia Solórzano), Carmen Salinas (Doña Tí), Tito Vasconcelos (Susy), Margarita Isabel (Silvia), Victor Carpinteiro (Rubén), Cheli Godínez (Tere), Daniel Rergis (Carmelo), Adyari Cházaro (Perla), Blanca Guerra (Colorada), César Sobrevels (Chucho), Mikhail Kaminin (Russian sailor), Rodrigo Gómez (Malena), Sergio Colmenares (Karla), Ángel de Valle (Yadira), Martha Navarro (witch). **Crew:** María Novaro (director, co-writer, co-editor), Beatriz Novaro (co-writer), Rodrigo García (cinematographer), Nelson Rodríguez and Sigfrido Barjau (co-editors), Dulci Kuri and Jorge Sánchez (producers), Pepe Luis and Felipe Pérez (music), Marisa Pecanins and Norberto Sánchez (production designers), Andrés Vargas (set decorator), Amado Domínguez and Carlos Rodríguez (set designers), Monica Neumaier (costume designer), Nerio Barberis (sound), Moisés Ortiz Urquidi (assistant director).

Otoñal (Autumnal)

Production of IMCINE-DIDECINE. Released in 1992. Color, 35mm. Running time of 6 minutes. Based on an idea by Quino. **Cast:** Delia Casanova, María Rojo, Sofía Cabrera, Alicia del Lago, Miguel Ángel Rodríguez. **Crew:** María Novaro (director), Dharma Reyes (writer), Lucía Olguín (cinematographer), Sigfrido Barjau (editor), Adalberto Ayala Martínez and Gerardo Grijalva Juárez (music).

El jardín del Edén (The Garden of Eden)

Production of Fondo de Fomento a la Calidad Cinematográfica, Instituto Mexicano de Cinematografía (IMCINE), Macondo Cine Video, Ministère de la Culture de la Republique Francaise, Ministère des Affaires Étrangères, Société Générale des Industries Culturelles du Québec (SOGIC), Téléfilm Canada, Universidad de Guadalajara, Verseau International. Released in 1994. Color, 35mm. Running time of 104 minutes. **Cast:** Renée Coleman (Jane), Bruno Bichir (Felipe), Gabriela Roel (Serena), Rosario Sagrav (Liz), Alan Ciangherotti (Julián), Joseph Culp (Frank), Jerónimo Berruecos (Sergio), Ana Ofelia Murguía (Juana), Ángeles Cruz (Margarita Luna), Denisse Bravo (Lupita), José García (Felipe's brother), Lucero Sánchez (Paloma), Xavier Bautista (El Maleno). **Crew:** María Novaro (director, co-writer, co-editor), Beatriz Novaro (co-writer), Eric Alan Edwards (cinematographer), Sigfrido Barjau (co-editor), Thomas Garvin, Dulce Kuri, Lyse Lafontaine, Richard Magnien, Jorge Sánchez (producers), José Stephens (music), Brigitte Broch (art director), Salvador Parra (set decorator), Pat Escobar (costume designer), Yvon Benoît, Marcel Pothier, Hans Peter Strobl (sound), Federic Henocque (assistant director).

Cuando comenzamos a hablar (When We Began Talking)

Production of Filmoteca de la UNAM, Instituto Mexicano de Cinematografía (IMCINE), Producciones Amaranta. Released in 1998. Color, 35mm. Episode in documentary anthology *Enredando sombras* (*Entangling Shadows*), running time of 90 minutes. **Crew:** María Novaro (director), Patricia Coronado and Jorge Sánchez (producers), Suzanne Crim (costume designer), Leon Sandoval (sound), Vanessa Hernández (production coordinator).

Sin dejar huella (Without a Trace)

Production of AltaVista Films, Fondo para la Producción Cinematográfica de Calidad (FOPROCINE), Tabasco Films, Televisión Española (TVE), Tornasol Films, Vía Digital. Released in 2000. Color, Super 35mm. Running time of 109 minutes. **Cast:** Aitana Sánchez-Gijón (Ana), Tiaré Scanda (Aurelia), Jesús Ochoa (Mendizábal), Martín Altomaro (Saúl), José Sefami (El Chaparro), Juan Manuel Bernal (Saúl's cousin), Silverio Palacios (Heraclio Chuc), Santiago Molina (Billy), Edmundo Sotelo (Juan), Roberto "Raki" Ríos (Trigger Happy), Gerardo Taracena (Niko), Cristina Michaus (Lolis). **Crew:** María Novaro (director, writer), Serguei Saldívar Tanaka (cinematographer), Ángel Hernández Zoido (editor), Mariela Besuievsky, Francisco González Compeán, Gerard Herrero, Dulce Kuri, Tita Lombardo, Mónica Lozano (producers), Lynn Fainchtein (music), Patrick Pasquier (art director), Hania Robledo (set decorator), Macarena Folache (costume designer), Maribel Romo (hair stylist), Karmele Soler and Carlos Sánchez (makeup artists), Juan Borrell, Nerio Barberis, Mario Martínez Cobos, Eduardo Vaisman (sound), Alejandro Vázquez (special effects coordinator), Miguel Lima (assistant director).

Las buenas hierbas (*The Good Herbs*)

Production of Axolote Cine, Fondo para la Producción Cinematográfica de Calidad (FOPROCINE), Instituto Mexicano de Cinematografía (IMCINE). Released in 2010. Color, 35mm. Running time of 117 minutes. **Cast:** Úrsula Pruneda (Dalia), Ofelia Medina (Lala), Ana Ofelia Murguía (Blanquita), Cosmo González Muñoz (Cosmo), Gabino Rodríguez (Gabo), Miriam Balderas (Ana), Alberto Estrella (Luis), Luisa Pardo (Citlali), Rodrigo Solís (El Rot). **Crew:** María Novaro (director, writer, producer, co-editor), Gerardo Barroso (cinematographer), Sebastián Garza (co-editor), Julio Bárcenas and Eric Reid (producers), Lorenza Manrique (art director), Leticia Palacios (costume designer), Iñaki Legaspi (makeup artista), Alejandro de Icaza (sound), Alejandro Valle (visual effects), Lisa Tillinger (digital colorist), Lucero Sánchez Novaro (set dresser).

Tesoros (*Treasures*)

Production of Axolote Cine and FOPROCINE. Released in 2017. Color, 35mm. Running time of 95 minutes. **Cast:** Dylan Sutton Chávez (Dylan), Andrea Sutton Chávez (Andrea), Lucas Barroso Tillinger (Lucas), Jacinta Chávez de León (Jaci), Julieta Bárcenas Nava (Julieta), Jazmin Bárcenas Nava (Jazmin), Matilde Hernández Guinea (Mati), Fabiana Hernández Guinea (Fabi), Aranza Bañuelos Garcia (Aranza), Michel Lucas Organis (Michel), Mara Sutton Chávez (Dylan's mother), Martin Sutton (Dylan's father), Santiago Chávez Novaro (Jaci's father), Judith de León (Jaci's mother), Zindu Cano (Zindu), Howin Albarrán Bañuelos (Uncle Owen), Avimael Cadena Bañuelos (Avi the teacher). **Crew:** María Novaro (director, writer, producer, editor), Gerardo Barroso and Lisa Tillinger (cinematographers), Paula Astorga, Julio Bárcenas, Pamela Guinea, Joaquín Ruano (producers), Alettia Molina (art director),

Igor Figueroa, Fernando Heftye, Roberto Lazzeri (music), Fabiola Gutierrez (wardrobe), Josue Hernández (visual effects), Valeria López Mancheva (sound), Lisa Tillinger (colorist), Lucero Sánchez Novaro (second unit director), Julio Bárcenas (assistant director).

Notes

Biographical Profile

1. Seth Fein, "From Collaboration to Containment: Hollywood and the International Political Economy of Mexican Cinema after the Second World War," in Hershfield and Maciel, *Mexico's Cinema: A Century of Film and Filmmakers*, p. 128.
2. Chloe Roddick, "Deep Focus: The Golden Age of Mexican Cinema," *Sight and Sound*, July 25, 2019.
3. Linda B. Hall, *Dolores del Río: Beauty in Light and Shade*, p. 197.
4. Carlos Monsiváis, "Cantinflas and Tin Tan: Mexico's Greatest Comedians," in Hershfield and Maciel, *Mexico's Cinema: A Century of Film and Filmmakers*, pp. 72-73.
5. *A Visual History with María Novaro, Director and Screenwriter*, video interview conducted by Lourdes Portillo, September 25, 2015.
6. Erik Larson, *The Splendid and the Vile: A Saga of Churchill, Family, and Defiance during the Blitz*, p. 225.
7. *A Visual History with María Novaro* video interview.
8. Ibid.
9. Robert Ellsworth, "María Novaro Interview," *Venice Magazine*, September, 1992.
10. Hall, *Dolores del Río*, p. 263.
11. *A Visual History with María Novaro* video interview.
12. Ibid.
13. Ibid.

14. Ibid.
15. Ibid.
16. Ibid.
17. Ibid.
18. Ibid.
19. Tim Golden, "'Danzón' Glides to a Soft Mexican Rhythm," *The New York Times,* October 11, 1992.
20. Elissa J. Rashkin, *Women Filmmakers in Mexico: The Country of Which We Dream,* pp. 68-69.
21. *A Visual History with María Novaro* video interview.
22. Ibid.
23. Ibid.
24. Rashkin, *Women Filmmakers in Mexico,* p. 63.
25. *A Visual History with María Novaro* video interview.
26. Ibid.
27. Gerald Martin, *Gabriel García Márquez: A Life,* p. 451.
28. *A Visual History with María Novaro* video interview.
29. Ibid.
30. Ibid.
31. Kevin Thomas, "A New Generation of Filmmakers from Mexico Dances into the Scene," *Los Angeles Times,* October 16, 1992.
32. *A Visual History with María Novaro* video interview.
33. Ibid.
34. Isabel Arredondo, "María Novaro on the Making of Lola and Danzón," *Women's Studies Quarterly,* Spring-Summer 2002, pg. 208.
35. Ibid., p. 209.
36. *A Visual History with María Novaro* video interview.
37. Piers Handling, "Lola," Fifteenth Toronto Film Festival Program, 1990.
38. "Lola," *Weekly Variety,* January 17, 1990.
39. *A Visual History with María Novaro* video interview.

40. Alejandro Leal, "María Novaro es descarada feminista y antimachista," *El Universal*, October 4, 1992.
41. Arredondo, "María Novaro on the Making . . . ," *Women's Studies Quarterly*, pp. 199-200.
42. *A Visual History with María Novaro* video interview.
43. Arredondo, "María Novaro on the Making . . . ," *Women's Studies Quarterly*, p. 208.
44. Ellsworth, "María Novaro Interview," *Venice Magazine*.
45. Coco Fusco, "Dance and Remembrance," *Village Voice*, August 27, 1991.
46. Janet Maslin, "A Melodious Variation on Feminist Awareness," *The New York Times*, September 25, 1992.
47. Michael Wilmington, "Exhilaration, Charm and Grace in Musical Romance 'Danzón,'" *Los Angeles Times*, F8, October 16, 1992.
48. Golden, "'Danzón' Glides to a Soft Mexican Rhythm," *The New York Times*.
49. James Ulmer, "In Transit: Novaro helping lead Mexican film comeback," *The Hollywood Reporter*, August 11, 1992.
50. María Novaro, Sony Pictures Classics *Danzón* press packet.
51. Ulmer, "In Transit: Novaro helping lead . . . ," *The Hollywood Reporter*.
52. Arredondo, "María Novaro on the Making . . . ," *Women's Studies Quarterly*, p. 211.
53. *A Visual History with María Novaro* video interview.
54. Interview with author.
55. Ibid.
56. *A Visual History with María Novaro* video interview.
57. Ibid.
58. Ibid.
59. Ibid.
60. Ibid.
61. Ibid.

62. Ibid.
63. Ellsworth, "María Novaro Interview," *Venice Magazine*.
64. David Rooney, "Leaving No Trace," *Weekly Variety*, October 9-15, 2000.
65. Elvis Mitchell, "A Festival of Latin Films That Go Many Different Places," *The New York Times*, August 9, 2001.
66. *A Visual History with María Novaro* video interview.
67. David R. Maciel and Joanne Hershfield, "Women and Gender Representation in the Contemporary Cinema of Mexico," in Hershfield and Maciel, *Mexico's Cinema: A Century of Film and Filmmakers*, p. 250.
68. *A Visual History with María Novaro* video interview.
69. Ibid.
70. Rashkin, *Women Filmmakers in Mexico*, p. 183.
71. *A Visual History with María Novaro* video interview.
72. Ibid.
73. John Hopewell, "Mexico's María Novaro on 'Tesoros,' Mexicans' Joie de Vivre," *Daily Variety*, March 10, 2017.
74. David R. Maciel, "Cinema and the State in Contemporary Mexico, 1970-1999," in Hershfield and Maciel, *Mexico's Cinema: A Century of Film and Filmmakers*, p. 223.
75. Anna Marie de la Fuente, "IMCINE Director María Novaro Ramps Up Outreach, Diversifies Incentives," *Daily Variety*, October 24, 2019.
76. *A Visual History with María Novaro* video interview.

Lola

1. *Lola* commentary, DVD release, Zafra Video/Facets Video, 2007.
2. Óscar Robles, *Identidades Maternacionales en el cine de María Novaro*, p. 91.
3. *Lola* commentary, DVD release, Zafra Video/Facets Video.

4. Ibid.
5. Ibid.
6. Traci Roberts-Camps, *Latin American Women Filmmakers: Social and Cultural Perspectives*, p. 42.
7. Diane Sippl, "Al cine de las Mexicanas: *Lola* in the Limelight," in Robin and Jaffe, *Redirecting the Gaze: Gender, Theory and Cinema in the Third World*, p. 43.
8. Arredondo, "María Novaro on the Making . . . ," *Women's Studies Quarterly*, p.197.
9. Ibid.
10. Ibid., pp. 197-98.
11. Roberts-Camps, *Latin American Women Filmmakers*, p. 41.
12. *Lola* commentary, DVD release, Zafra Video/Facets Video.
13. Ibid.
14. Ibid.
15. Ibid.
16. Sippl, "Al cine . . . ," *Redirecting the Gaze*, p. 52.
17. *Lola* commentary, DVD release, Zafra Video/Facets Video.
18. Ibid.
19. Romy Sutherland, "Journeys and Destinations: The Films of María Novaro," *Senses of Cinema*, December, 2002.
20. Rashkin, *Women Filmmakers in Mexico*, p. 189.
21. *A Visual History with María Novaro* video interview.
22. Roberts-Camps, *Latin American Women Filmmakers*, p. 44.
23. Arredondo, "María Novaro on the Making . . . ," *Women's Studies Quarterly*, p. 207.
24. Ibid.
25. Ibid, p. 208.
26. *Lola* commentary, DVD release, Zafra Video/Facets Video.
27. Ibid.
28. Ibid.
29. Ibid.

30. Thomas, "A New Generation of Filmmakers . . . ," *Los Angeles Times*.
31. *Lola* commentary, DVD release, Zafra Video/Facets Video.
32. Ibid.
33. Ibid.
34. Ibid.
35. "Actress Martha Navarro dies and the curse of the 3 deaths is fulfilled," *Mundo Hispanico*, December 30, 2020.
36. *A Visual History with María Novaro* video interview.
37. Ellsworth, "María Novaro Interview," *Venice Magazine*.

Danzón

1. Wilmington, "Exhilaration, Charm and Grace in Musical Romance '*Danzón*'," *Los Angeles Times*.
2. *Danzón* commentary, DVD release, Zafra Video, 2007.
3. Laura Mulvey, "Visual Please and Narrative Cinema," in Mulvey, *Visual and Other Pleasures*, p. 19.
4. Roberts-Camps, *Latin American Women Filmmakers*, p. 45.
5. Rashkin, *Women Filmmakers in Mexico*, p. 177.
6. Maciel and Hershfield, "Women and Gender Representation . . . ," *Mexico's Cinema*, p. 259.
7. Robert Farris Thompson, *Tango: The Art History of Love*, p. 4.
8. *Danzón* commentary, DVD release, Zafra Video.
9. Ibid.
10. Ibid.
11. Rashkin, *Women Filmmakers in Mexico*, p. 177.
12. *Danzón* commentary, DVD release, Zafra Video.
13. Ibid.
14. Maciel and Hershfield, "Women and Gender Representation . . . ," *Mexico's Cinema*, p. 259.

15. Arredondo, "María Novaro on the Making . . . ," *Women's Studies Quarterly*, p. 202-03.
16. Kimball Lockhart, "Michelangelo Antonioni," in Sarris, *The Saint James Film Directors Encyclopedia*, p. 22.
17. Arredondo, "María Novaro on the Making . . . ," *Women's Studies Quarterly*, pp. 202-03.
18. Ibid, p. 204.
19. *Danzón* commentary, DVD release, Zafra Video.
20. Ibid.
21. Rashkin, *Women Filmmakers in Mexico*, p. 173.
22. *Danzón* commentary, DVD release, Zafra Video.
23. Arredondo, "María Novaro on the Making . . . ," *Women's Studies Quarterly*, p. 208.
24. Rashkin, *Women Filmmakers in Mexico*, p. 176.
25. *Danzón* commentary, DVD release, Zafra Video.
26. Ibid.
27. Ibid.
28. Ibid.
29. Arredondo, "María Novaro on the Making . . . ," *Women's Studies Quarterly*, pp. 206-07.
30. *Danzón* commentary, DVD release, Zafra Video.
31. Arredondo, "María Novaro on the Making . . . ," *Women's Studies Quarterly*, pp. 209-10.
32. Ibid., p. 210.
33. Ibid., p. 200.
34. Ibid., p. 201.
35. "María Novaro llegó hasta la cumbre de su gran carrera," *Cine Mundial*, June 1, 1992.
36. Results summarized in Rashkin, *Women Filmmakers in Mexico*, pp. 181-83.
37. Quoted in Rashkin, *Women Filmmakers in Mexico*, p. 180.

El jardín del Edén

1. Mariam Haddu, "Welcome to Tijuana . . . space, place and identity in María Novaro's *El jardín del Edén*," *Journal of Romance Studies*, Winter, 2006, p. 4.
2. Alma Guillermoprieto, *The Heart That Bleeds*, p. 255.
3. Haddu, "Welcome to Tijuana . . . ," *Journal of Romance Studies*, p. 8.
4. Tomas Pérez Turrent, "Los milagros de Juan Soldado," *Revista Siempre*, October 19, 1995.
5. Amy Kaminsky, "Identity at the Border: Narrative Strategies in María Novaro's *El jardín del Edén* and John Sayles's *Lone Star*," *Studies in Twentieth-Century Literature*, Winter, 2001, p. 27.
6. Robles, *Identidades Maternacionales en el cine de María Novaro*, p. 190.
7. Ibid., p. 183.
8. Kaminsky, "Identity at the Border . . . ," *Studies in Twentieth-Century Literature*, p. 94.
9. Ibid.
10. Victor Bustos, "María Novaro, un clavado en la frontera," *Dicine*, January-February, 1996, p. 25.
11. Haddu, "Welcome to Tijuana . . . ," *Journal of Romance Studies*, p. 9.
12. Rashkin, *Women Filmmakers in Mexico*, p. 189.
13. Roberts-Camps, *Latin American Women Filmmakers*, p. 47.
14. Rashkin, *Women Filmmakers in Mexico*, p. 190.
15. Carla Olson Buck, "Gender/Ethnicity/Authenticity: Recirculating Domination in *El jardín del Edén*?," *Letras Femininas*, Summer, 2006, p. 240.
16. Roberts-Camps, *Latin American Women Filmmakers*, p. 47.
17. Haddu, "Welcome to Tijuana . . . ," *Journal of Romance Studies*, p. 4.

18. Norma Iglesias, "Reconstructing the Border: Mexican Border Cinema and Its Relationship to Its Audience," in Hershfield and Maciel, *Mexico's Cinema: A Century of Film and Filmmakers*, p. 233.
19. Ibid., pp. 234-35.
20. Interview with author.
21. Ibid.
22. Olson Buck, "Gender/Ethnicity/Authenticity . . . ," *Letras Femininas*, p. 246.
23. Emmanuel Levy, "The Garden of Eden," *Weekly Variety*, May 30, 1994.
24. Interview with author.
25. Ibid.
26. Ibid.
27. David Hunter, "The Garden of Eden," *The Hollywood Reporter*, June 16, 1995.
28. Levy, "The Garden of Eden," *Weekly Variety*.
29. Hazel-Dawn Dumpert, "Hecho en Mexico: Contemporary Mexican Cinema," *L.A. Weekly*, June 9, 1995.
30. Al Goodman, "The Movie Guide: El Jardín del Edén," *International Herald Tribune*, August 4, 1985.

Sin dejar huella

1. Roberts-Camps, *Latin American Women Filmmakers*, p. 49.
2. Ibid., p. 50.
3. Rashkin, *Women Filmmakers in Mexico*, p. 187.
4. Ibid., pp. 187-88.
5. Arredondo, "María Novaro on the Making . . . ," *Women's Studies Quarterly*, p. 202.
6. David Bordwell, *Reinventing Hollywood: How 1940s Filmmakers Changed Movie Storytelling*, p. 199.

7. Susan Hayward, *Key Concepts in Cinema Studies*, p. 318.
8. Arredondo, "María Novaro on the Making . . . ," *Women's Studies Quarterly*, p. 205.

Las buenas hierbas

1. Robert Koehler, "The Good Herbs," *Daily Variety*, March 23, 2010.
2. Deborah Young, "The Good Herbs: Film Review," *The Hollywood Reporter*, November 9, 2010.
3. Haydn Welch, "Women This Week: Ten Women and Girls Killed Each Day in Mexico," Council on Foreign Relations *Women Around the World* blog, September 24, 2021.
4. Young, "The Good Herbs: Film Review," *The Hollywood Reporter*.
5. Maciel and Hershfield, "Women and Gender Representation . . . ," *Mexico's Cinema*, p. 259.
6. Robles, *Identidades Maternacionales en el cine de María Novaro*, p. 33.
7. Sutherland, "Journeys and Destinations . . . ," *Senses of Cinema*.
8. Alec King, "The Two Childhoods in the *Immortality Ode*," in Cowell, *Critics on Wordsworth*, p. 100.
9. *A Visual History with María Novaro* video interview.
10. Koehler, "The Good Herbs," *Daily Variety*.
11. *A Visual History with María Novaro* video interview.
12. Ibid.
13. Ellsworth, "María Novaro Interview," *Venice Magazine*.
14. Hayward, *Key Concepts in Cinema Studies*, pp. 122-123.
15. *A Visual History with María Novaro* video interview.
16. Ibid.
17. Ibid.
18. Ibid.

Tesoros

1. Ana Morgenstern, "In *Tesoros* adventures create the basis for community: A Miami Film Festival review," *Independent Ethos*, March 4, 2007.
2. Debbie Olson, "The Hitchcock Imp: Children and the Hyperreal in Hitchcock's *The Birds*," in Olson and Scahill, *Lost and Othered Children in Contemporary Cinema*, p. 288.
3. David Thomson, *The New Biographical Dictionary of Film*, p. 883.
4. *Danzón* commentary, DVD release, Zafra Video.
5. John Hopewell, "Mexico's María Novaro on '*Tesoros*,' Mexicans' Joie de Vivre," *Daily Variety*, March 10, 2017.
6. Ibid.
7. Ibid.
8. Elisabeth Malkin, "Guerrero at war: chronicling southern Mexico's forgotten conflict—photo essay," *The Guardian*, November 16, 2020.
9. Ibid.
10. *Danzón* commentary, DVD release, Zafra Video.
11. Pablo Neruda, "El mar" from *Memorial de isla negra* in *Five Decades: Poems 1925-1970*, p. 297.
12. Arredondo, "María Novaro on the Making . . . ," *Women's Studies Quarterly*, p. 202.
13. Ibid., p. 203.
14. Ibid.
15. André Bazin, "De Sica: Metteur en scène," in Curle and Snyder, *Vittorio De Sica: Contemporary Perspectives*, p. 66.
16. Ibid.
17. Hopewell, "Mexico's María Novaro on '*Tesoros*,' Mexicans' Joie de Vivre," *Daily Variety*.
18. delarue, "Ampersan Play Dreamy, Cinematic Tropical Psychedelia in Their New York Debut at Lincoln Center," *New York Music Daily*, October 20, 2017.

Conclusion

1. Rashkin, *Women Filmmakers in Mexico*, p. 189.
2. Roberts-Camps, *Latin American Women Filmmakers*, p. 38.
3. Fusco, "Dance and Remembrance," *Village Voice*.
4. Robles, *Identidades Maternacionales en el cine de María Novaro*, p. 215.
5. Roberts-Camps, *Latin American Women Filmmakers*, p. 52.
6. Ibid., p. 36.
7. Robles, *Identidades Maternacionales en el cine de María Novaro*, p. 215.
8. *A Visual History with María Novaro* video interview.
9. Haddu, "Welcome to Tijuana ...," *Journal of Romance Studies*, p. 9.
10. Ibid., p. 2.
11. Ibid.
12. *A Visual History with María Novaro* video interview.
13. Sippl, "Al cine ...," *Redirecting the Gaze*, p. 40.
14. Golden, "'Danzón' Glides to a Soft Mexican Rhythm," *The New York Times*.
15. Ellsworth, "María Novaro Interview," *Venice Magazine*.
16. Rashkin, *Women Filmmakers in Mexico*, p. 190.
17. Kaminsky, "Identity at the Border ...," *Studies in Twentieth-Century Literature*, p. 102.
18. Ibid.
19. Ellsworth, "María Novaro Interview," *Venice Magazine*.
20. Arredondo, "María Novaro on the Making ...," *Women's Studies Quarterly*, p. 203.
21. Sutherland, "Journeys and Destinations...," *Senses of Cinema*.
22. Ibid.
23. Thomson, *The New Biographical Dictionary of Film*, p. 652.
24. *A Visual History with María Novaro* video interview.
25. *Danzón* commentary, DVD release, Zafra Video.

26. Arredondo, "María Novaro on the Making . . . ," *Women's Studies Quarterly*, p. 205.
27. *A Visual History with María Novaro* video interview.
28. Arredondo, "María Novaro on the Making . . . ," *Women's Studies Quarterly*, p. 205.

Sources

"Actress Martha Navarro dies and the curse of the 3 deaths is fulfilled." *Mundo Hispanico*, December 30, 2020.

Arredondo, Isabel. "María Novaro on the Making of *Lola* and *Danzón*." *Women's Studies Quarterly*, Spring-Summer 2002, Vol. 30, No. 1/2, pp. 196-212.

Bazin, André. "De Sica: Metteur en scène," in Howard Curle and Stephen Snyder (eds.), *Vittorio De Sica: Contemporary Perspectives*. Toronto: University of Toronto Press, 2000.

Bordwell, David. *Reinventing Hollywood: How 1940s Filmmakers Changed Movie Storytelling*. Chicago: The University of Chicago Press, 2017.

Buck, Carla Olson. "Gender/Ethnicity/Authenticity: Recirculating Domination in El jardín del Edén?" *Letras Femininas*, Summer, 2006, pp. 237-49.

Bustos, Victor. "María Novaro, un clavado en la frontera." *Dicine*, January-February, 1996, pp. 24-25.

Cato, Susana. Review of *Danzón*. *Proceso*, June 24, 1991.

Coleman, Renée. Interview with author, July 27, 2021.

Danzón commentary, DVD release, Zafra Video, 2007.

"*Danzón*, María Novaro, Mexico." Montreal World Film Festival Program, 1991.

"*Danzón*." *Weekly Variety*, April 29, 1992.

de la Fuente, Anna Marie. "IMCINE Director María Novaro Ramps Up Outreach, Diversifies Incentives." *Daily Variety*, October 24, 2019.

delarue. "Ampersan Play Dreamy, Cinematic Tropical Psychedelia in Their New York Debut at Lincoln Center." *New York Music Daily*, October 20, 2017.

Dumpert, Hazel-Dawn. "Hecho en Mexico: Contemporary Mexican Cinema." *L.A. Weekly*, June 9, 1995.

Elena, Alberto and Marina Díaz López, (eds.). *The Cinema of Latin America*. London: Wallflower Press, 2003.

Eller, Claudia. "Orion Gets Spanish, Aussie Pics." *Daily Variety*, October 11, 1991.

Ellsworth, Robert. "María Novaro Interview." *Venice Magazine*, September, 1992.

Fein, Seth. "From Collaboration to Containment: Hollywood and the International Political Economy of Mexican Cinema after the Second World War," in Joanne Hershfield and David R. Maciel(eds.), *Mexico's Cinema: A Century of Film and Filmmakers*. Wilmington, Delaware: Scholarly Resources, 1999.

Feinstein, Howard. "Entangling Shadows: One Hundred Years of Cinema in Latin America and the Caribbean." *Weekly Variety*, May 11-17, 1998.

Franco, Jean. *Plotting Women: Gender and Representation in Mexico*. New York: Columbia University Press, 1989.

Fusco, Coco. "Dance and Remembrance." *Village Voice*, August 27, 1991.

Galeano, Eduardo. *Open Veins of Latin America: Five Centuries of the Pillage of a Continent*. New York: Monthly Review Press, 1973.

Garcia, Alberto. "Premieres and Special Events: Danzón." Sundance Film Festival Program, 1992.

Glantz, Margo. "Danzón: Los pies de las mexicanas." *Nitrato de Plata*, 1994, Vol. 17, pp. 18-21.

Golden, Tim. "'Danzón' Glides to a Soft Mexican Rhythm." *The New York Times*, October 11, 1992.

Goodman, Al. "The Movie Guide: El Jardín del Edén." *International Herald Tribune*, August 4, 1995.

Goodridge, Mike. "Altavista's Heart leads slate." *Screen International*, October 6, 2000.

Goodwin, Betty. "Red, White and Sexy Shoes." *Los Angeles Times*, November 20, 1992.

Guillermoprieto, Alma. *The Heart That Bleeds: Latin America Now*. New York: Vintage Books, 1995.

Haddu, Miriam. "Welcome to Tijuana... space, place and identity in María Novaro's El jardín del Edén." *Journal of Romance Studies*, Winter, 2006, Vol. 6, Issue 3, pp. 1-11.

Hall, Linda B. *Dolores del Río: Beauty in Light and Shade*. Stanford, California: Stanford University Press, 2013.

Handling, Piers. "Lola." Fifteenth Toronto Film Festival Program, 1990.

Hayward, Susan. *Key Concepts in Cinema Studies*. London: Routledge, 1996.

Hopewell, John. "Berlinale FiGa Films Acquires Berlin Generation Kplus Player 'Tesoros.'" *Daily Variety*, December 23, 2016.

_____ "Mexico's María Novaro on 'Tesoros,' Mexicans' Joie de Vivre." *Daily Variety*, March 10, 2017.

Hunter, David. "The Garden of Eden." *The Hollywood Reporter*, June 16, 1995.

Iglesias, Norma. "Reconstructing the Mexican Border Cinema and Its Relationship to Its Audience," in Joanne Hershfield and David R. Maciel(eds.), *Mexico's Cinema: A Century of Film and Filmmakers*. Wilmington, Delaware: Scholarly Resources, 1999.

Kaminsky, Amy. "Identity at the Border: Narrative Strategies in María Novaro's *El jardín del Edén* and John Sayles's *Lone Star*." *Studies in Twentieth-Century Literature*, Winter, 2001, Vol. 25, No. 1, pp. 91-117.

King, Alex. "The Two Childhoods in the Immortality Ode," in Raymond Cowell (ed.), *Critics on Wordsworth*. London: George Allen and Unwin Ltd., 1973.

King, John. *Magical Reels: A History of Cinema in Latin America*. London: Verso, 1990.

Koehler, Robert. "The Good Herbs." *Daily Variety*, March 23, 2010.

Larson, Erik. *The Splendid and the Vile: A Saga of Churchill, Family, and Defiance During the Blitz.* New York: Crown, 2020.

Leal, Alejandro. "María Novaro es descarada feminista y antimachista." *El Universal,* October 4, 1992.

Leñero Franco, Estela. "Entrevista con María Novaro." *Nitrato de Plata,* 1992, Vol. 12, pp. 3-5.

Levy, Emmanuel. "The Garden of Eden." *Weekly Variety,* May 30, 1994.

Lockhart, Kimball. "Michelangelo Antonioni," in Andrew Sarris (ed.), *The Saint James Film Directors Encyclopedia.* Detroit: Visible Ink Press, 1998.

Lola commentary, DVD release, Zafra Video/Facets Video, Mexico, 2007.

"Lola." *Weekly Variety,* January 17, 1990.

Maciel, David R. "Cinema and the State in Contemporary Mexico, 1970-1999," in Joanne Hershfield and David R. Maciel (eds.), *Mexico's Cinema: A Century of Film and Filmmakers.* Wilmington, Delaware: Scholarly Resources, 1999.

Maciel, David R. and Joanne Hershfield, "Women and Gender Representation in the Contemporary Cinema of Mexico," in Hershfield and Maciel (eds.), *Mexico's Cinema: A Century of Film and Filmmakers.* Wilmington, Delaware: Scholarly Resources, 1999.

Maldonado, Veronica. Review of *El jardín del Edén. Dicine,* January-February, 1996.

Malkin, Elisabeth. "Guerrero at war: chronicling southern Mexico's forgotten conflict—photo essay." *The Guardian,* November 16, 2020.

"María Novaro llegó hasta la cumbre de su gran carrera." *Cine Mundial,* June 1, 1992.

Martin, Gerald. *Gabriel García Márquez: A Life.* New York: Alfred A. Knopf, 2009.

Maslin, Janet. "A Melodious Variation on Feminist Awareness." *The New York Times,* September 25, 1992.

Matsumoto, Jon. "Light Danzón: Mexican Film Fails to Take the Tough Steps." *Village View*, October 16-22, 1992.

Menell, Jeff. "Film Review: Danzón." *The Hollywood Reporter*, September 25, 1992.

"Mexican Auteurs: Patricia Riggen, Issa Lopez and María Novaro." *Weekly Variety*, March 5, 2019.

Mitchell, Elvis. "A Festival of Latin Films That Go Many Different Places." *The New York Times*, August 9, 2001.

Monsiváis, Carlos. "Cantinflas and Tin Tan: Mexico's Greatest Comedians," in Joanne Hershfield and David R. Maciel (eds.), *Mexico's Cinema: A Century of Film and Filmmakers*. Wilmington, Delaware: Scholarly Resources, 1999.

Morgenstern, Ana. "In *Tesoros* adventures create the basis for community: A Miami Film Festival review." *Independent Ethos*, March 4, 2017.

Mulvey, Laura. "Visual Pleasure and Narrative Cinema," in Laura Mulvey, *Visual and Other Pleasures*. Bloomington, Indiana: Indiana University Press, 1989.

Naremore, James. *Acting in the Cinema*. Berkeley, California: University of California Press, 1990.

Neruda, Pablo. "El mar" from *Memorial de isla negra* in *Five Decades: Poems 1925-1970*. New York: Grove Press, 1974.

Noble, Andrea. "'Yendose por la tangente': The Border in María Novaro's *El jardín del Edén*." *Tessarae: Journal of Iberian and Latin American Studies*, December, 2001, Vol. 7, No. 2, pp. 191-202.

Novaro, María. Sony Pictures Classics *Danzón* remarks included in press packet housed at Margaret Herrick Library, Academy of Motion Picture Arts and Sciences, Beverly Hills, California.

Olson, Debbie. "The Hitchcock Imp: Children and the Hyperreal in Hitchcock's The Birds," in Debbie Olson and Andrew Scahill (eds.), *Lost and Othered Children in Contemporary Cinema*. New York: Lexington, 2012.

Perez Turrent, Tomas. "Los milagros de Juan Soldado." *Revista Siempre*, October 19, 1995.

Rashkin, Elissa J. *Women Filmmakers in Mexico: The Country of Which We Dream*. Austin: University of Texas Press, 2001.

Rich, B. Ruby. "The West Indies." *The Nation*, February 26, 2001.

Roberts-Camps, Traci. *Latin American Women Filmmakers: Social and Cultural Perspectives*. Albuquerque: University of New Mexico Press, 2017.

Robles, Óscar. *Identidades Maternacionales en el cine de María Novaro*. New York: Peter Lang Publishing, Inc., 2005.

Roddick, Chloe. "Deep Focus: The Golden Age of Mexican Cinema." *Sight and Sound*, July 25, 2019.

Rooney, David. "Leaving No Trace." *Weekly Variety*, October 9-15, 2000.

Sarabia, Carlos Fabián. "El jardín del Edén". *Nitrato de Plata*, 1994, Vol. 17, pp. 22-26.

Sippl, Diane. "Al cine de las Mexicanas: Lola in the Limelight," in Diane Robin and Ira Jaffe (eds.), *Redirecting the Gaze: Gender, Theory and Cinema in the Third World*. Albany: State University of New York Press, 1999.

Stein, Elliott. "Aztec Camera." *Village Voice*, June 30. 2004.

Stevenson, William. "Mexico's 'Danzón' Cops Top Prize at Gotham Latino Fest." *Daily Variety*, August 28, 1991.

Sutherland, Romy. "Journeys and Destinations: The Films of María Novaro." *Senses of Cinema*, December, 2002, Issue 23.

Thomas, Kevin. "A New Generation of Filmmakers Dances Into the Scene." *Los Angeles Times*, October 16, 1992.

_____ "On the Lam in Mexico." *Los Angeles Times*, July 26, 2001.

Thompson, Robert Farris. *Tango: The Art History of Love*. New York: Vintage Books, 2006.

Thomson, David. *The New Biographical Dictionary of Film*. New York: Alfred A. Knopf, 2002.

Torres, Edén E. *Chicana Without Apology: The New Chicana Cultural Studies*. New York: Routledge, 2003.

Toumarkine, Doris. "'Danzón', Sony Classics in Step." *The Hollywood Reporter*, July 21, 1992

Ulmer, James. "In Transit: Novaro helping lead Mexican film comeback." *The Hollywood Reporter*, August 11, 1992.

Vega, Patricia. "Entrevista con María Novaro." *La Jornada Semanal*, August, 1991, pp. 27-30

A Visual History with María Novaro, Director and Screenwriter. Video interview conducted by Lourdes Portillo in Mexico City on September 25, 2015. Part of "From Latin America to Hollywood: Latino Film Culture in Los Angeles 1967-2017," the Academy of Motion Picture Arts and Sciences contribution to *Pacific Standard Time: LA/LA* art project.

Welch, Haydn. "Women This Week: Ten Women and Girls Killed Each Day in Mexico." Council on Foreign Relations Women Around the World blog, September 24, 2021.

Wilmington, Michael. "Exhilaration, Charm and Grace in Musical Romance 'Danzón.'" *Los Angeles Times*, October 16, 1992, F8.

Winter, Jessica. "City Sickness: Latin Beat 2001—Recent Films from Latin America." *Village Voice*, August 14, 2001.

Young, Deborah. "The Good Herbs: Film Review." *The Hollywood Reporter*, November 9, 2010.

Index

Academy Awards, 20, 134
Alemán Valdéz, Miguel, 5
Altavista Films, 40, 137, 230
Altomaro, Martín, 160, 230
Alzheimer's disease, 3, 164-65
Antonioni, Michelangelo, 92
Arredondo, Isabel, 58-59, 92
Ariel Awards, 3, 20-21, 27, 31, 37, 41, 44, 49, 74-75, 77, 99, 105, 131-135, 137, 159-61, 184-85, 225
Armendáriz, Pedro, 6
Arredondo, Isabel, 58-59, 92
Arroyo, Conchis, 19, 227
auteur theory, 207
Ávila Camacho, Manuel, 5
Aztec Codex, 165, 172, 174, 177, 181-82, 215
Azul celeste, 2, 22-23, 25, 36, 76, 159, 227

Balderas, Miriam, 170, 231
Banco Cinematográfico, 22
Barberis, Nerio, 161, 228, 230
Barjau, Sigfrido, 33, 36, 76, 103, 135, 228-229
Barroso, Gerardo, 43, 45, 185, 204, 231
Barroso Tillinger, Lucas, 204, 231
Bazin, André, 205-206
Bergman, Ingmar, 207
Bernal, Juan Manuel, 160, 230
Bichir, Bruno, 35, 37, 105, 130, 132, 134, 159, 229
Bichir, Demián, 35, 132-133, 159

border films, 130, 214
Bordwell, David, 150
Borrell Soldevila, Juan, 161, 230
Broch, Brigitte, 133-134, 229
Buck, Carla Olson, 125, 132
Buenas hierbas, Las, 42, 44, 46, 87, 132, 162-187, 196-97, 208, 211-12, 214-15, 217-18, 221-25, 231
Buñuel, Luis, 7
Bustos, Victor, 240

cabaretera, 7, 28, 30, 103, 130, 214, 217
Cahiers du cinéma, 207
Calderón, Felipe, 198
Camus, Marie-Christine, 18-20, 22, 227
Cannes Film Festival, 1, 31, 79, 105, 159
Cano, Zindu, 205-206, 218, 231
Cantinflas, 6, 8
Cárdenas, Lázaro, 8
Carrera, Carlos, 1
Cassavetes, John, 151
Castro, Dolores, 12-13
Castro, Fidel, 23
Cazals, Felipe, 1, 225
Centro de Capacitación Cinematográfica (CCC), 1-3, 22, 42, 76, 103, 185
Centro Universitario de Estudios Cinematográficos (CUEC), 1-2, 17-21, 24, 41, 185

Chávez de León, Jacinta, 45, 190, 192, 204, 231
Chávez, Mara, 17, 19, 34, 45, 185, 204, 227, 231
Chávez, Santiago, 16-17, 34, 43, 45, 185, 204-05, 218, 231
Ciangherotti, Alan, 133, 229
Cine-Mujer, 16, 18
Coleman, Renée, 35-36, 39, 112, 115, 130-31, 134-35, 229
Coppola, Francis Ford, 23
Cortés, Alberto, 21, 76
Cortés, Busi, 2, 47
Cruz, Ángeles, 133, 229
Cuando comenzamos a hablar, 38, 230
Cuarón, Alfonso, 1-2, 20, 33, 161
Culp, Joseph, 133, 229

Danzón, 3,7, 23, 28, 30-33, 44, 47, 50, 60 65, 76, 78-79, 84, 86-87, 89, 91-92, 94, 97, 100, 103, 105, 122-23, 125, 128, 130-31, 157, 159 161, 173, 197, 201, 206, 208-09, 211-12, 214-15, 217, 221, 223-24, 228
danzón (dance), 29-30, 43, 79-81, 83-84, 88-90, 93, 96, 98, 104
de la Madrid, Miguel, 70
de Lara, Maricarmen, 16
de León, Judith, 45, 185, 204, 231
del Rió, Dolores, 6
del Toro, Guillermo, 133
Demy, Jacques, 49
de Sica, Vittorio, 192, 205
Díaz Ordaz, Gustavo, 15
Díaz, Porfirio, 8
Dietrich, Marlene, 49
Donner, Richard, 49

Edwards, Eric, 36, 133, 229
Eisenstein, Sergei, 207
Ellsworth, Robert, 11
Enredando sombras, 38, 230
Estrada, Luis, 1, 20-21, 133
Estrella, Alberto, 184, 231

Fassbinder, Rainer Werner, 49
Félix, María, 6
feminism, 16, 19, 31, 103-04, 129, 146, 169, 212, 216
Fernández, Rosa Marta, 16
Fernández Violante, Marcela, 17, 20-21, 38
Figueroa, Gabriel, 7
Fondo de Fomento a la Calidad Cinematográfica (FFCC), 22, 228-29
Fondo para la Producción Cinematográfica de Calidad (FOPROCINE), 137, 162, 230-31
Fons, Jorge, 1, 135

Gabriel, Juan, 161, 218
Galeano, Eduardo, 198
García Márquez, Gabriel, 21, 23-24, 29, 31, 39, 43, 49, 76, 180
García, Rodrigo, 21, 26, 30, 40, 76, 102, 133, 228
Garza, Sebastián, 43, 185, 231
gaze, the, 82, 83-85, 125
Godard, Jean-Luc, 207
Godínez, Cheli, 23, 76, 227, 228
Golden Age of Mexican Cinema, 5-7, 12, 28, 30, 77, 214
Gómez-Peña, Guillermo, 109, 116-118, 127
González Muñoz, Cosmo, 172, 184, 211, 231
Group of Eight, 12

Guerra, Blanca, 100-01, 228
Guillermoprieto, Alma, 113

Haddu, Miriam, 112-13, 119, 128, 213
Hall, Linda B., 6, 12
Hayward, Susan, 155, 179
Hermosillo, Jaime Humberto, 1, 29, 75
Hernández, Julián, 1
Hernández Zoido, Ángel, 160, 230
Hershfield, Joanne, 42, 86, 91, 170
Historias de ciudad, 22, 227
Hitchcock, Alfred, 192
Hopewell, John, 46
Huijara, Leticia, 26, 57, 67, 72-74, 76, 217, 225, 228

Iglesias, Norma, 104, 130
Iñárritu, Alejandro González, 1, 33, 133, 160
indigenismo, 115, 172-73, 215
Infante, Pedro, 6, 71, 163, 178, 218
Inicial, Rosa, 38
Instituto Mexicano de Cinematografía (IMCINE), 13, 22, 27, 29, 35, 46-47, 49, 162, 228-31
International School for Cinema and Television (EICTV), 23
Isabel, Margarita, 100-01, 228
Isla rodeada de agua, Una, 2, 19-20, 22-23, 227
Iturbide, Graciela, 114, 128

Jardín del Edén, El, 23, 34-37, 43, 76, 105-136, 160, 173, 178, 182, 184, 207, 209, 212-13, 215, 216-18, 220-24, 229
Juan el soldado, 109, 116, 124, 128-29, 134, 215, 221

Kahlo, Frida, 109, 114, 116, 121, 127, 129, 183, 216
Kaminsky, Amy, 115, 117, 218
Keaton, Buster, 207
King, Alex, 172
Koehler, Robert, 173
Kuri, Dulce, 25, 35, 77, 105, 135, 228-30

Landeta, Matilde, 7, 47
Larson, Erik, 10
Leal, Alejandro, 28
Levy, Emmanuel, 133, 135
Lola, 2, 3, 23, 25-28, 33, 47, 49-78, 86, 100, 102-03, 130, 169, 172, 214, 216-17, 221, 224-25, 227
López Mateos, Adolfo, 13
López Obrador, Andrés Manuel, 46
López Rivera, Diego, 47
Lubezki, Emmanuel, 1, 20

Maciel, David, 42, 47, 86, 91, 170
Malkin, Elisabeth, 199
Malle, Louis, 187
Manrique, Lorenza, 185, 231
Marin, Alejandro, 19, 227
Mazursky, Paul, 24-26
Medina, Ofelia, 42-44, 162, 172, 174, 177, 182-84, 225, 231
melodrama, 7, 12, 86, 103, 134, 170, 175, 209, 214
Mendez, Rosa María, 18
Mexicanidad, 7, 30, 114-17, 146, 172-73, 196-97, 213-15, 217
Mexico City, 8, 10, 14-16, 21-22, 27, 29-30, 34, 37, 44, 49, 50, 55, 60, 63, 69, 77, 79, 81, 85-86, 91, 93, 95, 98-99, 105-06, 119, 135, 146, 159, 162, 164, 209, 212-14, 216-17, 219, 221, 224

Miller, Elisa, 42, 47-48
Mira, Beatriz, 16
Mitchell, Elvis, 41
Molina Rivera, Alettia, 206, 231
Monsiváis, Carlos, 7
Mora Catlett, Juan, 1
Motion Picture Association of America (MPAA), 12, 37
Mulvey, Laura, 83
Murguía, Ana Ofelia, 42, 44, 105, 132, 162, 170, 182, 184, 225, 229, 231

Navarrete, Santiago, 22, 227
Navarro, Martha, 75-76, 228
Neruda, Pablo, 199
North American Free Trade Agreement (NAFTA), 36-37, 148
Novaro, Beatriz, 11-14, 22, 27-29, 34, 36, 38, 40, 49, 77, 103, 130, 135, 160, 207, 227-229
Novaro, María, 5, 26, 28-29, 32-33, 38, 40, 48, 72, 73-76, 99-100, 102, 131-36, 159, 161, 162, 183, 207, 225-26
   administrative work and, 3, 13, 46-47
   awards of, 3, 20, 27, 31, 37, 41, 44, 45, 49, 77, 105, 135, 160, 182, 185, 187
   education of, 13-15
   family of, 7-15, 16-17, 34-35, 36, 39, 44, 101, 185, 204-05
   film themes of, 3, 14, 19, 23, 30-31, 34, 41, 43, 50, 55-64, 81-90, 111-21, 137, 143-49, 168-75, 191-99, 208-16
   Mexicanidad and, 30, 114-17, 146, 172-73, 196-97, 214-15, 217
   politics and, 15, 16, 17, 20, 43, 58, 70, 103-04, 113, 148-49, 173, 178, 198-99, 215-16
   professional training of, 2, 16-23, 24-25
   teaching and, 3, 13, 41-42
   visual style of, 19-20, 45, 64-72, 91-98, 121-30, 150-58, 175-82, 200-04, 216-24
Novaro, Octavio, 7-14
Novaro Peñalosa, Gabriel, 8, 11, 185
Novaro Peñalosa, Luis, 8, 10-11, 185
Novaro Peñalosa, Octavio Augusto, 8-10, 185
Novaro, Tito, 12

Ocampo, Yolanda, 19, 227
Ochoa, Jesús, 145, 160, 230
Office of the Coordinator for Inter-American Affairs (OCIAA), 5-6,
Olguín, Lucia, 33, 229
Olson, Debbie, 192
Ophüls, Max, 49, 96, 222
Otero, Silvia, 18-19, 227
Otoñal, 33, 76, 229

Passer, Ivan, 24
Paz, Octavio, 13
Pecanins, Marisa, 77, 228
Peckinpah, Sam, 191
Peña, Elizabeth, 25
Peñalosa Calderón, Javier, 12
Peñalosa, María Luisa, 8
Pervertida, La, 20-21
Pollack, Sydney, 24
Pontecorvo, Gillo, 23
Portillo, Lourdes, 47, 174

Pruneda, Úrsula, 42, 44, 170, 172, 174, 177, 182-85, 211, 225, 231

Quino, 33, 229

ranchera, 6, 12
Rashkin, Elissa, J., 16-17, 43, 63, 86, 90, 98, 100, 120, 122, 149, 207, 216
Ray, Satyajit, 192
Redford, Robert, 23-25, 39, 49, 73
Rergis, Daniel, 32, 89, 101, 228
Rios, Roberto, 160, 230
Ripstein, Arturo, 1, 225
Rivera, Diego, 116, 129
Rivera, Mauricio, 76, 228
Roberts-Camps, Traci, 57, 59, 66, 86, 120, 128, 145-46, 208, 212
Robles, Óscar, 50, 116-17, 170, 210, 213
Rockefeller, Nelson, 5
Roddick, Chloe, 5
Rodríguez, Gabino, 184, 231
Rodríguez, Nelson, 103, 228
Roel, Gabriela, 23, 36, 106, 131, 225, 227, 229
Rojo, María, 29, 31-33, 43-44, 79, 84-85, 87-90, 98-100, 102, 104, 159, 183, 208, 224-25, 228-29
Rotberg, Dana, 2, 47
Rulfo, Juan, 19

Sagrav, Rosario, 115, 131-32, 229
Saldívar Tanaka, Serguei, 41, 160-61, 230
Salinas, Carmen, 79, 87, 100, 225, 228
Salinas de Gortari, Carlos, 70

Sánchez-Gijón, Aitana, 40-41, 138, 143, 145, 147, 155, 158-59, 225, 230
Sánchez, Guadalupe, 18, 228
Sánchez, Jorge, 27, 32, 35, 39, 46, 77, 105, 135, 228-30
Sánchez Novaro, Lucero, 25, 34, 36, 42-43, 45, 133, 185, 205. 229, 231-32
Scanda, Tiaré, 41, 143, 147, 155, 158-59, 225, 230
Schyfter, Guita, 2
Secco, María, 42
Sefami, José, 160, 230
Sin dejar huella, 39-41, 137-161, 162, 169, 182, 208, 209, 212-17, 219, 222-23, 225, 230
Sindicato de Trabajadores de la Producción Cinematográfica (STPC), 22, 25-26, 77
Sippl, Diane, 58, 62-63, 214
Solanas, Fernando, 23
Solis, Rodrigo, 184, 231
Sosa, Roberto, 27, 74, 228
Sotelo, Edmundo, 160, 230
Stabat Mater, 60, 63, 65, 71, 74, 217
Sundance Institute, 24-25, 41, 49, 73, 105, 137
Sutherland, Romy, 63, 171, 219, 220
Sutton Chávez, Andrea, 45, 190, 204, 220, 231
Sutton Chávez, Dylan, 45, 204, 231

Tamés, María Eugenia, 16
Taracena, Gerardo, 160, 230
Tesoros, 44-46, 87, 187-207, 210, 211, 213, 215, 218-20, 222-24, 231
Thelma and Louise, 39-40, 158
Thompson, Robert Farris, 88

Thomson, David, 192, 222
Tillinger, Lisa, 45, 185, 204, 231-32
Truffaut, Francois, 187, 192

Universidad Nacional Autónoma de México (UNAM) 8-9, 14-15, 22

Valdéz, Germán (Tin Tan), 7
Valenti, Jack, 37
Valle, Alejandro, 185, 231
Varda, Agnès, 207
Vargas, Alejandra, 26, 57, 67, 72, 74-75, 228
Vasconcelos, Tito, 79, 84, 100-01, 228
Vasquez, Angélica, 206
Vazquez, Alejandro, 41, 161, 230

Velasco, Maria Elena, 2
Vigo, Jean, 187
Vivaldi, Antonio, 60, 65, 74, 217
von Sternberg, Josef, 49

Weaver, Sigourney, 24
Welch, Haydn, 169
Welles, Orson, 185, 207
Wilmington, Michael, 31, 79

Young, Deborah, 169

Zapatista Army of National Liberation, 149, 215
Zaragoza, Javier, 78, 228
Zedillo, Ernesto, 38

www.ingramcontent.com/pod-product-compliance
Lightning Source LLC
Chambersburg PA
CBHW071426150426
43191CB00008B/1060